UNMAPPED

UNMAPPED

THE (MOSTLY) TRUE STORY
OF HOW TWO WOMEN LOST AT SEA
FOUND THEIR WAY HOME

Charlotte Getz

&

Stephanie Phillips

A MOCKINGBIRD PUBLICATION
CHARLOTTESVILLE, VA

For the wanderers,
which is to say, *all of us.*

Ninety percent of what's wrong with you
   could be cured with a hot bath,
says God from the bowels of the subway.
   but we want magic, to win
the lottery we never bought a ticket for.
   (Tenderly, the monks chant, embrace
the suffering.) The voice of God does not pander,
   offers no five year plan, no long-term
solution, nary an edict. It is small & fond & local.
   Don't look for your initials in the geese
honking overhead or to see thru the glass even
   darkly. It says the most obvious crap—
put down that gun, you need a sandwich.

                    Mary Karr
                    "The Voice of God"

   If grace is an ocean, we're all sinking.

                    John Mark McMillan

CONTENTS

INTRODUCTION

WE FIRST BECAME INTRODUCED TO each other, not in person, but as contributing writers for Mockingbird (mbird.com). Ours is your average modern-day (cyber), non-sexual love affair. As we read each other's extraordinary works of theological prowess, we realized we had a lot in common: namely that we were both severely struggling mothers with one eye on our failures and another, more reluctant eye on God's grace. We also realized that we were both about to be ripped from the comfort of our settled-ish lives to follow our husbands and their jobs to places we did not want to go; yet we were bound by both God and the government to do just that. What follows is the story of our friendship, and the complicated turns one takes to wind her way through the wilderness places—all at once lost and found. Consider yourselves properly warned that this narrative is not always reasonable or indicative of *exactly how things played out in real life.* THAT WOULD BE BORING. In the pages to come, we will speak to you from the mouths of our childhood selves, in essay, in verse, and more often than not from the salty decks of a vessel we never actually commandeered. But we believe that what we want you to know can only be rightly communicated *like this.* So get on board, k?

PART ONE

HOW TO
FIND A PADDLING PARTNER

SHIPWRECKED

Charlotte

WHEN MY HUSBAND ALEX AND I were due to have our first baby, we were stranded from any familial sanctuary; we lived in Savannah, Georgia, and our nearest kin were six hours away by car. This didn't seem all that significant, until our son Ford actually arrived. He was needy as hell. He didn't like to sleep, and his head bobbed around like one of those dime store trinkets. There was nothing I could do to make my delicate boy stop screaming…or puking, as if he were a hair-licking cat instead of a colicky baby. Ford's relentless need elevated our own relentless need. We didn't have enough hands or know-how. We were helpless, exhausted, and hormonally confused (at least on my part).

Suddenly, our families and the homes of our childhoods seemed like glistening mirages far, far in the distance—oases we were incapable of reaching, the desert sand thick around our ankles. We built these places up in our imaginations, blooming paradises in central Illinois and Alabama, where everything was easy like a Sunday morning, where we were known. We whispered about them during the endless newborn nights. We envied our friends and cousins who were already there. "Well of course her highlights aren't brassy—*she's in Alabama.*"

In Alabama, Alex and I could go on dates more often. In Alabama, there would be babysitters we didn't have to pay (i.e. Mom and Dad). There would be opportunity. There would be world renowned doctors to attend to my many and confusing "health issues." There would be pool access and a music scene. The water would taste better. The Holy Spirit would move. The skies would be bluer (and all other Lynyrd Skynyrd ascriptions). *Alabama.* Oh sweet home.

When Ford was two and Margot was an infant, Alex and I made what seemed like a colossal decision to migrate back to Birmingham, our land of milk and honey. The good Lord was bringing us home.

And we almost made it there.[1]

Several months before our supposed crossing, we could see it in the distance, feel the relief tingling in our fingertips, smell the ribs smoking over blinding magenta charcoal.

Alex had received an unexpected job offer from an impressive company out in Los Angeles, which at least meant he was professionally desirable and we wouldn't starve. The company thought they could locate us in Miami. If he didn't get offered a different job in Birmingham, at least we'd be in the South.

"Can you imagine moving to LA?" said Alex with an arrogant glint in his eye.

"I would literally die before raising my children in southern California." I had gone to undergraduate in Malibu—it was the greatest four years of my young life, *but that was*

---

1. We made it to Auburn, where Alex would attend grad school for a year before finding a job in Birmingham.

then. I'd seen shows like *Laguna Beach* and *The O.C.* Hell if I was about to drag my kids into that socially barbaric dystopia.

Several weeks later, Alex and I were reclining on chaise lounges in southern Florida—Alex was on spring break from graduate school—and we watched as our kids splashed around on the stairs of a sparkling blue pool. Clusters of coconuts swayed in a rhythmic breeze above us. The sun poured warmth over our winter-starved skin. If Birmingham wasn't heaven, this was.

"The Miami thing isn't going to work out," said Alex. "We're looking at California as our only option."

"What do you mean? You'll get a job in Birmingham," I assured him.

"The time limit on this job offer is about to expire, Charlotte. And I have to tell you, I think it would be a huge mistake to turn down the opportunity to work for a company like this," he said with a touch of worry edging through the cracks of his otherwise rock-steady character.

This was news to me. He was going to get an even better job in Birmingham. *We just needed to wait.*

But as the days drew nearer for the California offer to expire, and still on leave in Florida, Alex's phone sat idle and quiet on the nightstand. Our eyes were aimed south, but all the signs, common sense, and whispers began to abruptly shout, "WEST."

"We have kids now. We can't shoot the moon in these decisions anymore," argued Alex after a few days; always with the nauseating logic.

He was right, of course. We'd be idiots to risk saying no to such an opportunity, all in hopes that Birmingham would come through. But maybe with our wills—our long-waited for wants—we could *make* that phone ring with the news we'd been working toward for years.

Alabama.

By the end of the week, in the wet heat of southern Florida, the decision was upon us. But there wasn't a decision to make. All this time, California had been our fire by night, our cloud by day, and it was really the only way we could go—whether I wanted to or not. Alex accepted the offer.

There weren't enough Lime-A-Ritas in the world to get me through this new reality. I felt like I was gripping the trunk of a palm tree bent in the gales of a hurricane, taking sharp debris to the face all the while. This is what exile feels like—glancing over your shoulder at paradise, with only cold hard wilderness up ahead. What if I fall apart out there? What if my health declines? What if our salaries are not enough to live by or our kids get stuck in one of those crunchy preschools? What if they take up surfing one day? Or—God forbid—*boogie boarding?* WHAT ABOUT THE REALLY BIG ONE?![2]

Alex and I didn't talk, could hardly look at each other in those first 24 hours of plot twist. This was *his fault*, after all. *God, where are* You *in this?*

Life had already tried us because, well, life. And we had almost made it home. We stared it right in the face. Smelled its beer-drenched breath; that breath smelled like freedom, y'all. I felt helpless, afraid, alone—God's truth swirled around like shrapnel, impossible to grasp. There in the chaos, I picked up a book, Robert Morgan's *The Red Sea Rules,* and found a momentary lull in the storm:

---

2. It's a historically long-overdue, catastrophic tsunami/earthquake event, people. Look it up.

The Red Sea may roll before us; the desert may entrap us; the enemy may press on our heels. The past may seem implausible and the future impossible, but God works in ways we cannot see. He will make a way of escape for His weary, but waiting, children.

With our spring vacation nearing its end, our hearts filled with ache and dread—for an old dream unrealized and a new future unwanted. We sat back on those same chaise lounges, and Alex reached his hand out for mine. We were together. Always together in this. We watched our beautiful kids delight in the cool water of the pool. He said, "This is going to be our same weather, only less humidity." We looked up into the late afternoon sky, the palm trees dancing around us like a gospel choir, and for a moment, California sounded like an answer instead of a curse. I recalled a mighty God who fiercely loves His unlovable children (*Alex*); and sometimes, for reasons unknown to us, He also pulls His beloved face first into the raging storm.

I sat silent for a moment, breathing in the warm weather.

"So we're really doing this?" I asked.

"We're really doing this."

"You're positive?"

"I already accepted the job, Charlotte. This is not a drill."

"Ugh, fine."

ADRIFT, AGAIN

Stephanie

THE FIRST TIME IT HAPPENED, I was cooling down on the indoor track at my gym, comfortable in a settled life in suburban Atlanta, where my husband Jason and I, and our two boys, had finally made a home. There was the church that took four years to find. There was the school and the doctors and the therapists I'd locked in for our older son, diagnosed on the autism spectrum a year earlier. There was my tight-knit group of friends, a first in the life of my severely introverted self—the end of small talk, CHECK! Best of all, we were surrounded by family, particularly my sister. At twelve months apart, we'd been close all our lives but had lived apart going on ten years. It was time for us to drink wine and raise our kids together while trying not to become our beloved mom. Earlier that morning I had received a phone call from my sister. She had just discovered she was pregnant with her second child. I was thinking about a potential niece or nephew when my phone buzzed, and it was Jason on the line.

He never calls during the day. That's what texting is for.

We have agreed to these terms.

"So…" he began, immediately confirming my hunch that Something Was Up.

He went on to explain that the company he worked for had just acquired a business in Sydney. AUSTRALIA. I expected him to tell me they wanted him to take a trip there, and I was prepared to pout about anything longer than three days.

"They may offer me a position," he said instead.

For the second time that day, I asked the person on the other end of the line if they were joking. For the second time that day, I was assured they were not. I was out of words—well, sort of. And not really. I told Jason that it was batshit crazy to even consider moving across the world right now. Sure, we had considered overseas moves before, on long walks and during conversations fueled by wine and a willing suspension of disbelief in our own limitations. But even then, the furthest locale mentioned was London, a mere seven hours ahead at most. For God's sake, we'd barely survived the four-hour flight to visit Jason's family in California the previous summer with both kids in tow—how would we ever survive that plus fourteen hours *further* west?!

Not for nothing were the other concerns, which I held tightly within my heart…for now. What if our son regressed with all the changes brought on by an overseas move? What if *I* did, my mental health in these postpartum years having become a strange animal to me? Do they even have counselors in Australia?!

I can't remember what I said in response to Jason's news. All I know is that he said we'd talk about it later, we hung up, and I began to cry while continuing to walk around the track, stunned.

Later we did talk about it, on one of our long walks. We weighed the pros and cons, which consisted of my reciting to Jason all the reasons we had to stay where we were. Enough was enough: we'd both moved around incessantly, it seemed. Jason had lived all over the world by the time we met in New York City. For my part, I had covered some serious domestic ground. We had landed, finally, in Atlanta, where we both found jobs and had a family, and we had lived there for six years. It was time to continue putting down roots, not yank them out of the ground! I'd spent my twenties wandering through my own desert; if God was kind, wouldn't I close out my thirties on familiar ground, staying put in a Promised Land full of friends and family? Surely He would agree.

After months went by with no mention of Australia, I assumed the Almighty did agree, and I gave him a virtual high-five for the support.

Unsolicited advice: don't do that. And by "that," I mean assume that we *ever* really know what God is up to. Or that it couldn't defy our plans. Or that there is any limit to his willingness to interrupt our lives in order to love us.

THE SECOND TIME IT HAPPENED, I got an email from Jason during the day (dude had wised up and decided not to call). This was about eight months after that first phone call, and mere days after my niece was born.

Australia was on the table again.

Spoiler alert: our traveling had just begun.

CHARACTER
DESCRIPTIONS

STEPHANIE PHILLIPS is a 40-year-old ginger female who used to practice dentistry but was recently promoted to Co-ordinator of *Phillips Family Affairs: Sydney Edition*, due to a misunderstanding with God over what "living by the beach" means. She spends her days driving her kids around on the left side of the road in a car full of sand while trying (and failing) to avoid the local cupcake and wine shops.

CHARLOTTE GETZ is a 33-year-old genius. She was named one of *Time* magazine's "100 Most Influential People" at the age of 21, only carries fifty-dollar bills in her wallet (just because she can), and she invented post-its. Also *she lies*. CHARLOTTE GETZ is a 33-year-old accidental mother and reluctant chameleon, weary from both parenthood and re-locations that have taken her to just about every odd corner of America. She has long, tired brown hair and the sort of blue eyes you could tell would be pretty if she were wearing any make-up.

THE MEET-CUTE

INTERIOR: THERAPIST OFFICE—MORNING.

STEPHANIE PHILLIPS *and* CHARLOTTE GETZ *sit side-by-side on a plush beige couch—the sort of cheap-ish "luxury" piece one might find on clearance at a massage parlor masquerading as a furniture warehouse. The mauve drapery is drawn, the lights turned low, and a sound machine coos a soft, steady stream of ocean ambiance throughout the room.* STEPHANIE, *a young woman in her late 30s with bright, wondering eyes, wrings her hands in her lap. She is nervous but poised.* CHARLOTTE, *a younger but no less doe-eyed creature, sits cross-legged on the couch with her shoes tossed carelessly off of her feet. Across from the two girls, staring through the lenses of glasses which might be marketed specifically to librarians or mental health practitioners, is a 50-something* THERAPIST *who looks as if she's just smelled a rose.*

THERAPIST: Well, since we're all here, I suppose I should tell you why I brought you together this morning.

Both women shrug their shoulders and sheepishly catch eyes. STEPHANIE *gives a breathy giggle.* CHARLOTTE *smiles and blushes. The awkwardness is tangible.*

THERAPIST: Well, against my better professional judgement, it occurred to me that I had two patients going through very similar life circumstances...

CHARLOTTE (*to Stephanie*): You daydream about dropping your kids at a fire station and bolting?

THERAPIST (*cheery but still professional*): Remember, Charlotte, that's just your inner child at work.

STEPHANIE (*ignoring* THERAPIST, *she responds directly to* CHARLOTTE): Yes... (*She is amazed.*)

THERAPIST: Girls, that's really not what I—

CHARLOTTE (*to* STEPHANIE): You sometimes feel like you're watching this gigantic, slow-rolling wave hurtle towards you, but your feet are stuck to the ground? Or like you're being chased by a serial killer, some guy running at you with just a blow torch and a letter opener, and there are people everywhere who could help you, but you can't find your voice to scream?

STEPHANIE (*to* CHARLOTTE): Or like you've got to go to the bathroom—I mean, *it's an emergency*, right? And there's bathrooms on every street corner but no toilets, only sinks?

CHARLOTTE: YES!

THERAPIST: Wait. Girls. (*Clears the phlegm from her throat to buy some time.*) This is good. This is...all good. But, I was actually thinking more about the fact that you're both on the verge of making big moves with your families.

STEPHANIE: Oh!

THERAPIST (*to* STEPHANIE): Stephanie, Charlotte's husband's job is taking her family out to California. Charlotte, Stephanie's husband's job is taking her family all the way to Australia.

CHARLOTTE: Whoa!

THERAPIST: Yes, so you see there's a common-thread here.

STEPHANIE: Right? We both have jackholes for husbands!

CHARLOTTE: YES!

THERAPIST: Well…(*clears her throat again*)…now… Really I just thought you two might be able to, you know, support each other during this time. Especially since you'll no longer be under my care.

CHARLOTTE: Oh wow. So like, I could be her therapist?

THERAPIST: W-well I don't—

STEPHANIE: And I could be hers?

The girls crack up. THERAPIST *is second-guessing herself.*

THERAPIST (*laughs a very canned, operatic laugh*): Yes, yes girls, you'd both make *wonderful* psychiatrists! So spirited! But I was thinking more along the lines of…keeping each other company.

CHARLOTTE *and* STEPHANIE *size each other up.*

THERAPIST: It's just that, life is really throwing you both into the deep end right now. And, well, I thought it might help to have someone else along with you in "the lifeboat of life."

CHARLOTTE: Really? You're going with *lifeboat?*

THERAPIST: It's a good metaphor. You really need some help. You both do.

STEPHANIE: Like, to rub aloe on each other's sunburns?

CHARLOTTE: Yeah, or to pee on each other's jellyfish stings?

STEPHANIE: To lip sync duets into the flare gun-mic?

THERAPIST: Well, yes, to all of those things. But, also, you may need help rowing…

THE END/BEGINNING.

SCUBA DIVING

Charlotte

I HAVE NEVER UNDERSTOOD THE childlike draw to creatures like amphibians. I distrust almost anything that lacks at least some amount of fur. Not to mention (let's call a spade a spade) most amphibians look like prehistoric boogers that move; they dart around way too haphazardly for my taste.[3] *However*, there is something admittedly enviable about the amphibian. They are perfectly fluid in that they can live both on land and in water.

My earliest memories are in water: a bath or a pool or a lake or an ocean. In water I feel weightless, wild, otherworldly. The water quiets me, gives me space to think and breathe, and I've passed this blessed affinity on to my daughter.

When Margot was born, she (like Ford) suffered from acid reflux-induced colic. There were times in her first weeks and months when she would scream for hours on end, the type of scream that levitates every hair on your body, such that you would do anything short of petting an amphibian

---

3. If they aren't darting then they're *blending in*, which is equally as disturbing.

to make it stop. When she entered these horrible, inconsolable fits, in so much pain from the burn in her tiny esophagus, I learned of only one way to soothe her. I would strip us both bare, draw a warm bath, and lay her on my chest as the water enveloped us.[4] The sound of it drumming from the faucet made soft the lullaby I'd sing into her ears—"Tender Shepherd," my own mother's favorite. I'd drizzle the water on her back and with every passing second could feel both our breathing slow to calm. Sometimes she'd nurse. Other times she'd just let that otherworldly experience of a warm soak render her motionless and at peace. We'd stay like that until the water turned cool.

Margot, like her mother, has remained part fish ever since. Who knows, maybe it started in the womb. She jumps in every puddle, stays in her bath until I must forcibly remove her, and even at the age of one could splash around on the steps of a pool well past sunset.

I'm carrying this truth close to my chest as we look toward our coastal destiny. In Birmingham we are primarily terrestrial, landlocked on all sides. We are sealed by things like family, friends, and roots. At the same time, a principal element of the human experience—*separation*—leaves not one of us unscathed. Just walk into the lunchroom of any junior high school, pock-faced tweens frantic for the asylum of an open seat, and you'll remember what it's like to feel utterly other. Or just pick up and move across the continent, away from everyone and everything that makes home feel like home.

Who will I be in California if not *other*?

At least there will be water.

---

4. If you're freaking out about the safety of this beautiful ritual, Alex always chaperoned us from atop the closed toilet.

✽

WHEN I AM OVERWHELMED by these thoughts, deluged in both reasonable and unreasonable anxieties, my inner child usually blunders into the scene.

LIL C *is a chubby, unkempt fourth grader who almost exclusively wears stirrup leggings with an oversized flannel shirt. She slouches back on the kitchen stool with her dirty Keds propped up on the counter.* CHARLOTTE *wears her pre-baby designer jeans (which are noticeably too tight), paired with the same shirt she wore yesterday. She puts down the dish she's cleaning and the cool water settles her anxious breathing. She is resentful for having to do dishes at all, and also stuck in what her therapist calls "obsessive thoughts" about her future.*

CHARLOTTE: We're leaving in a week! I AM NOT READY FOR THIS.

LIL C (*casually licking a spoonful of peanut butter*): I don't know what you're so worked up about. It's not like you haven't done this before.

CHARLOTTE: It's different this time. We have kids! I'm comfortable here! And how disappointing is Christmas going to be with *palm trees* and *sunshine* all over the place?

LIL C: You have a point.

CHARLOTTE: How am I going to make friends? What if people don't "get" me on the West Coast?

LIL C *is scared about this too, but she plays it cool, always in pursuit of saving face.*

LIL C: Dude, you're going to be fine! You'll meet other

moms at the playground and the gym and stuff.

CHARLOTTE: It's not that easy anymore.

LIL C (*preoccupied, digging at the bottom of the peanut butter jar*): When you *do* meet someone, just make sure you start out strong. Like, tell them how to be a better mom or something.

CHARLOTTE: What? I don't do that, do I? That's awful. No.

LIL C (*moaning in frustration*): Uggghhh, but you seem so smart and worldly when you give advice!

CHARLOTTE: No, I just want to be *myself* out there.

LIL C (*sits up straighter*): Whoa whoa, hang on now! You're starting to worry me. You want to be *yourself? Please* just hear me out before you go and do something you'll regret.

CHARLOTTE (*a little offended*): O-kay…

LIL C: First of all, you've *got* to be funny. Like, *hilarious*. At all costs. People love it when you're funny! And definitely work your accent.

CHARLOTTE: What accent?

LIL C: Next, talk about how *cute* and well-behaved your children are, and how *perfect* your marriage is!

CHARLOTTE (*beginning to come around*): Yeah. I guess I could do that.

LIL C: And then you close the deal with your travels. Allll the places you've been.

CHARLOTTE: But doesn't that sound a little braggy?

LIL C: No, no, you're just painting a picture of who you are.

CHARLOTTE: You make it sound like a sales pitch.

LIL C: Well, isn't it kinda?

CHARLOTTE (*starting to panic*): I think I'm going to puke.

LIL C: You're being dramatic.

CHARLOTTE: It's just that, I'm exhausted. I feel like I've completely lost authority over the kids. My underwear doesn't fit me anymore. Alex is never going to leave work once he starts this new job. And I'm just having a really hard time envisioning how all of *this* (*she gestures to herself*) is going to translate in California.

LIL C (*bored, makes a fart noise into her palm*): Come on, I hate it when you whine.

CHARLOTTE *sighs.*

LIL C: Okay, *this* (*she motions up and down to* CHARLOTTE) is only going to leave you all alone. Get control of yourself! Turn on that thing, what do you call it? Charm? Put on a smile, suck in your stomach, and go make us sparkle! I mean, you know, make us proud, make us some friends.

CHARLOTTE: You sound like our mom.

LIL C: Just...slow down when you talk, okay? You come off all sweaty and nervous when you talk fast.

CHARLOTTE *nods knowingly.*

LIL C: And *don't* talk about anything like your recurring rashes, *okay?*

When she's confident she's made her point, LIL C *loafs outside to see if she can catch the ice cream truck for a late afternoon Bomb Pop.*

CHARLOTTE *is left to ponder their conversation.*

GROWING UP, I always felt on the outside of something. I was not into things like cheerleading, or dolls, or the President's Physical Fitness test, or "fitting in" the way I thought I should. That perception of otherness even applied to Christianity, especially as I got older. Every Christian I knew looked like a walking Gap ad—perfect clothes, perfect life—the type of people who always seemed happy, the type of people who showered at least every other day. They had their junk together. I, on the other hand, struggled with an often debilitating depression and liked beer and cigarettes way too much to get in on that hoo-ha. I'm nearly four years' nicotine-free, and just writing that sentence makes me salivate a little.

Then I became a Christian—not because I realized right away that *they* actually didn't have it all together (which they didn't), but because it occurred to me that if *I* even had a shot at getting it together, then I couldn't do it on my own. I had all the strength of a corpse. I needed a God. Of course, now I realize that "having it all together" is an expectation of the human, not the divine. It wasn't the most cerebral thought process behind a conversion (and, as you might guess, the story is more complex than the last few sentences imply). It wasn't the whole tidy Gospel-package. But it was pretty close. It involved a profound understanding that I was not enough and a deep, even poetic longing for something more to intervene.

Prior to that conversion, even when I "didn't believe" God was out there, or "right for me," he would nag in the back of my mind—like the ex in Adele's "Hello," the shadow of someone you suspect you shouldn't have said goodbye to, the phantom of a person who could actually be *for you*. He seemed to pop up at the most inconvenient moments as if to say, "*HELLO*, what if you're wrong about me?"

Even after I started to identify as a Christian, I sometimes felt on the outside—not Christian-y enough. Hell, I still have those moments all the time. I swear too much, eat too much, think too highly of myself, don't get to church enough, or read my Bible as much as I should (and on and on and on); all at once too much and not enough.

I think a lot of people assume that after you become a Christian you get better, easier, lighter; once you become a Christian, you're on a Jesus high that never ends, footprints in the sand and whatnot.

Not always so.

Scenes from my life flash through my mind like a movie montage: crying about having no friends in my sixth grade home room—watching as the boy I liked held hands with my best friend—slamming the door on my mom, desperately wishing I could take it back, that she'd open it anyway—gazing out the window of my boarding school dorm room sophomore year, dreaming I had a boyfriend or the right friends or anything at all in common with these northern strangers—hugging the edge of my bed in anger, facing away from my husband, wondering who would budge first and apologize—being led not toward but far far *away* from my southern sanctuary, with a husband and two toddlers in tow no less. Scenes from the outside.

SEVERAL YEARS AGO Tim Keller wrote on social media, "The founders of every major religion said, 'I'll show you how to find God.' Jesus said, '*I am God who has come to find you.*'"

Our Immanuel. Our God with us. "Who shall separate us from the love of Christ?" Not funky brain chemistry or a life plan gone Hindenburg. And yet, this banishment to the Golden State still feels like a question mark. How will we breathe when we are underwater?

A FEW WEEKS AGO, Margot saw a scuba diver for the first time at the local aquarium. Since then, she has not stopped talking about the "Gooba Diber." Here was a person who had the ability, so to speak, to exist in two places at once: land and water. A human amphibian, the ultimate chameleon.

In California, we will deep dive whether we're ready to or not. There will be land. There will be water. We will be *there* and not *here*, and yet expected to move in and out of these two places with a certain amount of grace and ease. To do so, we will require things like external oxygen and a slick protective suit in order to survive in this space of the in-between, a space that might otherwise bring us death.[5]

There's good news on this front.

On Good Friday, Jesus—THE scuba diver[6]—died on a cross. The earth shook and the curtain of the temple was torn apart from top to bottom. This means—*apparently*—that no matter what we do or don't do, no matter where we go or how low we fall, we'll always have this improbable air to breathe.

Outside/Inside, Both/And, Water/Land. This is an amphibious life, but not one I've wanted or asked for.

Although I've likely just blown you away with this highly insightful metaphor, I am terrified of what lies ahead, of

5. Not *literal* death. You get the point.
6. Go with me here.

who I will be out there. Too much. Not enough. A prehistoric booger that moves, who has *perfect children*, the *sexiest marriage*, and has *traveled the world over*. My mask is fogged and I'm sure I have the bends.[7]

How will we survive? Inhale/Exhale, Inhale/Exhale.

I guess I'm taking God at his word—for now—this God with us.

---

7. Decompression sickness.

MOTHER (AND CHILD)
OF AN ADVENT

Stephanie

IT'S DECEMBER, 2016. My favorite time of year is approaching and with it, the reality that this will be our family's last Christmas as US residents…for a while, at least. I feel like we're teetering near the edge, like there's a huge precipice within steps of this holy holiday. But I'm trying to take comfort in the fact that it's not the first Christmas that has brought huge changes with it. After all, five years ago I was waiting not just for Christmas but for the birth of my first son. And about two thousand years before *that* momentous occasion was another one: different baby boy, different mother.

But *was* it that different?[8] Childbirth is an experience that is universally life-changing, disruptive, painful[9], and somehow also beautiful, along with bringing a drastic change in identity: the death, of sorts, to the children we were before

8. Of course it was. But stay with me.
9. Unless you deliver in a pool and document it to Instagram, of course. Then it's just #blessed.

our own children came along. I think about Mary, by all accounts around age fourteen when Jesus was born, and compare her stunted childhood to my extended one. I gave birth twenty years later than she would have, at age thirty-four. In those intervening years, I had the chance to make huge mistakes, chalk up regrets, set a course and watch it disintegrate into what actually happened—you know, *life*. Life mixed in with lots of therapy. Mary was a child herself when Jesus was born. Did this make her more intimidated, or less—was ignorance bliss, or was it complicated for her too?

Take the journey to Bethlehem. At fourteen I was still sitting in the backseat of my parents' boxy white Volvo, a.k.a. The Marshmallow, whining "Are we there yet?" while fighting with my sister and interpreting my dad's impatience as a lack of love. I'm guessing Mary didn't take a lot of road trips. And becoming a mother as a young teen doesn't leave a lot of time for therapy, or delving into deep-seated feelings from atop a donkey on a dirt road. *Or does it?*

I used to love how the carol "Silent Night" captured my image of the Advent season: peaceful, expectant, hopeful. Then I became an adult, and a parent, and Christmastime became anything but serene. I found myself singing words like "all is calm, all is bright" while looking around at other faces, wondering, "Does anyone actually believe this nonsense?" When God saw fit to give me my own swaddled baby boy—then another—I related to Mary more than ever and felt that someone must speak up for her, because if I know anything about Christmas with a newborn (and I do; my kids were two weeks and two months old, respectively, at their first Christmases), it is anything *but* calm and bright, and heavenly peace is a vanishing vapor.

I bet Mary second-guessed herself and her ability to, you

know, raise the son of GOD and all. I bet she was sweaty on Christmas night. I know *I* am this year, and not just from the Santa panic. Hello... WE ARE MOVING ACROSS THE WORLD. We're being evacuated from our comfortable life and sent packing. I mean, I know it's not the same as becoming the vessel through which our Lord and savior forever and ever amen enters the world, but still. *Stress.*

Being evacuated from a familiar home into a new place is a fitting metaphor for motherhood: the dawn of a new era, the end of one chapter and the beginning of another. It's funny, though, the things that persist from the old era, the former chapter. I remember my surprise when Therapist mentioned the concept of the Inner Child to me—that, much like an appendix, a vestigial remnant of my child self remained embedded within me and, like an appendix, it was only noticeable when it hurt. That this Inner Child could be interfering with my decision-making, my emotions, my parenting. That she could even be calling the shots a lot of the time!

So what was I going to do about this brat who didn't even know how to fold laundry but could totally screw with my mental health?

Well, according to Therapist, I could—and should—listen to her. And talk back. So, leading up to our move, that's what I decided to do.

STEPHANIE: (*rifles through suitcases, throwing out clothes and folding them again, frantic*): Where is that stupid sweater? Do I even need it? Do they even call them sweaters in Sydney? I NEED A XANAX!

LIL STEPH, STEPHANIE's *inner child, emerges from behind*

STEPHANIE *and stares up at her.* LIL STEPH *is about seven years old. She wears pigtails, a smocked dress, and white Mary Janes.*

LIL STEPH: Are you mad at me?

STEPHANIE (*sighs deeply; upon remembering to breathe, tries to convert the sighing to breathing deeply*): Oh God. No. I'm not mad at you, sweetie. Remember how I told you that just because someone uses a harsh or irritated tone in your presence doesn't mean it's about you? It may just be whatever they're dealing with at the moment.

LIL STEPH: You seem scared. Now I'm scared. Why do we have to move?

STEPHANIE: Because…I'm married now. And because it's for our own good. We're being…stretched. We could make some new friends! Or…(*under her breath*) *this could all go horribly wrong and lead to gastric distress and abject humiliation.*

LIL STEPH: What did you say?!

STEPHANIE: Nothing, dear. NEW FRIENDS! New experiences! See, sometimes you have to do hard things because of the good they could lead to. Sometimes you have to choose to pursue joy instead of just avoiding fear. Sometimes you have to take a risk—

LIL STEPH: Did you get that from Oprah?

STEPHANIE: Oh no honey, she's been off the air for years. I think I read it in a mom blog. Like I was saying, sometimes the road is dark until you take the first step, and it's always darkest before the dawn, and without pain there's no new life—

LIL STEPH: I'm scared again. (*Begins to whimper.*)

STEPHANIE (*rolls her eyes while turned away from* LIL STEPH): It's going to be fine. FINE! Either way, whether we love Sydney or not, we'll come out the other side… alive. Yes, let's make that the standard: WE WILL LIVE. Okay let's do some mindfulness exercises to center us in the present! We'll wash our hands and feel the warm water spraying over them or something.

LIL STEPH: I WANT TO STAY HERE! (*Begins stamping her feet on the ground while crossing her arms tightly over her chest.*) I DON'T WANT TO LEAVE AND I'M TIRED OF YOU BRINGING ME TO PLACES I DON'T LIKE! I WANT TO STAY HOME AND READ MY BOOKS AND JUST BE ALONE!

STEPHANIE (*sighs deeply again; begins to feel like she might hurl*): Look, *dear heart*, I can't let you run the show all the time. You've made me scream at my kids, like, twice this week already just because I was minorly embarrassed in public over little things they did that made *you* feel small. So you're going to have to roll with this one. We have to step out of our comfort zones now and then. So please, for the love of God, *put a lid on it.*

LIL STEPH (*under her breath, out of* STEPHANIE*'s earshot*): I'm not going to put a lid on it. I'm going to do whatever it takes to make this move unsuccessful so we can *come back here.*

STEPHANIE, *meanwhile, continues to frantically unfold and refold laundry, wondering why she can't just calm down and* be present.

FEARFUL LIL STEPH IS COMING with us on this trip. So is rebellious Teenage Steph, and bad-decisions-Twenties Steph, and Anxious Mom Steph. (Self-awareness leads to *so* much more packing.) When we start this next chapter, I'll be bringing my history: every precipice over which I've stood, every corner I've turned. The evacuations that have piled up over the years: my children from me, my own plan for a new story. Which, I know from experience, is life—not a placid float down a lazy river but, more often, a turbulent ride to new locales. Via hospitals, planes, donkeys, boats. Uncertainty becoming familiarity, goodbyes becoming hellos, death becoming life.

Can I remember this as we step forward? Or is it a lesson I'm doomed to keep repeating, learning over and over? Doomed, or blessed (no hashtag)? My clothes land next to my sons' in the suitcase and I zip it, barely believing that the next time I open it we will be on Australian soil. Whether I believe it or not, whether I'm ready or not, new life is happening. We will be ejected from our old home into a new one.

And SCENE. For now.

RECOVERED TRANSCRIPTS FROM LIFEBOAT 815

EXTERIOR: NIGHT—SOMEWHERE IN THE PACIFIC.

The PHILLIPSES *and the* GETZES *are aboard a smoothly sailing ship—something like a spring break party cruise. With little warning, the oversized ship begins to sink. Sirens blare and ship employees dash around, frantically herding passengers toward the lifeboats. This is not a drill.*

STEPHANIE: What's going on??

CHARLOTTE: No idea. Doesn't really feel like the right temp for icebergs.

STEPHANIE: I was totally just thinking the same thing!

CHARLOTTE: So do you want to head straight for the lifeboat or—

STEPHANIE: *Pillage.*

CHARLOTTE: YASSS!

The women run down the hallways of Deck 4 and begin throwing open whatever cabin doors are unlocked. They scour the place for necessities they might need on their own lifeboat.

STEPHANIE: WAIT! Where are the kids??

CHARLOTTE: They're en route to the Lido with Jason and Alex.

STEPHANIE: Will they be allowed on the lifeboat without us??

CHARLOTTE: THIS ISN'T *THE TITANIC*, STEPH!

STEPHANIE: Right.

STEPHANIE *stuffs things like Twizzlers and mini-cans of Pringles into her purse.*

CHARLOTTE (*tossing some condoms and tampons into a spare pillowcase*): What are we even going to need out there??

STEPHANIE: I'm not exactly sure, but I feel like you've missed the ball a bit with the contraception.

CHARLOTTE: Toilet paper?

STEPHANIE: Dammit, we have to grab stuff for the kids and Jason and Alex too, don't we?

CHARLOTTE: You KNOW they didn't do it themselves.

STEPHANIE: Screw it, Jason's not getting any underwear. But I do need child-sized toothbrushes for the boys...

CHARLOTTE (*sarcastic*): Oops, I "forgot" Alex's contact solution.

They move into another cabin and ransack the place like convicts on the lam.

CHARLOTTE (*cont'd*): Oh, look at this pink jumper! This

would be great for Margot if she didn't prefer Ford's clothes.

STEPHANIE: What about this atlas?

CHARLOTTE: Too heavy. Hard pass.

STEPHANIE (*walking over to a desk*): Seriously, who brings a typewriter on a cruise?

She dings a few of the keys.

CHARLOTTE: PACK THAT!

STEPHANIE: Really, dude?

CHARLOTTE (*shrugging*): You never know.

STEPHANIE: Fine. Then we're bringing the atlas too.

The women continue through the hallway, grabbing anything and everything until their arms are overflowing.

STEPHANIE (*lugging the typewriter and all manner of spoils*): My arms are already tired.

CHARLOTTE: I feel like a pack mule. *There's* something that's not new AT ALL. Hello, *motherhood.*

STEPHANIE: Tell me about it. I almost had to choose between sunscreen for the kids and my antidepressants a second ago.

CHARLOTTE: How'd you make room?

STEPHANIE *turns to* CHARLOTTE, *her blister-pack of meds shoved between her teeth, and raises her eyebrows, muttering "SEE?" around the meds.*

CHARLOTTE: Ooh, good idea.

CHARLOTTE *starts tearing open packages of cashews and pretzels and stuffing the contents into her mouth for safe storage.* STEPHANIE *grabs another handful of Combos and tries to work them around her meds.*

CHARLOTTE (*muffled from all the snack food*): Head to the lifeboats?

STEPHANIE, *in a similar predicament, nods in agreement.*

The women arrive at the Lido deck and quickly spot their families, who are huddled near a lifeboat. Screams of "MOMMY!" and "I have to pee!" are coming from the children while Alex and Jason are engaged in a conversation about football. CHARLOTTE *and* STEPHANIE *hand off their luggage and loot to the men, who toss it aboard the boat. Next, they help the women aboard, then hand the kids off one at a time.* CHARLOTTE *and* STEPHANIE *settle each child into his or her own spot with a snack and an iPad. The men climb aboard next, and soon the boat is lowered into the water alongside many others.*

CHARLOTTE: So...anyone know where we're going?

THE SERMON WE'RE PREACHING TO OURSELVES (AND YOU)

IT'S ONLY BEEN AN HOUR or so, but we've been thinking *a lot* in those 60 long minutes. With no other outlet on board (our kids glaze over whenever we start talking poetically about "the journey"), we thought we'd pen some words that might give us comfort along the way.

Atlanta to Sydney. Alabama to Los Angeles. Depending on the size of the map you're studying, these pairings can be inches (centimetres) or feet (metres) apart. In any event, on any map, these locations are what cartographers would call "not even close, dude."[10] Which brings us to a question we've uttered countless times before in our all-over-the-map existences:

What is the deal, God?

Let's be honest: we're not super fond of reading maps (we are, after all, women; we can just stop and ask for directions). Lists are more our thing, and we have run our lives hinging on them: to-do lists, goal lists, resumes, lists of resolutions; you name it, we've had a list for it. But where a list won't suffice, a map is a handy addendum because they both

---

10. No actual cartographers were consulted to obtain this quote.

serve the same purpose: they put us in the driver's seat and preserve our illusion of control. *We know where we're headed.* And as long as that's true, we can maintain a level of calm and peace.

Right? Oh wait…WRONG.

We're convinced that the effort we've spent keeping our lists together, and our maps secure—even when they were tattered and in pieces—is much of what has left us so anxious in the first place. That, and some chemical imbalances, and some inborn genetic predispositions. It's complicated, you know? But we have a confession: we're starting to suspect that we have been listening to what might be lies about God, lies that tell us his primary agenda is disaster and rudeness. We want to believe his agenda is actually one of *rescue*, but the whole out-to-sea ordeal could make a person wonder…

We wake up in the morning to the delightful coos (or high pitched, nasally, and ungrateful gripes) of our children, and sometimes it feels like a personal injustice that the poop in kid #2's diaper will only disappear if *we* wipe that precious tush. *God* filled that diaper. Just like he signed off on the throw-up bug last week and the flat tire before that and, oh yeah, paved a way not homeward but way way *way* westward.

Instead of this way forward seeming like a yellow brick road leading toward some emerald city, it looks a lot more like the green mile towards our certain and deserved deaths.

We think the poor, sweet Israelites knew a little something about this. God delivered them from Egypt (yay), and instead of taking them directly to Canaan (which some people think would have taken a week), God took them the long way. He led them right to the edge of a body of water—all so he could part it for them.

And then they jaunted around in the desert for 40 years, making their long and labored way toward and away from, sometimes near, other times far, and finally to their Promised Land.

When we first read about the Israelites and their lack of basic directional sensibility, we honestly felt a little sad for them—like the same way we'd feel sad for the type of person who'd walk head first into the same glass door two times in a row (not us). They doubt, they make their own way, they get it wrong; they stop, shiver, shake, fail, and then they move forward again. Looking at it like that, maybe they aren't such sorry bozos after all.

You might be asking yourselves why the 40 years instead of the week? We're asking ourselves the same question.

A.W. Tozer said, "To the child of God, there is no such thing as an accident. He travels an appointed way... Accidents may indeed appear to befall him and misfortune stalk his way; but these evils will be so in appearance only and will seem evils only because we cannot read the secret script of God's hidden providence." Dear Lord, please let this be true.

Westward-ho.

PART TWO

HOW TO
ROCK CAPTIVITY

RECOVERED TRANSCRIPTS
FROM LIFEBOAT 815

EXTERIOR: LATE, LATE AT NIGHT—SOMEWHERE IN THE PACIFIC.

The GETZES *and the* PHILLIPSES *have officially launched their boat from the sinking mothership. They are out to sea.* CHARLOTTE *and* STEPHANIE *look to* ALEX *and* JASON *for direction.*

STEPHANIE: So, where to?

JASON (*takes a minute to assess*): The closest land is probably that way.

There are boats all around, but not one of them seems to have a clear direction.

ALEX: Might as well give it a shot?

CHARLOTTE: Here's an idea, babe—maybe we *look at a map* before we up and go rogue?

ALEX *and* JASON *both shrug and then resume talking about football.*

CHARLOTTE (*under her breath, eyes cutting to* STEPHANIE): *Seriously?!*

STEPHANIE *rolls her eyes. She pulls the atlas from their stash of supplies.*

STEPHANIE: Pretty handy, right?

CHARLOTTE: But we don't even really know where we are *right now...*

The women open the book anyway and expertly go about trying to ascertain their exact whereabouts.

STEPHANIE: I have no effing clue.

CHARLOTTE (*looking around*): Literally, all I see is darkness and water.

STEPHANIE: Maybe the guys were right?

CHARLOTTE: I mean, we can't just sit here...

STEPHANIE *grabs a paddle and hands the other to* CHARLOTTE.

STEPHANIE: I could swear the ship was heading that way (*she points to her right*), but it looks like everyone else is headed in the other direction.

CHARLOTTE: I mean, look at who's paddling for most of them...

They both glance around and see men holding oars on the majority of the boats.

CHARLOTTE *and* STEPHANIE *nod to each other knowingly. They turn the boat around.*

STEPHANIE: We've got this.

CHARLOTTE: We've *so* got this.

STEPHANIE: I feel better already.

CHARLOTTE: It'll be like a vacation!

STEPHANIE: Some quality time with the fam, a few rays, maybe a good book or two...

CHARLOTTE: And you can't beat the seafood!

STEPHANIE *winces.*

CHARLOTTE (*cont'd*): What?

STEPHANIE: Jason and I hate seafood.

CHARLOTTE*'s eyes widen.*

CHARLOTTE: What about, like, fried calamari??

STEPHANIE: Do you realise that most calamari in America is actually pig's anus?

CHARLOTTE: Stop.

STEPHANIE: It's true.

CHARLOTTE: Why would you say something like that?

STEPHANIE: I'm telling you, I read it somewhere.

CHARLOTTE: No.

STEPHANIE: Look it up. Anyway, the Phillipses will prevail, sans pig anus, calamari, or any other aquatic cuisine.

CHARLOTTE: Dude, I'm concerned. The Combos are only going to get you guys so far...

STEPHANIE: Why *didn't* we aim for more nutritious foods in The Great Pillage?

CHARLOTTE: Heat of the moment, man.

STEPHANIE: I already miss that soft-serve ice cream machine from the ship.

CHARLOTTE: Because soft-serve is nutritious? Get your head out of your ass, Stephanie.

STEPHANIE (*ashamed*): I know.

CHARLOTTE: We should have raided the liquor too. *What were we thinking?*

STEPHANIE: Huge oversight.

CHARLOTTE: We could *literally* have made a swim-up bar and cashed in on this disaster.

Flies start to swarm around the boat.

STEPHANIE (*swats angrily, almost dropping her oar*): There are flies ON THE OCEAN?

The sun begins to peak over the horizon.

CHARLOTTE (*squinting*): I feel like an umbrella would be useful right about now.

Both women look around with expressions of disgust and uncertainty. They continue to row nonetheless.

STEPHANIE: What exactly did we pack that *will* be useful?

CHARLOTTE: Tampons?

They fist bump, as FORD saunters in their direction.

FORD: Mamma. Mamma. Mamma. Mamma.

CHARLOTTE: Sweetie, Mamma is a little busy right now. What is it?

FORD: Ummm uhhhh uuhhhhh ummmm.

CHARLOTTE: Ford?

FORD: Uhhhhh. How many more minutes are we going to be on this boat?

CHARLOTTE: I really don't know, honey. It might be a while.

FORD: How many minutes?

CHARLOTTE: I have no idea, baby.

FORD: Five?

CHARLOTTE: No, probably a lot longer than that.

FORD: Four?

CHARLOTTE: Well—

FORD: HOW MANY MINUTES?!

WILL: Mommy, James HIT ME.

MARGOT (*crying and wagging her arms up to* CHARLOTTE, *who is still trying to row*): Mamma I need you! I need you!

STEPHANIE: Will, go talk to your daddy. Mommy's working, okay? *JASON?*

JASON *and* ALEX *have their heads together, working out some elaborate star chart, although it is now fully morning.*

JASON: Hang on, I think we're onto something!

MARGOT: I need you! I need you! I need you!

WILL: MOMMY!!!!!

The women exchange desperate glances. They put down their paddles and tend to their little ones.

STEPHANIE: Dude, we need to get ourselves out of this predicament like now.

CHARLOTTE (*starting to hyperventilate*): I can't (*strained breath*) breathe.

STEPHANIE: Eeeaaasy girl. Head between your knees. There you go (*gently rubbing her back*).

CHARLOTTE (*bent over*): Was this boat always so tiny?

STEPHANIE: Seemed like a yacht an hour ago.

CHARLOTTE: THIS IS A DINGHY, STEPH!

STEPHANIE: At least we'll be sunkissed?

CHARLOTTE: And eaten alive by these flies.

STEPHANIE: Oh God, *is that possible?*

CHARLOTTE: Probably.

STEPHANIE: NO.

She looks around the boat, pushing their supplies aside.

STEPHANIE (*cont'd*): You'd think a boat like this might come stocked with some essentials. Like bug spray, for instance.

CHARLOTTE (*muffled*): And *wine*.

CHARLOTTE (*cont'd*) (*with her head still between her knees*): Hey. HEY! I think I found something!

STEPHANIE: What is it?

CHARLOTTE (*grasping a box in her hands*): Looks like some supplies! It was shoved in my corner over here.

She places the box between them and they open it together.

STEPHANIE: Is that what I think it is?

CHARLOTTE: Oh sweet Savior it's red wine...and in the back here—bread!

STEPHANIE: What's that label on the bread package say?

CHARLOTTE: It says it's divided into rations of one day each. Ugh, what good is that when we feel like carbo-loading?

STEPHANIE: Looks like the wine doesn't have instructions. Maybe that's to use at our discretion? Oh thank God! WE GOT PROVISIONS NOW, Y'ALL!

CHARLOTTE (*nudging Steph, whispers*): Let's just keep the wine between us. We can be in charge of distributing, you know?

STEPHANIE: Good idea. I bet there's more where that came from!

They pick up their oars and begin to row again.

STEPHANIE: What do you think? This way? (*She nods to her left.*)

CHARLOTTE: Why not?

TRAPPED IN ELEVATORS AND EXPECTATIONS

Stephanie

LONG BEFORE I EVEN MET my husband, a friend with a young son told me about a clock she kept in his room that told the time in red when it was too early to get out of bed; the numbers transitioned to green when he was allowed to leave his room in the morning. *What a great idea!* I thought, adding this product to my growing list of Parental Hacks. Cut to my bed every single morning, with a six-year-old planted firmly atop the comforter. *He's* the clock. And his and his brother's diets, despite the all organic, sugar-free food I envisioned? Wretched. The other night I actually uttered, "Eat more of your bread and you can have a cookie." All the "pleases" and "thank yous" I planned for my son to master before age two were hurled to the backburner when he didn't speak until age four, as were so many other comparably minor considerations when he endured spinal surgery and faced innumerable challenges afterward.

And me? I would have parented *so confidently* were it not

for this desecration of my expectations. So confidently, efficiently, and awfully.

When your kid is born almost a month early, gets surgery at 1 and 2 and a spectrum diagnosis at 3 and has no words until 4, your expectations take a flying leap. And for this, my younger son gives thanks. *As do I.* The Mother I Would Have Been has died a slow death, and with her all the fear-motivated, law-abiding gracelessness that would have characterized her relationship with her children.

The Mother I Would Have Been did not have the grace to see how complicated parenthood, and people, actually are. The Mother I Would Have Been would have been too busy trying to conform her children to a perfect image to see them as messy individuals like herself. The Mother I Would Have Been exhausts me and saddens me…and occasionally makes guilt-inducing visits via her ghost.

Let me take you back to summer 2016, right before I got the email from Jason about Australia being back in play. The last time I felt trapped in a small place and suspended in time and space: in an unventilated elevator with a four-year-old in the hundred-degree heat.

It is July in the South, and all I can think about is how pissed I am at PETA. Heat, claustrophobia, irrational anger: a perfect snapshot of motherhood for me. The elevator in question is the one my son, the four-year-old in question, has glommed onto like a new best friend, begging to ride about every fifteen minutes at the condo where my parents live and where we are "vacationing." Although I think we all know that when kids are along for the ride, there's no such thing as *vacation* as much as there is *relocation of our typical lives to another venue.* "Trapped" may also be a misnomer, as this hotbox is functioning, but it certainly feels like a prison when there is a beach nearby and I'm not on it, sipping a frozen alcoholic beverage. Which brings me to my beef with PETA, a tenuous argument at best, but in this moment my anger feels profoundly justified: why are they so concerned with the mistreatment of wild animals when all around them, human beings (mothers) are trapped and caged and *no one does a damn thing about it?*

It's possible that the lack of ventilation is affecting my sanity. It's also possible that motherhood is.

While this stainless steel contraption hurtles me up five floors and back down again and my son grins in rapt wonder at the red digital numbers, I have a moment to think. I consider my healthy, happy young boys who love nothing more than a good elevator ride, a carb-laden meal, a long nightly cuddle, and a seat in front of the toilet while I pee. They ask for so much and so little at the same time. They drive me mad and keep my heart beating. I asked for them, and they were granted, and our relationship, unbeknownst to them, is unendingly fraught.

Or maybe, like *vacation* and *trapped* and all the other misapprehensions I've garnered since becoming a parent, I've called this one wrong, too. Maybe it's my relationship with *myself* that's hit a rough patch the size of Australia.[1]

While the elevator keeps moving and the sweat drips down various crevices and PETA remains annoyingly unconcerned with my plight, I pause for spasms of thought between spurts of emotion. Images from my life appear in my mind like a themed Instagram feed: #priorcaptivity. The shot of myself as a kid surrounded by books instead of friends. The shot of myself in Alabama year after year despite trying

---

1. See, 10th grade English teacher? I *do* understand dramatic irony! I think…

to escape out-of-state for higher learning. Then there was the freedom that finally arrived when I fled in a U-Haul to New York out of desperation. "The bravest thing I've ever done was to run away and hide," sang the Barenaked Ladies from the U-Haul as I drove.[2] A final shot: Jason proposing on his roof. #freedom?

Within the span of a year, my beloved and I went from being single in New York to being married expectant parents in Atlanta (*expectant* being a word with layers of meaning). Marriage seemed easy until our son arrived, bringing with him sleepless nights and power-brokering over child-care responsibilities. Within weeks of his birth, I found myself sitting on the couch sobbing for reasons I couldn't articulate as an infant slept in my arms (it was daytime, so of course he was sleeping) and my husband sat a few feet away, wondering what happened to the carefree woman he'd met in New York.

I wondered too.

I began wondering a lot of things: whether I was the same person I'd always been or had fundamentally and irrevocably changed. Whether I liked the changes that had occurred. Whether I had the emotional resilience to parent a child in such a scary world—a world where I could often be part of the scariness. Whether this was motherhood or torture. Whether our marriage would survive. I think, deep down, I knew the answers to all these questions, but I didn't like how close those answers were to an edge that I now felt perilously close to, a matter of inches separating me from the person I'd always told myself I was and the person I was turning out to be.

2. That's not true—I heard that song later and inserted it into my life's soundtrack. Carry on.

Which brings me back to the elevator, where PETA has not shown up and I am still "trapped." But help never, after all, shows up in the way we expect, or even ask for…does it?

The doors open and light floods in. My son tosses a grin back at me and runs out into the open-air hallway, assuming I will follow him. Because I am his mother, I do. He stops at the railing a few feet away, where a breeze ruffles his hair, then mine. He stares ahead, and I see the ocean twinkling a half-mile away in the midday sun. He looks back at me, smiles, and says, "Water." He was not speaking a word nine months ago. I grin back at him, nod, and repeat. "Water. Ocean," I add. "Ocean," he echoes, turning back to the water with that expression of wonder that only kids can pull off. I have forgotten, in this moment, the heat and the sweat and the absent ventilation and the way PETA won't take my calls. Instead, I'm now captivated by this view that I never would have taken in had my child not led me to it. A view I never expected.

The next day, my husband and I will drive to spend a night in a hotel on the beach while the kids stay with my parents. I will be in that ocean, feeling the waves roll over me and realizing that freedom from my children only transfers me into concern for their safety and a longing to be with them again. I will know that either I will never be truly free, or that freedom must have a different definition now.

Love has an annoying way of redefining both freedom and captivity, of placing boundaries that first seem constraining but, with more time and deeper examination, may actually be escape hatches to a different way of living. My choices in life haven't done such a good job of setting me "free"—not according to what I thought freedom meant. Then again, maybe I'm not such a wild and roving creature as I thought. Maybe this identity "crisis" is self-discovery. Maybe, in these elevators and with this family, I am finally home…and being freed from expectations.

Little do I know that within days, I will hear about the possibility of Australia, and all of these musings will be re-shuffled and scattered along with the boundary lines of our existence. Once again I will feel stuck in transition, wondering where—and *how*—I will end up. And I will learn that I am, indeed, less wild and roving than I thought—but that the winds of grace scattering those boundary lines are de-cidedly not.

the getz family

cross country move

Los Angeles

THERE'D BE DAYS LIKE
THIS, MAMMA SAID

Charlotte

As of two days ago, we have officially relocated. We took off in 100-degree humidity, and landed in 75-degree paradise. The minutiae of preparing our family of four to get from Point A to Point B in this cross-continental transition was overwhelming to say the least. How could we choose a preschool for our children when we were 3,000 miles away? How could we convince the shrewd California landlords to let us rent their houses when we could not be there in person to show them how approachably charming we were? What about a church? Or a babysitter? We worked our skin to the bone trying to set up these things in advance, but as our move date neared one thing became remarkably clear: a move like this, in our current phase of life, was a lot like having your very first newborn. You could prep all you wanted, but no amount of pre-purchased nipple shields could actually prepare you for the predatory jaws of a newborn.[3]

The sum total of my mother's early education to me

3. Newborns are terrifying.

about child-rearing was, "You'll figure it out when the baby gets here!" And so we must similarly plant ourselves in southern California—not in advance, but in real time. I only hope that I'll adapt to the west quicker than I have taken to motherhood.

Ford is now three, and Margot is one-and-a-half. They're here. The both of them. *All the time.* They never leave. And damn if they don't constantly need something from me. Three years I've been a mother and whatever "it" my mom referred to in the beginning has yet to be "figured out." I think it takes more than arrival for things to fully make sense.

LAST SUNDAY, we made it to church.[4] It was our last service in Alabama.

On the way home, Ford began to sing a song he'd evidently learned in Sunday School that morning: "And the rains came down and the floods came up." He sang it over and over. Only problem? He couldn't remember any more of the lyrics than those. At first it was cute, because what mother's heart doesn't turn into a pile of pink Silly Putty when their children first start to at least *sing* about Jesus? However, after about five minutes of "The rains came down and the floods came up, and the rains came down and the floods came up," the car suddenly felt very small, like a hot tiny box. I began to sweat behind my knees and beneath my bra and so rolled down the window for some air. Ford's refrain began to feel freakishly like the soundtrack to both my life as a mother, and also my life as a mother who was about to haul her kids into the wilderness[5]: The rains-a-comin'

---

4. These days, a miracle on the level of Lazarus.

5. Blame Alex, not me.

down and the waters quick-to-rising. Your move, Lord Jesus. Help.

Motherhood (not unlike moving to a strange new place)—after all of the snuggles and kisses and wide-eyed curiosity—really does sometimes feel like being padlocked inside a hot tiny box, which is something I'm familiar with...

Growing up, Hide and Seek was a family staple. If all else failed in afternoon entertainment, there was ever the prospect of wedging oneself into an impossible space and waiting to be found. My brother, Bruce, frequently bore the brunt of being chosen as the first "Seeker."

On one such occasion—I was eleven and Bruce was seven—I was looking to entertain my friend, Virginia, and Hide and Seek seemed like the most appealing option. Bully for us, the game required more than two willing participants in order to yield any amount of fun. Bruce was the only available third that afternoon but, when propositioned with the venerated privilege of starting as Seeker, he fell into one of his pitiful moods and refused to play.

"I'll be the Seeker," Virginia offered sweetly.

"No! It must be Bruce..."

As his older, more cunning sister, I suspected that the easiest way to change his mind was to hide anyway and wait for curiosity to get the best of him. "Why did everything get so quiet?" he'd suddenly wonder while robotically collecting sticks by himself in the driveway. "Where did everyone go?" he'd ask himself. Fear of abandonment—a fear I'd long been planting in his mind with suggestions like "maybe you were adopted"—would begin to take root. "If I don't find them, who will?" Hook—line—sinker.

Virginia was skeptical that he'd go for it.

Sure that this tactic would work, I decided to hide in

my camp trunk, a navy blue box only barely large enough for me to curl into a sideways ball and squeeze in. I hugged my knees tightly to my chest, took in one last big breath for good measure, and closed the lid. "Lock it! Lock it!" I whispered feverishly (nearly mad-scientist-cackled) to Virginia. So she did exactly that and then found a hiding place for herself in a nearby nook.

And we waited for curiosity to best Bruce.

It's important to mention now that my trunk, with camp still several weeks away, resided in our unventilated attic. It's also important to mention that it was currently mid-June in Alabama with a record-breaking heat index. Finally, I should tell you that Virginia did not go to camp herself, and so had little experience with trunks (much less securing a smallish child into one). So when I told her to "lock it," that's what she did. What I meant (and anyone who's ever been to camp would know this) was to *latch* it. There's a difference.

The difference being that to unlock a latch, one merely needs to flip it.

Duh.

To unlock a lock, one needs a key. A key that neither I, nor anyone in my family, had ever seen. Meaning it was probably disposed of upon purchase.

After a while, things got very hot and good oxygen was hard to come by. It was clear that Bruce was perfectly content to sulk in the driveway collecting twigs. He hadn't taken the bait. We'd lost.

"Okay, Virginia, he isn't coming, unlock me."

"Okay. Where's the key?"

"What key?" I said.

"The key, Charlotte."

"Just unlock it!"

"Yeah, but where's the key?"

Things went on like this for several more minutes before I understood the sinister reality of the situation at hand. I was *locked* in a trunk…in a sauna of an attic…and I'd wasted what precious oxygen I had left debating about a non-existent key.

"Get my mom…" I tried not to panic, but my lungs were crunched with little room to expand. "Breathe slowly," I assured myself. "Mom will know what to do." Moments later, I heard two sets of footsteps tearing up towards my new petite place of residence. Mom had apparently brought a hair barrette, hoping to jimmy the lock open. "Just stay calm," she said softly. "I'm really making progress…" But the barrette was proving futile, and I could hear it in both my mom's tentative voice and the obstinate dinky tweaks and clicks occurring only centimeters away from my face.

I only remember seeing spots and beginning to lose all hope. *But I hadn't left a will and testament! Was there such a thing as heaven? If I went there, would I at least get to make day-trips back to the States?* In the face of my own death, I felt unprepared, and began to cry a frantic, get-me-the-hell-out-of-here cry. So Mom, in complete control, firmly uttered the word *"hammer,"* as if the stoic surgeon to her attending nurse. And I heard Virginia efficiently disappear down the stairs and then up again. With just two or three harsh bashes to the lock, the lid was opened and I was free. Mom was on her knees, panting. Dressed in a smart navy skirt-suit from an earlier meeting, she pulled me out of the trunk. Tears streamed down her now-flushed face, but there was not a single run down her tidy ecru panty hose.

Mom's relief morphed quickly into venomous rage from

the terror I had just given her and poor Virginia, mortified from her classic blunder as a non-camper. But I was *alive*.

I now know that this—being trapped inside a camp trunk in a sweltering attic—is what it actually feels like to be a mom sometimes: total claustrophobia, nothing but darkness, difficulty breathing, and no way out except at the assistance and rescue of someone smarter and more competent than myself.

I'M CONSTANTLY having to manage my expectations in motherhood and in life. I always thought I would be a footloose and fancy-free burgeoning artist (or some other sort of sexy creative-type). I'd travel. I'd stay out late talking about important things with important people at important places, drinking drinks I can no longer pronounce the name of (unless it's *wine* or *beer*). Honestly, I'd probably just be staying up late in my flannels watching syndicated *Golden Girls* on the cable, but still. At least it would be on *my* terms. From the minute Ford was conceived, everything changed. He was an accidental baby, conceived only days or weeks after Alex and I got married.

They say there are two reasons a woman gets married, right? Either she wants a husband, or she wants to start a family. While I love my kids dearly, I fell into the first category of brides. What little I knew of babies came mostly from movies like *Look Who's Talking* and *Look Who's Talking Now*. I had never actually *cared* for one. For instance, I still don't understand why mothers offer for other people to hold their newborns.

"Do you want to hold her?" the mom always says, as if she thinks she has read my mind.

"Um, sure, you have something else you need to be doing or what?"

She flashes me a look of confusion, while preparing to hand me her baby.

"Are your arms tired?" I ask.

The mother shrugs off these irrational questions and passes over her kid, as if she's doing me some large favor by letting me hold it.

I'm still perplexed, but I awkwardly hold the thing anyway, bouncing it a little, assuming something important, something crucial must be transferring between the two of us during this stiff physical exchange. Unfailingly, the baby starts wailing at once, and I am thankfully relieved of my duties.

Before Ford was born, I thought motherhood would pretty much look exactly like my life did pre-baby, only I'd have this quiet, angelic offspring to pass into the arms of any unsuspecting friend or stranger. And then I woke up one morning to my first grueling labor contraction, and it occurred to me I may have been a little off-base.

This was not what I expected. My sweet, colicky boy cried and cried, so uncomfortable outside of my cushy womb. In the first weeks, my husband and I would resort to late-night car-rides listening to smooth jazz/hip-hop (think makin' luv on an animal-skin rug by a fire in a ski chalet—*that* kind of smooth jazz). Forget "Jesus Loves Me" or his mother's loving embrace; raunchy slow jams were the only means to lull my innocent little bundle to sleep. But every time he stopped screaming at me for a minute, I would take a look at him—a real look—and I knew he couldn't be mine at all; he'd been shaped and molded by something heavenly. He was the most beautiful thing I'd ever seen.

In the following weeks and months of motherhood, my expectations were limited to the next minute or hour. "Can I convince this baby to breastfeed?" "Am I capable of laying him down to sleep 'drowsy but awake' like the book said?" "Am I holding him too much, or not holding him enough?" "Do I change his diaper before or after the late-night feeding?" "It's 6PM. Why has nobody mentioned that I have my pants on backward?" It was like a firework show that gets lit all at once. Ford was the first newborn I had ever held. Needless to say, I wish I'd practiced more.

Now that I've been a mother for three years, I've gotten better at managing expectations. It's like a science to me. For example: waking up in the morning. Some people burst out of bed like an angel kissed by the sun-stroked clouds, ready for whatever delightful surprise life throws at them that day. I am not one of those people (now or ever). I wake up looking and feeling like I've survived a bar fight. I hear those first "Hellooooo, I'm awake!!! Come get me!!!!!!!!!" sounds from the baby monitor, and my stomach drops like I've just realized drunk Voldemort is in the house. In a matter of about three minutes, I must go through all five stages of grief.

1. DENIAL: "Maybe they'll fall back to sleep…"

2. ANGER: Mostly directed at my husband for impregnating me, then at myself and my nearly supernatural fertility, then at Alex again for leaving the house at 4:30AM every morning with this new job, then at my children for being awake at such a godawful hour (usually about 6:30AM which, I'm aware, is a totally reasonable hour for a child to awaken).

3. BARGAINING: I talk back to them in the monitor in my sweetest mommy-voice: "I'll give

you a sucker…or what about *Toy Story*, you can watch *Toy Story* this morning…just go back to sleep for a liiittle bit longer."

4. DEPRESSION: I think I have it worse off than those starving children in Ethiopia. At least they can probably sleep whenever they want to.

5. ACCEPTANCE: I finally actually crack open my eyes. It's a little clouded over outside, which I always like in the morning—it's like the weather is mirroring my emotions, the sun itself not quite ready for full-swing. My kids, who now share a room, begin to giggle hysterically through the monitor, and I think, "This life is a good one, Lord. Holy Spirit fistbump."

It's not a science you can learn right away, but I do feel like understanding how to grieve, in a way, has been an all-around survival tactic for me. I have to grieve for the old, long-gone, pre-children me, I have to grieve for the me just-as-I-am, and then I think I also grieve the person I thought I'd be. But I think—*I hope*—that grief has a lot to do with acceptance, and acceptance has a lot to do with joy.

WHAT A STRANGE THING, to be needed like this. It's like nothing I've ever known. I crave it and reject it all at once. Motherhood is hard. In one sense, I want to do my own thing *all the time*. I am often bitter at my children for keeping me from whatever that "own thing" is (pedicures and reruns of *Dawson's Creek* and…oh yeah…*world stardom*). Motherhood has brought me to my knees because I am face-to-face every day with this vicious and outrageous tug-and-pull: is it going to be me or them today? Me or them? Victim or culprit? It's the hardest role I've been picked to play in my life, breathing inside this tiny hot box with a key that no one can find.

If I look at the camp trunk story from the vantage-point of my own mother, I think she might have understood my present conundrum. She had just come home from work that day, and was probably doing "her own thing" downstairs, happy to be breathing some kid-free air. It was likely an annoyance when Virginia first tiptoed into her office, until she realized what was at stake: her darling. Because in spite of that urge that always lures us deeper into ourselves, motherhood, in a way, doesn't give us an option. It's always *them*, whether or not we go willingly or kicking and screaming. What comes right into all of that bitterness and self-loathing is this immense love for these tiny, pitiful humans. This love has a gospel tune. We created them, we carried them, and then we brought them into the world. Knowing what I know now, my mom wasn't just trapped in motherhood that day, she was also trapped with me in the trunk. She was on her knees, praying for her own survival by way of *my* survival. It is strange, how our lives and emotions become so inextricably linked to our children's the very moment we become a parent (even in utero, if you want to go there).

I FIND MYSELF in impossible situations quite often. I've been stuck on top of a basketball hoop, stuck on top of the monkey bars, locked in a hospital waiting room, stranded on a highway on Christmas Eve, fired from a job, and then I did not plan to become pregnant. Now, my family has unwillingly hauled our whole brood cross-country and, if moving were an Olympic event, we would definitely *not* have made air-time. We need help. I need help.

Were I a psychologist, which I am not, I would note that somewhere deep down in the complex and sometimes [most of the time] disturbing machine of Who I Am, I seem to seek out, even crave these impossible situations.

"But why would I go looking for a disaster? I could have died!" I ask psychologist-me, annoyed at her pretentiousness.

Psychologist-me jots a few notes down in her legal pad and then looks up at me, pausing to adjust the clasp on her uncooperative necklace. "You weren't looking to almost die," she hesitates, only slightly sure of where she is going with this. "You were looking to be rescued."

> *The foolish man built his house upon the sand,*
> *The foolish man built his house upon the sand,*
> *The foolish man built his house upon the sand,*
> *And the rains came tumbling down!*
> *The rains came down and the floods came up,*
> *The rains came down and the floods came up,*
> *The rains came down and the floods came up,*
> *And the house on the sand went SPLAT!*

WE HAVE OFFICIALLY relocated—as if marooned—from Alabama to California. And I have to admit I'm surprised (and grateful) to find Ford and Margot such eager participants in this wild and scary story. Our house sits a block away from the beach where I should note, there is no small amount of sand[6] and we are technically in a flood zone.[7] The house we've rented is tiny on a good day. There is no air conditioning, so the heat can be stifling. In this place we are all at once home, still lost, and—as ever—we wait for rescue.

---

6. See above song.

7. See above footnote.

RECOVERED TRANSCRIPTS
FROM LIFEBOAT 815

EXTERIOR: DAY — SOMEWHERE IN THE PACIFIC.

STEPHANIE *has taken a break from rowing and obsessively scrolls through her iPhone.* CHARLOTTE, *rowing solo and on only one side of the boat, notices that they are beginning to go in small circles.*

CHARLOTTE (*irritated*): What are you *doing*?

STEPHANIE: What does it look like?

CHARLOTTE: How are you even charging that thing? Are you about to *cry*?!

STEPHANIE: Shut up. I'm looking through old photos.

CHARLOTTE (*shimmies closer to where* STEPHANIE *is resting against the side of the lifeboat*): Are these pre-kids pics?

STEPHANIE (*not paying attention*): Huh?

CHARLOTTE (*Looks into the sky, reminiscing*): When our self-esteem and our boobs were higher...

STEPHANIE: They're from James's first birthday party.

CHARLOTTE (*squinting at the screen*): Why is there so much alcohol?

STEPHANIE: We like to treat our kids' parties as parties for ourselves, too. You know—another year of keeping them alive, pass the wine!

CHARLOTTE: Solid.

STEPHANIE: But this is so weird, man. Looking at these brings back all the feelings I had then.

CHARLOTTE: Blurred vision? Wine giggles?

STEPHANIE: Duh. But also...that moment when they're supposed to stick their face in the cake? You know?

CHARLOTTE: What?

STEPHANIE: You know, because they're babies and don't know what cake is?

CHARLOTTE: So they stick their face in the cake? Is this an Australia thing?

STEPHANIE: Just let it go, k? Their faces are supposed to be all messy, right? So at James' party I sat there, camera poised, and when he gingerly touched his cake with the tips of his fingers, it was like...I felt a sense of failure. Like...oh no, he's doing this wrong.

CHARLOTTE: Because...he was supposed to put his face in it?

STEPHANIE: YOU KNOW WHAT I MEAN.

CHARLOTTE: Sorry, yes. Go on. We're being serious now.

STEPHANIE: Anyway, I had this, like, existential crisis. Like, what does it all *mean*?

CHARLOTTE: Well to be fair, he'd been through so much already, right? You had concerns. I'm sure that was playing into it.

STEPHANIE: Yeah, but...I think even without that, I expected parenthood—that is, *my kids*—to adhere to some sort of cookie-cutter path, to look a certain way. And so much of actual parenthood has been breaking me of that. Which has been *painful.*

CHARLOTTE: Preaching to the choir. It really is an exercise in insanity.

STEPHANIE: And identity displacement. They should make a board game based on parenting and call it that. *Identity Displacement.*

CHARLOTTE: Hell yeah. Move one space back if you wore white jeans expecting not to get them stained by your kid's snot.

STEPHANIE: Move one space back if you felt shame over the shitty cupcakes you bought from Target for his birthday at school and decorated to look homemade.

CHARLOTTE (*her laughter turns crazy*): Yeah, and move like ten spaces back if instead of finally settling your children in the land of their ancestors, you just uprooted them approximately one million miles to the other side of the country.

STEPHANIE: Or world!

Both girls pause for a moment as that sinks in.

CHARLOTTE: I feel like this game would be largely composed of steps backward.

STEPHANIE: We'll work out the kinks later.

They continue to look at the screen, huddled together as the boat rocks gently on the water.

THIS IS
THE DIARY OF:
CHARLOTTE GETZ

PRIVATE!

Do Not Open!
Read this at your own peril!

No, really.
I mean it…

DEAR DIARY,

Today we went to the local aquarium. Thank God for those tiny fish that completely mesmerized my kids. The beach has been a real lifesaver, too. With my toes in the sand, the Pacific thunders in rhythm before me. And a sea of sunbathers, and fishermen, and other tired people like me swarm its banks. On the beach, I think to myself, "I can be grateful." Because when you notice the faces of your two babes, wide-eyed in wonder at new surroundings and things like Pacific sunsets—when an ocean wind blows brisk like that on your face, it doesn't just make your hair stick to your lip gloss; it feels like it blows all the bad attitude and homesickness right out and through you. I am grateful for the wind.

Dear Diary,

It's 8:45 in the morning here, the sun is shining but it's jean weather outside (yeah, in August), and I'm sitting in a Coffee Bean *alone*. No kids. No familiar, distracting faces. That's right, today is day #1 with "the babysitter." She's coming two mornings a week so that I have some time to get my work done. This means I've finally been given that moment of freedom I've so longed for—freedom to "do me." And yet instead of working, all I can think to do is write in my diary like some sad middle schooler about how lost I feel.

Our culture separates the "stay-at-home mom" and the "working mom" with such differentiating vigilance that I suddenly don't know where I fit in. Working moms are (apparently) heartless escape-artists who care more about their careers than raising their children, and stay-at-home moms just never cut the cord. But I am both of these things, or rather somewhere in the blurry in-between. And I'm feeling that grayness of "stay-at-home-work-from-home" hard, like my arms are being stretched wide and unbending in two oh-so-different directions. I miss my kids. And yet there is much to be done! I wonder what they're up to, if this babysitter will know that Margot needs to hold *both* of her blankies when she's upset. I've been in this "mudblood" gig for over a year and I almost feel like I've betrayed them by abandoning them in a location where they expect me to be (home, as opposed to preschool); I plopped them on the floor with crayons and a red-headed stranger and tip-toed out the door like a guilty bandit in the night.

I'm going to get over this right?

Dear Diary,

Today is a good day. I've finally figured out some level of childcare/momcare balance, during which I can get my work done and also be a B+ mom. Basically, everything is perfect now and I should win some kind of major award.

Dear Diary,

Here's how I'm failing right now:

- We moved from Alabama to California two weeks ago, and I am trying my best to settle us in, to establish a routine, to make it clear that we are home, but I feel pretty sure my kids are going to be in therapy alongside those army brats who went to like 400 different high schools every month.

- In full knowledge, I put Ford to sleep last night with sand all in his hair.

- I still feed my kids veggie packs. That's right. I said it. They won't eat veggies I cook, only the pureed crap with fruit and sugar mixed in to disguise the taste.

- Right now, I'm sitting holed up in my bedroom writing in this diary while Alex entertains our babies. I should be out there, right? Tossing them up in the air? Building forts? But what I really want to do is eat nachos and watch reruns of America's Next Top Model all day.

- Don't remember the last time I brushed the younger one's teeth.

- The mornings the babysitter comes have begun to feel like my sanctuary. I have a chance at survival because of her. I don't care how cute this girl is. I don't even care if I catch Alex checking her out (it hasn't happened, but I've seen the movies). She is taking my kids for four hours a day, two days a week, so that I can do my work, and I would literally pick lice out of her hair if she asked me to. She doesn't have lice, FYI. (NOTE: Alex has a full-time job, and did he have to spend hours upon hours on care.com weeding through psychopaths to find someone to watch our children so that he can get his work done? DID HE?!...seriously...I'm over it...)

- I have asked said babysitter to do the laundry and dishes, so that I can shirk these historically maternal responsibilities that I hate doing myself.

- I will spend half of my time while the babysitter is here visiting my own doctors because, apparently, I have the body of an 80-year-old. It feels sick all the time. This is new within the last few years. What is with that? I HATE DOCTORS. AND MY BODY.

- I let Margot get away with murder. She just looks at me with these big Bambi eyes and all of my good-intentioned disciplining goes out the window.

I feel tired and anxious and never up to par.

Everything in me is saying, "Work harder. Be better. Vacuum the freaking floors yourself."

But I'm grateful for baby kisses. Margot—sometimes in the heat of a frenzy, other times for no reason at all—will just lean her head up for a kiss, as if she were a Disney Princess or something. It's as if a kiss from me is all she needs to stay sane. And when I give it to her, I realize that her sweet little drool-soaked lips are actually all *I* need to stay sane.

MESSAGE IN A BOTTLE

To Whom It May Concern,

First and foremost, whoever you are, SEND HELP. There are eight of us stuck on a small lifeboat. We've been out here for a week. Our coordinates are approximately THE MIDDLE OF NOWHERE but we think the sun is setting to our west, if that helps.

Once you're done flagging down the coast guard, consider this: if you are a male, or a mother already, or a small child, then the rest of this note is really unnecessary. Leave the bottle on the beach. Move on. This is not for you.

Now, to the young woman who is certain to eventually find this, *you're welcome*. Being on this tiny boat for a week, fighting for our lives alongside our kids, has given us a sort of sage glow. It seems a shame not to let some of our wisdom rub off on you.

Here's the thing, gurl. Sometimes you are physically displaced—like in the case of a refugee or, say, a dutiful wife following her precious husband's career pursuits. And sometimes you become someone completely different than you were. As in, you *were* an artist, you *are* a homemaker. This can happen overnight. It's terrifying.

We used to be *the most impressive* moms. You know,

before we had kids and everything.

Our pretend kids ate all their vegetables and never embarrassed us in public. They potty trained immediately, and until then, we carried their accessories in the cutest designer Coach bags, which *never* emerged from a bathroom with smears of poop.

Oh, and our marriages were perfect, sexy like in the movies, because fighting over stupid things and being too tired for sex is for losers. And our careers? Fulfilling! So there we were, these women (much like you) who had managed to #haveitall, smiling beatifically and non-judgmentally down at the rest of the world from our skyboxes of perfection. Our imaginary kids slept through the night from eight weeks until forever; we deftly managed our part-time jobs with the type of work/life harmony that most only dream of; our marriages were like a tasteful porno, and our identities were super likeable and founded in all the right places (Jesus, duh).

Then…we actually *had* the babies.

I don't think either of us expected to engage in hair-pulling fights with her two-year-old. Or to put a decade-in-the-making career on the *way* back burner so that her husband could take the reins on her student loan repayment and she could stay home with her kids. Which sometimes feels a lot more like indentured servitude than a cherished and time-honored tradition to uphold. It's even possible that while her kids were at school today one of us ate lunch in her car after a shopping outing just for the sheer quiet solitude of it.

This is not a good look, by most standards: picking through a takeaway box inside a car, hair unwashed and unstyled, gym clothes mocking the lack of an actual gym visit, and the unmistakable scent of unshowered flesh (combining with food) to create an atmosphere of general stank.

But this is, for us, more often our picture of motherhood than the one we (and *you*) planned, which looked more like this...(cue swirly dream screen):

IDEAL BODY	ACTUAL BODY
• Pilates	• Cheese
• Smoothies	• Wine
• Tanktops	• Stretchy pants
• Razors	• All the hair
• Bikinis	• Repeat
• Soul cycle	
• Self-control	

IDEAL STYLING	ACTUAL STYLING
• Appearance of professionally applied airbrushing	• Forgot deodorant
• Mascara	• Google: "contouring" (as seen on teenage girl's hit Youtube channel)
• Self-tanner	• Stretchy pants
• Eyeliner	
• Daytime lipstick	
• Concealer	
• Hair blown dry and smelling delightful	

IDEAL CAREER

- Full-time career woman
- Kids in daycare
- Pant-suits
- Meetings
- Conference calls
- Headset phones (is that still a thing)
- *Power*
- *Control*

ACTUAL CAREER

- Stay-at-home/work-from-home mom
- Multiple-boss situation
- No-wage situation
- Constantly slammed for slacking on the job
- Stretchy pants

IDEAL PARENTING

- Baby will sleep, *all the time*
- When baby is born, maternal instinct will go off like a grenade and we will just know what to do
- Lunch dates with baby
- Life will be exactly like it is now, but add a baby
- Baby will just crawl up to boob and teach itself how to nurse
- Will read more
- Lots of down time while baby entertains itself and sleeps more
- We will be, like, really good at this

ACTUAL PARENTING

- [Insert laugh/cry emoji]
- Disney Jr.

IDEAL CAR

- Two-doors (baby sits shotgun because, #coolmom)
- Sleek
- Leather
- Shiny
- Always newly washed
- Interior clean and smelling fresh because
- No food or drink allowed in car
- Latest hip music wafting through speakers
- No noticeable dings or dents
- Windows down

ACTUAL CAR

- Huge scratch on side from run-in with pillar in parking deck
- Small animals foraging in trunk
- Unidentifiable crumbs scattered throughout upholstery and underneath mats and ESPECIALLY buried in crevices of car seats
- Roach infestation
- Windows up because three-year-old "doesn't like wind"
- Mixture of body odor/ dog odor/a little pee/and Chinese-takeout-smell ever-lingering (because windows are up)
- Sticky remnants of spilt OJ in cupholder
- Raffy tunes blaring from speakers because *it's never loud enough*
- Appropriately-sized SUV because we just can't with the mom-van

IDEAL FASHION

- Form-fitting and freshly washed jeans
- Silk tunic
- Dangly earrings
- High heels
- Designer bag

ACTUAL FASHION

- Stretchy yoga pants that have never actually been used for yoga, and if they had, would likely have been see-through in certain poses (we're looking at you, "Happy Baby")
- Old, unwashed-for-weeks t-shirt with remainder of kids' breakfast and possibly vomit on the sleeve
- No jewelry other than wedding ring (usually, unless forgotten) which some days resembles tiny handcuff
- Sneakers with hole in toe
- Backpack you got for free at the gym you never go to (filled with diapers, Ninja Turtle undies, hand sanitizer, wipes, Legos, unidentifiable crumbs, and emergency Imodium)

IDEAL GENERAL DEMEANOR	ACTUAL GENERAL DEMEANOR
• Calm	• Still recovering from the shock
• Assured	• Not sure if we're effing these kids up
• Fun	• Frazzled about finances and whether or not to save for the kids' college or their therapy
• Spontaneous	• Remember to breathe
	• Remember to blink
	• Stop sending the husband SOS texts throughout the day
	• Women have been doing this since the dawn of time
	• So why are we so bad at it?
	• Go on a date with your husband!
	• Have sex with him!
	• Stop talking to yourself!

THIS IS A BITTER TONIC to taste. We know. You'll recover in a minute.

The weird thing about our Future-Self vision is this: we were never really all that swanky to begin with. Our inner selves have long betrayed our actual selves: high strung, messy, wine-loving, comfort-loving, TV-loving, SUV-driving wackadoos. Oh, and go figure, we were actually made for this mom stuff. So what if it looks like a five-alarm-fire in Russia most days? *That's just how it is okay?!* We need reminding, every minute of every day, that our kids aren't the rotten ones—*we are*. Somehow, remembering this—how pitifully in need of God and grace and love and rescue *we are*—actually fuels our own tanks to rescue and give to and love our kids. This is a weird identity that feels new because, in some ways, it has robbed us of the *possibility* to be anyone different: calm, well-fed, in control, and sober. There's no time or energy left for self-salvation projects like a vacuumed car (or a Clorox-wiped lifeboat).

So who are we now that we are stuck in our exactly-as-we-are-ness?

We're a lot like our kids: bossy, needy, helpless, whiny as hell, growing like weeds, and loved. What *doesn't* God do when our hands are tied?

SINNER IN THE HANDS
OF A RUDE
BUT PRESENT GOD

Stephanie

December 27, 2016.

I'm working on a List of Things I'm Grateful For: Culture Shock Preparation Kit Edition. It's WAY incomplete, but I'm packing for a trip across the world that will relocate our lives to Sydney, and I need to reassure myself that we're going to be okay. So here goes anyway. I am grateful for:

- Ryan Reynolds' Twitter account (accessible from Sydney)
- *Hamilton* soundtrack and mixtape (goes with me)
- Netflix's steady domination of cinema and television, here and abroad
- Lexapro and other mood-stabilizing drugs that don't dampen my crying reflex
- my crying reflex, which has led to many emotional epiphanies

- Nick Jr, for raising my children and existing on Sydney's Foxtel cable
- free childcare at churches, here and abroad
- free childcare at gyms, here and abroad (I checked, it's called Fitness First)
- warehouse wine stores (the one in Sydney is called Dan Murphy's; I will be their most reliable patron)
- Costco (yep—in Sydney; they sell kangaroo meat, yikes)
- earbuds that allow me to listen to podcasts while my kids are watching Disney Jr.
- Xanax
- hormonal fluctuations that allow me to blame mood swings on something other than being legit insane
- all the boyfriends I had before getting married... for NOT ending up as my husband
- the shitty relationship I was in before moving to New York, that motivated me to move to New York
- the downfall of my Good Girl identity that occurred during said shitty relationship that also led me to move to New York
- the five years I spent in exile in New York that taught me I could make it there...(you know the rest)
- the fact that I can make it anywhere?
- wait a second...am I about to have an epiphany set to a musical montage of my life's detours that turned out for good?
- are we going to be okay in Sydney?!

And Jason just texted me that Amazon is setting up an out-post in Australia.

Are you there, Stephanie? It's me, God. STOP MAKING EXCUSES. I'm GOING WITH YOU.

ON THE WINGS OF LOVE?

Stephanie

MY HANDS ARE GRIPPING THE armrests, but fear of flying is not the culprit. That particular phobia has been dethroned by another one, not so briefly named and way bigger: Fear of Flying our Family to Another Country and Ruining Our Lives. Technically, it would be Jason ruining our lives, but I feel like pointing that out, at this stage in the game, would not be beneficial to our marriage. Neither would screaming, "Why are we doing this?!" or "I want to go back!" or "When do they start serving alcohol?!"

I am utterly out of control. The thought dawns on me with alarming clarity and with it arrives a strange release. It's like I'm back on my childhood swing, but no longer able to control my distance from the ground by slowing the pumping of my legs. Now, the arc is huge and I'm not alone and there is nothing to do…but let go. I could never do that on the swing.

The boys crashed (yikes—poor word choice) as soon as

they settled into their seats, their exhaustion the result of a flight to Los Angeles yesterday and our 11PM takeoff tonight, which still feels like 2AM to their East Coast body clocks. My own clock, if it even operates anymore, has hands swinging wildly. I am adrift between time zones, continents, hemispheres…yet strangely stationary in this metal tube that houses everything, every*one*, who matters most to me.

We are utterly out of control.

And trapped: in this decision we have made, in this plane, in this seatbelt. There is nowhere to go—not for the next fourteen hours, surely, and not for awhile—but forward, into this new life. There is no in-flight entertainment that will distract me from the monumental move we're making (although this series about a *Bachelor*-style reality show looks interesting…), no amount of wine that will make me forget how irrevocably we could be changing our lives (but props to the actual *bar* situated at the front of this Virgin Australia flight). May as well settle in: this plane only moves in one direction.

But my thoughts? They're all over the place, in-flight entertainment be damned. For example, what if we love it in Australia? Then we'll be pulled between two places, yet again. My heart still isn't fully over New York and never will be. Maybe we'll never have one true home—we'll always just feel displaced between two or more locations, wandering around, unsettled. Then I imagine my boys with Aussie accents and am all, well, *there's* a silver lining…

Fourteen hours later, my children are still sleeping (file that one under "Miracle" right next to "Watching an Entire Season of *Unreal* on the Flight"). I glance out the window and see the sun rising. I look down and see new land approaching—our land. I see the curving edge of the Eastern

Australia coastline and feel an instant connection to its jagged wandering. And I notice: we will be surrounded by water. I can't help but think: this is like a baptism.

Sydney, here we come.

RECOVERED TRANSCRIPTS FROM LIFEBOAT 815

EXTERIOR: DAY—SOMEWHERE ON THE OCEAN.

The women gather their kids on the side of the boat where the men are not napping. CHARLOTTE *brushes the tangles out of* MARGOT's *hair while* STEPHANIE *adjusts* WILL'S *sunhat.* STEPHANIE *has her phone out to document the journey but the kids are proving unwilling to make it easy.*

CHARLOTTE (*under her breath to* STEPHANIE): Why can't we get just *one* good picture?

STEPHANIE: This is hell. Pure hell. You'd think we were telling them to smile for a firing squad.

CHARLOTTE: I think this may have been ill-conceived.

STEPHANIE: Of course it was. We got the idea from social media, which is where bad ideas go to spawn. Still doesn't change the fact that everyone wants updates from our Trip from Hell, and I don't want them seeing the boys peeing off the side of the boat while Margot does her shirtless belly drums.

CHARLOTTE: Don't get me wrong—I'm all for creating a facade when necessary. But this is *exhausting*.

STEPHANIE: I'm pretty sure Ford just grabbed something out of the water and ate it.

CHARLOTTE: Yeah, that might have been a jellyfish.

STEPHANIE: At least he's pretending to smile, though. James keeps trying to dive for the iPad. He won't even look over here.

CHARLOTTE: I say we just take a crap picture and be done with it. Sort of, "this is our life right now. Deal with it."

STEPHANIE: Ugh, I *so* wanted this to go better.

CHARLOTTE: Aaand Margot just dropped a deuce.

STEPHANIE: Will is pulling his pants down. You know what? Screw it. Let's just take the damn thing and call it a day. It's happy hour anyway.

CHARLOTTE: It's already two? SMILE, KIDS!

THE NEXT DAY, *the girls are at their wits end with their gaggle of unruly kids.*

CHARLOTTE (*flustered on* STEPHANIE'S *iPhone*): Dude. Does Pandora not work out here?

STEPHANIE: You're trying the Disney station again, I hope. Seriously, at this point, I just feel like we're being punished. Even though they wouldn't stop listening to that damn *Moana* song all day yesterday, I'd give my last pair of clean underwear to have it back again if they'd *just stop whining.*

CHARLOTTE: Right, but can we discuss how annoying it was for four small children to be belting out "We Know the Way" in *these* circumstances? Um, hello, WHAT WAY?!

STEPHANIE: Yeah, more like "Poor Unfortunate Souls."

CHARLOTTE: I am *such* an Ursula.

STEPHANIE: This morning, I yelled at the kids for brushing their teeth wrong. Granted, they were using saltwater, but still. I'm teetering on the edge, man.

CHARLOTTE: I just know if I have to moderate one more game of Duck Duck Goose I'm going to start holding my breath underwater to see if I can pass out.

STEPHANIE: When I was a kid, my mother told me that if I was bored she'd "find something for me to do." And you know what that something never was? Playing Duck Duck Goose with me.

CHARLOTTE: Yeah, parenting is so *all-in* these days. We would have done better back when all you had to do was cook up a pitcher of Tang and unlock the backdoor.

STEPHANIE: I used to wander the neighborhood until sunset!

CHARLOTTE: YES.

STEPHANIE: Except—

CHARLOTTE: You'd be too worried now?

STEPHANIE: I mean, hello, I've coated my children with sunscreen no less than five times each today. I never let them take off their lifejackets. I so did *not* mean to become a helicopter mom.

CHARLOTTE: Yeah, but here we are.

STEPHANIE: Yep. Here we are. God knows where, but here.

PART THREE

HOW TO
DEPLOY
"SURVIVAL MODE"

RECOVERED TRANSCRIPTS
FROM LIFEBOAT 815

EXTERIOR: DAY—SOMEWHERE IN THE PACIFIC.

STEPHANIE and CHARLOTTE have been rowing for weeks. The two pull through the water in perfect sync and chit chat to pass the time. The sun beats down on their shoulders. Across the lifeboat, their kids play on iPads and their husbands halfheartedly attempt to fish.

CHARLOTTE: I don't know how you handle the role of mother to a special needs babe with such grace.

STEPHANIE (*wipes her forehead with the back of her hand*): Dude, motherhood is just a bomb that keeps going off, day after day. The sizes of the bombs change, but they never stop detonating.

CHARLOTTE: Okay, that wasn't quite as inspirational as I was hoping for. Yesterday, our new pediatrician announced Ford had a heart murmur.

STEPHANIE: Bomb.

CHARLOTTE (*out of breath*): She said it was probably nothing serious, but he needs to see a pediatric cardiologist just to be sure. *Yesterday,* I was cool as a damn cucumber: *"Tell me what we need to do, doctor. We trust you!" (imitating a stronger version of herself).*

STEPHANIE: And today?

CHARLOTTE: Last night, when everyone else was asleep and I could hear the soft breathing of my precious babes through the monitor, I started to crumble. *What the hell does this woman know?? She belongs to a practice called "Surf City Pediatrics." Get serious, people! There are lives in your cheeky little hands!* I tried to think of other things. But the pediatrician's chipper voice kept bursting through: "He has a heart murmur!" As if she were delighted to have discovered it.

STEPHANIE: Be serious. Nobody is delighted about a heart murmur.

CHARLOTTE: Maybe. But my next thought was, *What if this is another divinely-inspired booby trap? What if this is just the beginning of a whole new life-narrative: Son with Heart Problem. What are you trying to teach me now, God? Why don't any of your lessons involve doughnuts and getting skinnier without trying?*

STEPHANIE: Oookay, head through your knees again. Deeeep breath.

CHARLOTTE *(bent over)*: I mean, why aren't you freaking out more about your own kids?!

STEPHANIE *(placing her paddle beside her and leaning down to yell into* CHARLOTTE's *ear)*: I AM ALWAYS WORRIED ABOUT MY KIDS.

CHARLOTTE: I'm literally sitting right next to you.

STEPHANIE: Sorry.

CHARLOTTE: But I mean, look at you. You're barely even breaking a sweat.

STEPHANIE: That's because I'm dehydrated, Char. I'm running out of sweat to break. On the other hand, I am never *not* worrying. I think it's my method of self-protection. Like, if I worry as though the worst things will happen then they won't? Why do I think it's all up to me?

CHARLOTTE: It's the *waiting* that is bearing on my shoulders like one of those jam-packed, first-day-of-school book bags. And it's been one day. You've dealt with this for *years*.

STEPHANIE: This is my reality. It's just a way of being that I've had to get used to—like how the gray hairs are going to keep showing up, not magically disappear, and my knees often hurt for no reason—or because it's going to RAIN. What the hell am I, a barometer?

CHARLOTTE: Hello, can we discuss chin whiskers?

STEPHANIE: But, on my good days, I think that God has—graciously and meanly it seems sometimes—been pushing me into a place of trusting him that I never would have chosen on my own. I guess the alternative is just going insane, and changing my identity in a real-life version of *Gone Girl*. But I'm so tired. And I wouldn't be able to stay at nice hotels.

CHARLOTTE (*taking a bite of a Twinkie*): And all that fast food? How could Amy let herself *go* like that?

STEPHANIE: Exactly. Most nights I can't even fall asleep without medication. The truth is, I'm not strong. What if it's not about *my* strength, though?

CHARLOTTE: Are we getting spiritual now?

STEPHANIE: What if the whole point is that I'm weak? And that there's nowhere else for me to turn but to God?

CHARLOTTE: Kind of reminds me of our tiny California apartment...because it's so small, so cramped, *there's nowhere for him to hide.* (*She pauses, clearly spotting something over* STEPHANIE's *shoulder*) Am I hallucinating or is that a spot of land I see ahead?

STEPHANIE (*bolts to standing and shades her eyes, squinting into the distance*): You're not hallucinating. Oh wow. What does this mean? Are we almost done with this maritime nightmare? Will our feet finally feel firm ground again?

CHARLOTTE (*more quietly*): What if it's...different, though? What if the water tastes funny and the wine is all moscato and—

STEPHANIE (*nodding*): —It has that old-place smell like mothballs and the people say things like "Fri-yay!"

CHARLOTTE: Maybe we don't paddle for awhile and just see if we float in that direction? I mean, it *is* almost happy hour...

STEPHANIE: I'm fine with that.

CHARLOTTE: Yeah, no need to rush. We'll get somewhere eventually, right?

ON THE OTHER SIDE OF NUCLEAR APOCALYPSE

Charlotte

I DO NOT HAVE AN obsession with cockroaches. Blanket statement. While we're on the subject, though, I think it's important to note that roaches have been hanging around Earth for something like 4 million years. The first species even close to resembling a human only came on the scene 2.3 million years ago. Cockroaches can survive just about anywhere, and eat anything from beer, to leather, to hair, to glue. They have legs, wings, and a tough, sophisticated exoskeleton that is brown and easily camouflaged.

Sometimes I think God made an error in giving humans such thin skin. Otherwise I'd be able to weather the most basic daily annoyances, like running out of ground coffee or adjusting to a new "life situation" that's laden with too many wellness establishments and rollerbladers.

Roaches: 1

Humans: 0

A few years ago, Alex and I took a guided tour of the

Museum of Modern Art in New York City. Our leader, a renowned art historian, remarked that the wildly expressionistic paintings of artists like Matisse or Picasso could almost appear as the product of error. The strange images depicted, the rough and messy strokes of the paintbrush, seemed more like rushed sketches in the art climate during which they were created. Now we call them "masterpieces." Sometimes, when I see those childlike scenes played out on canvas, I wonder if the artists didn't actually have some shrewd insight into the human race. Maybe I too am a product of error. I have "body issues" in both the *Cosmo* and the medical sense. Maybe I am just an eccentric accident, an experiment or a crude joke gone wrong—with three eyes, four fingers, two faces, and geometric blue hair.

My schizophrenic perspective on the human body, and the fear of what lurked within, was formed at the ripe age of five. I was a kindergartener, older than my brother and sister, and so fancied myself something of a Commander in Chief. The Leader of the Gang. One day, the three of us were meddling around upstairs in the playroom—which was really just an attic-like space stocked with a few Mr. Potato Heads and some leotards. After a while, I broke away from the group and wandered downstairs to check out the goings-on in another part of the house. The TV was on in the den, but no one was there. My dad, a doctor, had been watching a surgical video of an appendix being removed but he left the room before I walked in. There I stood, frozen in the doorway, transfixed by the site of this pink, slimy, golf ball-sized lump being sliced and airlifted out of some poor soul's abdomen. For the next two years, the fear of an Appendix Attack[1]—of surgical dismemberment—would be my 'Nam.

1. Highly technical medical terminology.

Any small twinge or cramp occurring above my knees and below my shoulders would be cause for a Hail Mary and a hurried trip to my parents' room to double check that I wasn't dying.

Even then, as a five-year-old, I remember feeling ashamed of my fear. If I had only come downstairs five minutes later on that fateful day, or not stood there like an imbecile and actually watched the medical procedure, maybe I would have been spared. Maybe then I could sleep.

If only I were tougher, impervious, more adaptable to my circumstances.[2]

COMPREHENSIVE BODY PORTRAIT
of a Real Life Mrs. Potato Head:

Astigmatisms
Back pain (lower, infrequent)
Birthmarks (seven total)
Breast reduction surgery
Broken wrist
Bronchitis
Bruises like a peach
Carpel tunnel syndrome
Cavities
Chicken pox
Common cold
Cuts (various accidental)
Ear infection
Fever
Flu (seasonal)
Flu (swine)
Gestational high blood pressure

2. La cucaracha.

Goiter in thyroid
Hair cut
Hair dye
Head lice
Insomnia
Nodes in goiter in thyroid
Orthodontic braces
Piercing (ears)
Piercing (ears, second holes)
Piercing (nose)
Pregnancy
Scrapes (various)
Shaving (anything exposed by a bathing suit)
Snagged pinky toe
Sphincter of Oddi Syndrome
Strep throat
Stress fractures in shins
Sunburn (bad–very bad)
Swollen lymph nodes
Swollen salivary glands
Tattoo (henna)
Tattoo (stick-on)
TMJ
Torn ligaments in ankle
Torn MCL
Waxing (eyebrows, etcetera)
Wisdom teeth removal
Zits

JUNE, 2015: EMERGENCY GALLBLADDER AT-
TACK/SURGERY. Okay so the gallbladder is not the appendix, but we can all agree it's precariously close.

SINCE MOVING, the fear has only worsened. I find myself overwhelmed with terrifying, often unlikely fears (ranging from SIDS to secondary drowning to allofasudden having the urge to join a Bikram yoga class). I look around at my sun-kissed, kale-fed California peers and think *these people are taller and stronger than me.* My insides continue to ride me post-cholecystectomy, and my son for sure has a heart murmur.

This swell of fear gives way to an unquenchable urge to make sense of other people and things that I do not understand. Aside from self-scrutiny, my investigations are mostly limited to people like serial killers or the Kardashians. This thirst for understanding has actually become a real quandary. Case in point, Alex recently banned me from Google—even threatened to enforce Parental Controls on our Internet—ever since the "Jeffrey Dahmer Incident."

The Incident began just as all occurrences of this nature do—a Small Seed of Intrigue (SSI). That particular SSI implanted itself one night when Alex was out for a beer with his buddies, and I caught a glimpse on Netflix of the cover art for a 2002 biopic entitled *Dahmer.* For as much as I already knew about a slew of other celebrity killers, Dahmer remained a mystery to me. This was unacceptable. Unbeknownst to Alex, I spent the next three hours ingesting the Jeffrey Dahmer story into my very soul, by way of various Internet chat sites and loner blogs.[3] When Alex came home later to find me cuddling with my stuffed animals and watching *Babe* with every light on, he immediately

3. It's incredible that (as far as I'm aware) the FBI hasn't tapped my phone lines yet.

suspected foul play.

"I'll do it, I'll call Comcast and have them block Wikipedia!" he scolded. Hostile clichés like "curiosity killed the cat" and "this is the last straw" were batted around.

"No! No! It was an accident…a chance encounter on Netflix! You know those stories are like catnip to me. I promise I'll be fine." But by 4AM, and nearly finished with *Babe: Pig in the City* (*Babe*'s less impressive sequel), I still couldn't bring myself to reach over to the bedside table and turn out the lights. And every time I needed to use the restroom, I woke a begrudging-but-willing Alex to accompany me the seven-odd feet and then stand guard while I went.

Only after I'd parsed the traits, habits, and possible deviant sexual habits of every person I had ever met, to be sure there wasn't a killer lurking in our midst (a Word of Caution: it's always the suspiciously attractive man with a limp), did I finally fall asleep. This routine continued for a week. A year later, I still don't look too closely when I open refrigerators, lest I spot a cluster of knuckles in a Ziploc bag or a rasher of human smiles delicately encased in frosty clean Tupperware.[4]

---

4. As a part of my graduate studies, I actually dared to dabble in a photography project based on serial killers. THE PROJECT: I appropriated photographs of various renowned killers (John Wayne Gacy, Jr., Aileen Wuornos, Ted Bundy, etc.) and then on top of those I layered images of their victims. I aligned their eyes, noses, and mouths as best as biology allowed. Finally, I lowered the opacity of each of these layers so that some blurred, warped single face emerged from the killer and all of his or her victims. Ted Bundy turned out looking like a woman with long hair. John Wayne Gacy, Jr. looked like a young boy. Aileen Wuornos just looked tormented. Then, as if you aren't freaked out enough, I made resumes for each of the killers. The resumes depicted whatever I could find of their actual employment, familial, and educational history. I was trying to

My need to make sense of things that frighten me is rooted in the method by which I overcame my fear of tornadoes as a kid. In Birmingham, we got the fat-as-a-city-block kind of tornadoes. Therefore, the slightest shift in the wind, or a rogue dog barking down the street would send me into a deranged panic—after which I would move directly into enacting The Tornado Plan.

The Tornado Plan: In the event of a tornado, all present members of the household, related or otherwise, are to take residence in Dad's windowless closet. Necessary things to grab along the way: flashlight, cordless radio, dogs.

Should the plan be executed carelessly, or not at all, our mangled corpses would surely be found scattered about the city on various rooftops and trees.

I was in the ninth grade when my mom so wisely remarked: "We fear what we do not understand."[5] She reasoned that if I could understand tornadoes, predict them, know the very scent of a cumulonimbus cloud, then I would

---

understand these people. There had to be some common thread—an abusive parent, a mental illness, etc. But in the end, there weren't enough straight lines or answers. What I can confirm is that a lot of killers are men. And most killers have a "type" of victim. After a while, I ended up scaring the shit out of myself and dropped the project, although it was perhaps the best received of all of my graduate photography work. "What was so scary that you forewent high accolades from your peers and professors to move on to another project," you ask? It's like the Sufjan Stevens song about John Wayne Gacy, Jr.: "And in my best behavior I am really just like him, look beneath the floorboards for the secrets I have hid." Maybe that bent toward wrong is buried somewhere in all of us.

5. She was unknowingly quoting Nobel Prize winning scientist, Marie Curie.

be able to mentally conquer them. And so I went to the library and wiped out the entire meteorology section.

Stemming from my mom's/Marie Curie's imparted wisdom, I have spent our first weeks in California scouring every preschool and playground within a 40-mile radius of our home. I've researched doctors, counselors, Zagat recommendations, purchased a subscription to *Sunset* magazine, contacted several long-lost sorority sisters to ensure adult friendships, interviewed babysitters, and read up on housing codes and earthquake emergency procedures. I'm even on the verge of purchasing rollerblades.

I'm not scared, you're scared.

These vital concerns have me clock-watching all hours of the night. As you can imagine, this is nothing altogether new. Here are the major fears that have kept my cortisol spiking over the years:

- appendicitis
- sirens
- that my heart would stop beating
- that ghosts would lock me in my room
- that my parents would go on a date, or out to dinner with friends, and never return
- little girls in nighties
- neighborhood gypsies
- people with flat eyes
- leaky faucets
- tornadoes
- questionable shadows
- 3:15AM (the devil's hour)
- of being the last person to fall asleep (which, inevitably, I am)

- *The Exorcist* (the Director's Cut version)
- *Hocus Pocus* (any version)
- dolls
- basements
- attics
- any empty room
- mirrors
- windows
- any reflective surface
- the fear of being afraid
- sleep talkers
- sleepwalkers
- that I might wake up, aware of having sleep talked or walked…
- antiques
- dismemberment
- driving at night by myself (S-curves through the woods and men with limps and whatnot)
- public restrooms that echo
- Etc.
- Etc.

WHEN ALEX IS TRYING TO COMFORT ME during those nights of great horror, he will sometimes lovingly whisper unhelpful things in my ear like, "I'm not going to let anything happen to you," or "I'm right here," or "We'll be back in Alabama in no time!" But these well-meaning platitudes are all too familiar. See my fear-filled childhood alongside my equally loving (paranormally-naïve) dad. "We're right downstairs. Just scream and we'll be here in a jiffy"—as if a jiffy weren't just enough time for the lethal reflection of Bloody Mary to torment me well into adulthood. Much like the solution of sawing an achy tooth in half (as opposed to removing it altogether), the problem with these jejune consolations is that they don't get at the root of my terror. Am I *actually* afraid that a masked man with a chainsaw is going to sneak into my house and terrorize me? Not really. Do I *truly* worry that I will become possessed by the devil, helpless to stop myself from doing a backbend down the stairs and then puking green sludge all over the foyer right in the middle of my parents' fancy cocktail party? No. That only happened the once.[6]

At the root of my terror is a proneness towards over-visualization or, medically speaking, an "Imagination Overload."

As a child, I was the type of student sent home with nondescript words on my report card like "bright" and "well-meaning." Although my mother denies all evidence to the contrary, I am positive that talk of medication for Attention Deficit Disorder occurred at many of my parent/teacher conferences. This was before it was such a hot diagnosis. I recall once getting reprimanded in the middle of a history class for singing, which I literally had no awareness I was doing. I would go through entire lectures from my sixth grade teacher without processing a single word, lost in daydreams. Upon reaching an age when I understood what ADD was and that I probably had it, I confronted my mom, asking why she and my dad insisted that I struggle unmedicated through this fog of inattention. She immediately became defensive: "You do NOT have ADD. You JUST have an Imagination Overload!"[7] I wonder if she didn't recognize some of my own odd habits in herself.

6. No it didn't. It happened in *The Exorcist*.

7. The subject of medication would not come up again until I was in my twenties.

Eventually, my parents did take me to the pediatrician to be sure something wasn't *really* wrong. That's when my mom reported that the doctor had offered the diagnosis of Imagination Overload. Prescription: no caffeine after noon, frequent reading of the *Children's Story Bible*, and a nightly doodle in a drawing journal (to wear down my malfunctioning imagination). I don't know what crack degree that doctor boasted, but I suspect it involved at least a morsel of the creative pedagogy of Nina Botsford (Alias: Dr. Mom).

IT ISN'T THE FEAR of an actual horrible event occurring that is so debilitating. It's the *picture* of it; like the *picture* of me being scalped by a ghost, or the *picture* of me lying dead on the floor with my children crying over me because I've had a blood clot and Alex STILL HASN'T LEFT WORK.

It's pictures like these that led me down the stairs, tail between my legs to my parents' room at least several times a night to report in: "I can't sleep," code for "I'm scared" or "*Help*." Maybe I hadn't doodled enough. Or perhaps God was waiting until I'd memorized every story in the *Children's Story Bible* before He would intervene.

Wordlessly, dad would roll out of bed and then ask me what was wrong as he followed me back to my bedroom.

DAD'S MOST WINNING ATTRIBUTE: there is literally no worry too absurd to approach him with. He always, *always* finds a way to respond with concern, thought, and logic.

Panting from running down the stairs, "Daaad, I think my heart stopped beating!"

"Oh, that does sound bad! Let me get my stethoscope."

"Daaad, the sky looks weird…"[8]

---

8. This was a frequent observation.

"Why don't we turn on the Weather Channel, just in case."

"I think I heard the front door open, Dad!"

"I'll get the fire poker!"

But as the years went by, I grew weary of laying out the whole convoluted story every night. Unless it was something really pressing like, "A suspiciously attractive male stranger is limping up the driveway," I would come forth with a simple, "I'm just scared." He'd lie there with me while I anxiously awaited the moment I thought he'd probably leave again. And when he did, I'd ask him to check on me in a little while, and then make a pastime of counting down the minutes until he kept his word. After that, I'd usually go wake up my sister, Din, and make her sleep in my room (this became a nightly thing around the second grade and lasted until I married Alex at age 28). Finally, I'd wear myself out from the pageantry of it all, and pass out in a puddle of my own sweat.

I WONDER WHEN California will start to feel more like home and less like an anthropological study on western natives or an endurance test of the marital vow. In the midst of trying to survive and also not traumatize our children, we are eager to build a community and, namely, to find a church. The right church will fix everything. Right? If God sees us going to church, he'll bless us. That's how it works!

Every Sunday growing up, my family went through the rigmarole of dressing in our Sunday best and screeching down the driveway to make it to church on time. Oh sure, Sunday School was alright—crafts and games and the contingent of boys I had crushes on. But the hows and wheres and whys of things like miracles and omnipotence were sort of lost on me. I would even go so far as to say I felt a bit resentful. If God was such a wizard and all, why couldn't He make it so that I could get some damn sleep? I had reached a dizzying place in life wherein I was actually afraid of being afraid. I have recollections of sitting in the last period of the school day feeling a rising pit in my stomach because that final bell meant nighttime was all the nearer—and thus my Routine of Encroaching Doom.

No matter how hard I attempted to pray that I wouldn't be scared, nothing changed. So how could there possibly be a God out there who claimed to be powerful and to love me?

Starting around the fourth grade, every socially minded girl in school was attending a weekly, after-school community Bible Study led by some older high school students. Twenty girls crammed into an average-sized living room did not make for an intimate setting, but there were snacks involved, so I went. More importantly, I hoped that frequenting the Bible Study would yield some kind of an answer to the unsolvable problem of my fear. This was more than a popularity thing—it was reconnaissance.

The insinuation from these weekly lessons was that I needed to be a better person and then good things would come my way. So every week while sitting in Bible Study, I frantically scribbled down notes, ideas that might lead to my emancipation:

"Be nicer"

"Stop talking about other people at all"

"Defend the orphans and the widows"

"Stop hiding in trunks"

"Take better care of my hygiene"

"Read the Bible at least three ~~or four~~ times a day"

"Don't judge"

"Tell everyone about how great Jesus is"

"Quit suggesting Bruce was adopted"

"Eat healthier"

"Exercise more"

"Pray more"

"Stop sinning altogether"

"Try not to be jealous of Din, who seems to accomplish all of these things with great ease"

Nothing worked.

One day though, the Bible Study lesson really got my attention, like a highway billboard lit up at night: "Ask Jesus Into Your Heart Today." A light went off in my head. I hadn't thought of this. I had no idea that Jesus needed a formal invitation! Brilliant! I took in the instructions like an eager teenager before her first time behind the wheel of a car. Seatbelt? Check. Parking Brake? Check. Adjust rearview mirror? Got it. LET'S DO THIS!

On the way home from Bible Study, I carefully replayed all of the necessary steps to invite the divine into my cardiovascular chamber. My mom must have been suspicious by my uncharacteristic silence, but beyond glancing over at me from time to time, she didn't pry.

She pulled into the garage and without waiting for her to put the car in park, I threw open the door and double jumped the stairs up to my bedroom.

I gently closed the door and tossed my book bag on the bed.

"Deep breaths. Clear your head, Charlotte. Focus. Focus."

I sat cross-legged in the middle of the room and clenched my eyes tightly together.

Hugging both the *Children's Story Bible* and my notebook

from Bible Study (for good measure) to my chest, I solemnly pressed my palms together, like a spiritually confused Buddha.

"Jesus, I invite you into my heart…"

…

Nothing.

I cautiously peeked one eye open and glanced around. Had I forgotten something? I jumped up and cracked a window, just in case He hadn't heard.

Three deep breaths.

"Jesus, I invite you into my heart…" a little louder this time.

…

…

"Répondez, s'il vous plaît, Jésus…"

Still nothing.

Was it my heart? I counted the beats. Nope, nope, pulse was still good.

"For real, Jesus, just get in here…" Now I was frustrated.

What was I supposed to feel upon Jesus' entry into my heart? I imagined some great gush of wind, like a sigh, or that all of the lights in my room would grow inexplicably brighter for a second or two. But none of this happened. Everything stayed exactly as it had been. No fantastic miracle. My heart seemed unaffected, *uninhabited*, if you will. And that night, I fell into the same routine, shuffling down the stairs with my head down, alone and afraid. God had heard my invitation (I mean, the freaking window was open) and had regretfully declined.

The important thing is that I didn't give up. I stuck with what I considered to be normal Christian routines, still optimistic that the fault was mine. I just hadn't tried hard enough, hadn't quite measured up to God's expectations of me. Of course, I told no one about my rejection. Sure that Jesus was happily indwelling in the hearts of each of my faithful friends by now (they had "the glow"), I just faked it. "He uses my towels, watches my TV, *and* He's cleaning out my refrigerator faster than I can stock it, y'all! What a guest, I tell you! What a guest!" The humiliation was just too great. I asked, He heard, He said no. But there was a code to be cracked and I was sure that I just hadn't discovered it yet.

I tried telling people about Jesus.

I wore a cross necklace.

I read *Chicken Soup for the Soul.*

I prayed harder.

I talked softer.

I tried to be nicer.

All of these seemingly logical steps had led to nothing but the same. I had done my part, but to no avail. And so my assumptions about God began to reconfigure. His love, generosity, and decision-making process seemed haphazard at best. He was unpredictable and, therefore, could not be trusted. I didn't violently turn away from religion or anything. But over time, God went from being my great hope to just another item on the long list of things I was suspicious of.

Meanwhile, nighttime fear continued to assail me. I felt completely abandoned, completely imprisoned, and that nothing or no one could set me free. Sort of like moving away from home; or like one of those ladies from *The Silence of the Lambs*, waiting in Buffalo Bill's hole in the ground to become another woman-suit for his twisted personal entertainment—"It puts the lotion on its skin!" my fear seemed to heckle over me. I was all but stuck in a hole beneath a hidden trap door, and nobody even knew I was missing. No one was coming to my rescue.

I THINK YOU CAN LEARN a great deal about a person according to how one arranges the contents of his or her bed when sleeping. For instance, some people sleep totally outside of the covers, facing the door, knife in hand, prepared to defend themselves to the death if need be. Others fall asleep to something soothing like Enya blasting through their headphones, barricading themselves in with a wall of pillows on both sides, sheets over their faces, blocking any line of site to all exits/entrances—blissfully negligent to any impending ruin. I tend somewhere towards the middle of these two extremes. As a singleton, I slept directly in the center of the bed, forming a small but secure hedge of pillows and stuffed animals on either side of me. These served as more of a fortress, or an obstacle to those with ill will. However, marriage, and incorporating another body into my sleep space, has added an unexpected layer of complexity to my practice. Alex alleviates any need for a left-side wall. But he, along with my dog Hercules, leaves scarce little room for me *and* the barricade to my right. I now find myself in this new and tiresome pattern of round-the-clock reconstruction and renovations.

Throwing children into the mix means that the barricade and all attempts at self-salvation are down the tube. I sleep at-the-ready, because there are now two adored babies to lay down my life for (should the horrific occasion arise).

I used to think that Alex slept soundly [carelessly], as one who does not think about these things at all. It seems as if he just passes out wherever/however he lands in the bed. But a few nights ago, he very solemnly sat me down to discuss how events would go down if anyone ever broke into our West Coast apartment.

Plan A: With a box-cutter hidden up his sleeve, Alex checks to see what's up, while I lock myself and our children in the master bedroom, pushing the heavy wooden dresser against the door. This plan irks me in several regards. First, it leaves Alex to fend for himself. Second, I feel that it assumes I'm the type of woman who might own a fainting couch or require smelling salts. Nonetheless, it comforts me to know that he has thought these things through. He has a plan—even if it does involve sparing the women and children first and at all costs. This says a great deal about Alex, and who he is at the heart of things.

The way I sleep, I think, says a lot about Who I Am. My methods reek of someone scarred with great fear in her life. I might be petrified beyond logic or reason, but I counter that emotion with dogged awareness and preparation. I need to understand the hows and whys and whats of it all.

You might be coming for me or my kids, but I'm ready. I've done all the research and heavy lifting, no stone unturned and whatnot. Bring it on.

Regardless of what actually happens, at least I know that I am good and practiced at screaming for help.

"Daaaad!"

CHAR AND STEPH WANDER THE DESERT

A Play by Charlotte Getz and Stephanie Phillips

ACT I

CHAR *and* STEPH, *two young-ish Hebrew women, work side-by-side in a field making bricks out of clay and straw. They are just two women amongst thousands, and the sun beats down on them all without a trace of shade in sight.*

CHAR (*wipes her forehead*): Damn it's hot.

STEPH: I'm so thirsty.

CHAR: What are the symptoms of dehydration again?

STEPH (*yells to no one in particular*): Can we get some water over here?!

CHAR: This day *literally* could not get any worse.

A deranged looking man—seeming terrified—runs onto the scene.

HEBREW #1: THE RIVER TURNED TO BLOOD!

STEPH: What did he say?

HEBREW #1: ALL THE FISH ARE DEAD!

CHAR: It's just Herm.

STEPH: Oh Herm...

CHAR (*to* STEPH): I spent two hours last night meal-planning for the week and FISH IS ON THE MENU, PAL.

STEPH (*snapping her fingers like a diva*): Ain't nobody gonna poopoo on my meal plan.

THE NEXT DAY...*the girls are side-by-side making more bricks.*

CHAR: So, do you want to talk about the whole river thing?

STEPH: That was weird.

CHAR: Super weird.

STEPH: Herm is almost never right.

CHAR: Literally, never.

STEPH: Who's with your kids today?

CHAR: Not sure. Last I saw, they were just running around.

STEPH: Yeah, me too. Told them to meet me when the sun starts to go down.

CHAR: Not a bad set up.

STEPH: Not bad at all.

The girls slap a high-five.

STEPH (*cont'd*): Just spitballing here, but are you worried at all that somebody will take them, or maybe they'll fall in the river and get diphtheria or something?

CHAR (*casually*): Not really...

STEPH: Yeah, me neither. I LOVE getting away from them, even if it's to make bricks all day.

CHAR: Okay, honestly, I'm terrified.

STEPH: I've literally cut holes in their pockets and filled them with matzo crumbs—just so I can follow them and see what they're up to.

SEVEN DAYS *after the water of the Nile turned to blood,* STEPH *and* CHAR *sweep up a host of dead frogs from around their brick-making site. The stench is overpowering, and they both gag as they work.*

STEPH: If I have to scrape another dead amphibian from the bottom of my shoe, I'm taking it up with the big guy himself.

CHAR: Pharaoh?

STEPH: No, Fat Albert. YES PHARAOH.

CHAR: PHA-WHOA, buddy. Chill out. It's not like we have any options. Moses said this would happen, so let's just push through and trust him. He's convinced God is going to come through for us.

STEPH: Dang, I can usually trust you to be more suspicious...

CHAR (*looks around to make sure nobody is listening*): Don't tell Alex, but I think Mo's stutter is kind of cute...

STEPH: Total dreamboat.

MANY DAYS LATER, *after the gnats, the flies, the live-*

stock, the boils, the hail, and the locusts, CHAR *and* STEPH *sit in the field in the middle of the day, but in total darkness. They continue to make bricks and their expressions are flat and hopeless.*

STEPH: Seriously, dude?

CHAR: There is literally no God.

SEVERAL DAYS LATER, *the girls stand side-by-side over a wobbly table in a small shanty, together with their four children. They are preparing a meal (if you could even call it that).*

CHAR (*chewing some bread while* STEPH *does a majority of the cooking*): Where's Jason?

STEPH: Off looking for a lamb. He keeps talking about how (*in a half-hearted impression of* JASON's *voice*) "it has to be without blemish and that'll make the search take longer," but I think he's just looking for excuses to have some alone time while I make another dinner the kids won't eat.

CHAR: Tell me about it. So far Alex has come home with *three* different lambs that he later returned to the field because once he got home, he realized they either had defects or were too old. He's out right now. I keep telling him to get a new pair of glasses, but noooooo.

STEPH: Why are our husbands so concerned with this whole sheep thing?

CHAR: Lamb.

STEPH: What?

CHAR: It has to be a lamb.

STEPH: Right, a lamb. I mean, God's not actually going to

kill anybody...will he?

CHAR: Literally, no chance.

THE NEXT DAY, *the girls sit solemnly caressing their eldest boys (who are more than a little confused, but also kind of enjoying the attention).*

CHAR (*to* FORD): I love you more than any mother ever loved any little boy ever.

STEPH (*to* JAMES): Me too.

CHAR (*to* STEPH): So, last night got real.

STEPH: I know, now I feel bad. Complaining about my kids while all the Egyptians have lost their (*she covers* JAMES' *ears and whispers*) *firstborn sons*! Not that they don't deserve it...I mean, they've been pretty awful to us.

CHAR: We literally don't have fingernails.

STEPH: Girl, you KNOW I can hold a grudge. But it just seems so...wrathful of God, you know? I mean, just when you think he's this grandfatherly figure in the sky, or your bro, he goes all Sodom and Gomorrah on an entire nation. And now we've got to hightail it out of here because everyone's freaking out!

CHAR: You realize that's a good thing, right?

STEPH: I know, I know, it's just that *this is our home.* And moving is such a hassle. Jason is all consumed with packing his *own* stuff up which of course leaves me to take care of the boys and myself.

CHAR: I think Alex has had us packed since the whole bloody river thing. That guy does not like a to-do list.

STEPH: What do you even pack for an exodus? I mean, like, how long will this trip *take*?

CHAR: A few days?

The women shrug their shoulders, unconcerned.

LATER THAT DAY, STEPH *and* CHAR's *families walk side-by-side in a mass of thousands of other Israelites. They carry only their essentials, including loaves of unleavened bread.*

CHAR (*gesturing to her satchel of unleavened bread and beginning to lose her calm*): I hate this stuff. I mean, we don't even have a minute to *bake* some damn bread before we leave? I read somewhere that unleavened bread can breed salmonella. Did you read that? Can you imagine if we got salmonella out here?? Not to mention that all this extra salmonella-bread weight is only going to slow us down. Did anyone pack anything that's *actually edible*? And where are we even going? Does anyone up there even have a map? WHAT IS THE PLAN, PEOPLE?!

STEPH: Maybe God is telling us to rely on Him for our provision?

The girls pause for a minute and then together, burst into laughter.

CHAR: No way he can pull this off without us.

STEPH: Not a chance.

SEVERAL HOURS LATER, *the herd of Israelites comes to a halt. Chatter begins to filter back toward where* CHAR *and* STEPH *stand tired and confused.*

HEBREW PERSON IN FRONT (*passes back the news*): God told Moses we should turn around, to go camp by the sea.

STEPH *and* CHAR *and* FAMILIES: WHAT?!

CHAR (*enraged, taking* HEBREW PERSON *by the tunic*): WHY AREN'T WE TAKING THE ROAD THROUGH THE PHILISTINE COUNTRY?!

People start to stare.

HEBREW PERSON (*shrugging his shoulders*): Jeez lady, I'm just passing on the info.

STEPH (*embarrassed*): Char, you're making a scene. Remember what you said before... *Trust Moses.*

CHAR: TRUST MOSES?! Forget that! (*To* ALEX) Alex, this is absurd, can you please talk to someone up front? Make sure you tell them I said *this doesn't make any sense...WE'RE GOING THE WRONG WAY.*

ALEX *obliges and hurries toward the front.*

CHAR (*to herself*): I mean what does Moses think we're going to do? Swim across an entire sea?

STEPH: I believe in you!

CHAR (*brushing her off*): Not now, Steph.

STEPH: But really, why *is* Moses the designated message-receiver? He can barely talk, and I heard he killed a dude back in Egypt. For reals.

ALEX *returns, and the look on his face says it all: bad news.*

ALEX (*out of breath*): God said.

CHAR: God said what?

ALEX: God said we have to go this way...

CHAR: Oh you talk to God now?

ALEX: No. Jeez. Padma said that Yaegar said that Aaron said that Moses said that... "*God said.*" As in, "Because he said so." Moses isn't budging on the route.

CHAR: Did you tell him what I told you to say?

ALEX: I did.

CHAR: Did you say it exACTLY how I said it?

STEPH: Just let it go.

CHAR: Maybe we should break away from the pack, go our own way...

STEPH: Now you've gone and lost your mind. Let's just stick with the group and keep following that cloud-pillar up there.

A FEW DAYS LATER, *as the Israelites camp alongside the sea,* CHAR *and* STEPH *lie awake whispering while their children sleep soundly on top of them.*

STEPH: Can you believe who Abra is walking with??

CHAR: I know, Ujarak?! She can so do better than Ujarak.

STEPH: Desperate times.

CHAR: Indeed.

STEPH (*pauses, noticing something over* CHAR's *shoulder*): What's that in the distance?

CHAR: What?

STEPH (*stands up and shrieks*): I knew it. EGYPTIANS!!!

LEARNING TO LAND BY WAY OF FLYING (ACROSS THE WORLD)

Stephanie

"My mind is a bad neighborhood I try not to go into alone." – Anne Lamott

FORGET MYERS-BRIGGS; I THINK YOU can judge just about all you want to know of a personality by the way an individual swings. Take, for instance, yours truly: the redhead on the playground whose arc on the swingset was small, manageable, and brief. The kids around me? Flying wildly toward the top of the structure before letting go and jetting through the air, no care at all about the landing awaiting them. Not this girl, though. Fear always kept me at a minimal distance from the ground.

I don't remember the first time I was afraid. Perhaps it was at birth? There are all sorts of psychological theories about birth trauma, though I'm not sure I believe any of them...[9] or that I want to, having been on both sides of birth—as the delivered and the deliverer, if you will. If birth can result in psychological trauma, I'm pretty sure both my two children and I will be lifelong strugglers of PTSD.[10]

I'd rather not add that to the already-stuffed baggage that is my concern for my children, or the hulking suitcase beside it labeled "My Own Disaster of a Psyche." I've dealt with fear and anxiety for as long as I can remember. It seems that any hope of wellness for me was doomed from the beginning—or, at least, around the time I was three months old and my mother noticed something freaky about my eyes.

She was sitting there feeding me, and when she looked down she realized that my beautiful newborn peepers were shaking back and forth rapidly. She took me to the doctor, who informed her that I have a condition called congenital nystagmus. *Congenital* meaning *from birth*, and *nystagmus* describing the vibrating-type movement of my tiny baby eyeballs. Relieved to know that I wasn't having a seizure, my mom took her shaky-eyed baby home, having no idea that this condition would be the first of many items on a long list that I would later title "Things I Hate About Myself."

Fear of people looking me in the eye became a daily companion as I grew up. Sometimes it would happen, and the person would ask me—in the way only children can—why my eyes were "doing that weird thing." Occasionally there would be added commentary subsequent to my explanation, offerings like, "Well it really freaks me out" or,

---

9. Read: I haven't read enough about them to render an educated opinion, and let's be honest, odds are slim that will ever happen.

10. This is not to imply that I am equating childbirth with fighting in a war. We all know no one is allowed to make those comparisons anymore (see: Gwyneth Paltrow).

"AAAHHH!!! Make it stop!" Rather than chalking such comments up to the ignorance (or cruelty) they revealed, I would allow them to make me feel worse about myself, to make me feel more different than I did before. And *different*, to a kid—After-School Specials, superhero movies, and educational campaigns notwithstanding—is anathema. To be avoided at all costs. The suggestion that I could control this phenomenon, *which I obviously couldn't*, planted a seed deep within me that there were other things I could and should control. I set about finding them.

Fear is the wallflower sister of control, the outward manifestation of an inward delusion that such control was within my grasp. I crept about my small world committed to that at which I excelled and avoiding everything and everyone that/who made me feel less capable. I became a straight-A student (and *Montgomery Advertiser* State Spelling Bee Winner 1989—thanks for the free milkshake, McDonald's!). In junior high, I decided to try ballet, and at the tender age of thirteen, when I was a head taller and about a half-decade older than everyone else in the role, I was cast as a tumbling gingersnap in the local ballet's production of *The Nutcracker*. Proud of my accomplishment at first, I realized quickly that I didn't have quite as much road ahead of me as my fellow ballerinas, having started late, and that the roles for older women in ballet—much like those for the same in Hollywood—were scarce. Plus, in four years I'd need to commit myself to a full-time college search. So I bailed on dancing and went back to my desk.

My Control Illusion caught up with me in the form of nausea-inducing daily headaches sometime in middle school. Occasionally I would puke and my mom would have to pick me up from school. We saw the pediatrician, who referred us to an ENT for an ECG. Nothing was found. Then we were referred to a neurologist for an MRI.[11] I remember being injected with the radiographic dye that would light up my brain for the doctors to interpret what was wrong with it. I'm still not sure if the dosage was off or I had a reaction, but once I was shuttled into the claustrophobic cylinder of the magnetic machine, I felt an overwhelming heat course through my body, to the point that I began to sweat profusely and wonder if I would have to pay for ralphing all over this clearly expensive device. The feeling passed, and the test came back normal. But when I went to the neurologist's office for the follow-up, he sat my mom and me down and asked a bunch of questions, mostly related to school. He finally gave his recommendation: that I step back from my studies, chill out a bit, and bring home some *C*s instead of *A*s as it was clear I was putting too much pressure on myself.

My mom and I nodded obediently, then hightailed it out of there without scheduling a return visit. *Cs?!* With that college search looming?! The possibility of mediocrity was horrifying: if all my hard work didn't end up separating me from the only world I'd ever known, and my never-fading sense of being out of place in it, then what had it all been for? *No way.* I decided to start controlling my headaches by choosing to forget about them. And, somehow, it worked. Maybe I just got distracted. Maybe they were a developmental thing. Either way, my illusion of control was bolstered.

✻

---

11. So many three-letter words…perhaps that's why I prefer the four-letter ones these days.

As I GOT OLDER and did away with childish things[12], the events I tried to (but couldn't) control loomed larger. They included:

- the guy I dated who didn't accept *no* for an answer
- the grade slippage during residency
- the preterm labor that landed me and my unborn son in the hospital at 31 weeks
- the scary mammogram when he was a year old that landed me on a sonogram table looking at the inside of my boob instead of the baby I was hoping for (talk about getting kicked when you're down—boobs are *not* as cute as babies)
- the second pregnancy that never took off but ended instead around seven weeks in a puddle of blood on the shower tiles
- the pregnancy that *did* take off, and the fear that accompanied it the entire time—fear of another miscarriage, fear of a cord around a neck, fear of similar spinal issues to his brother's, fear of never feeling like a good mom even after having done it once already
- the "Wake You Up at 3AM Fears"—of child safety, of shark attacks and secondary drowning and home invasions and electrocution and falls on the playground. Fears of health falling apart and one of the two of us abandoning the other with these kids. Fears of…well…*everything*.

I USED TO love flying. As a control freak, I counterintuitively enjoyed something about being trapped in the air at the

---

12. 1 Corinthians 13:11, though I'm pretty sure Paul was never as childish as I was. He always had bigger fish to fry.

full mercy of a machine and someone else's piloting skills.[13] Unlike the swing, if I crashed to the ground it wouldn't be my fault!

I noticed this changed after Jason and I began dating, and we were required to separate for a week due to spending Christmas with our respective families. I thought it a cruel fate, as we were in the throes of initial passion during which each is perfect to the other and the world looks and smells different and good. But I boarded my flight anyway, anticipating a restful time of reading and listening to music. What I found instead was total fear: as soon as the plane took off, all I could think about was what I would be missing out on if we crashed. Prior to Jason, that list was full of family but undercut by my own loneliness, poorly attenuated by bad dates and cheap wine.

By the time he and I were making out on a couch at the housewarming party of a guy we barely knew (after which I texted my sister that I would, in fact, be getting married after all), I could finally imagine a house in the suburbs and two cars and two kids and even a dog. I clung to the armrest of my seat and willed God to *not take this away from me*.

What I see now is that fear is deeply embedded with the idea of loss. And as one gets older, loss becomes less of an idea and more of a reality. How to navigate this unavoidable path without complete daily panic?

Well, there are anti-anxiety meds, because sometimes we all need a little extra help. It's more of a comfort than the loaded gun I kept while I spent the first summer after dental school "making it on my own" in Savannah.[14] Prescription

---

13. I have no piloting skills of my own, to be clear. Except in my dreams, in which I am a kickass pilot.

14. My dad taught me how to use it at my grandparents' country

help is a security blanket, a last resort for me when the day seems too long and my children have several more hours of awake time. It might turn into more one day; I might let the prescription run out altogether. Either way, it's nice to know it's there.

There's also the simple fact that my illusions of control have been utterly and brilliantly shattered. It's been a long and often painful process, this shattering, but it has been punctuated heavily by the births of both of my children. James came almost four weeks early, on a Saturday—the last day we'd ever sleep in until 9:30AM. I woke up to a bit of blood and the realization that I would be having a baby that day. Will showed up, characteristically, later and more loudly—after a day of contractions over which I was in denial, I stood up around 9PM to pee before bed and felt one swift, final kick—then my water broke all over our bedroom carpet. I barfed at the hospital, into a bucket rapidly provided by a nurse, and he was born around 1AM. For both boys, I was lying flat on a table, a scalpel opening me so they could emerge into the world. I was once again utterly out of control, and from that lack of control came two of the greatest, *hardest* gifts I've ever been given.

And every moment with them has been a reminder of just how little I have a say in the running of the universe, which not just I, but they, now inhabit. It's a much scarier one with them in it—these two beings whose lives I am charged to protect but not completely dictate, who I am supposed to teach but not control. Every news story is a threat to their well-being; every election colors their future;

---

property and then advised me to "shoot to kill" as I, illegally and terror-stricken, pulled the trigger—a great profile for a woman with a deadly weapon.

every visit to the playground carries physical and psychological implications that render me exhausted within a half hour. Everything feels designed to challenge my trust in a higher power who promises, ultimately, they will be okay. But there's a lot of wiggle room in *ultimately*. I mean, it's not guaranteed *right now*.[15]

But some afternoons, in our pre-Aussie life, we would head out to the swingset in the backyard, and sit, three-across, in its seats. Will would point to let me know he wanted me to swing too. So I did—haltingly at first, because my stomach dropped with each arc. *Did it always do that? Was it always this scary?* My movements were marked by hesitation more than freedom, a grudging slice through the air rather than the flying I remember observing during my youth. Then my boys would laugh beside me, and I would remember how to pump my legs, and I would go higher and higher, and they watched me and loved it. The chain held. And for a brief second, I was flying without fear.

Then I'd remember: we don't have a swingset in Sydney. But we will have plenty of time to fly, between continents, and homes.

Here's to smooth landings.

---

15. Are there better faith guarantees available in Australia? Note to self: check on this.

CHAR AND STEPH WANDER THE DESERT

ACT II

THE ISRAELITES *stand tightly packed together doubting, hating themselves, hating God, and saying their final goodbyes. Before them are the fearsome and enormous waters of the Red Sea. Behind them—drawing nearer by the second—is an army. There are murmurs of apprehension and downright terror buzzing throughout the group at a low hum that swells over time.*

CHAR (*holding* MARGOT *on her hip*): I always knew I'd go out theatrically, but this?

STEPH (*wistfully*): I always thought I'd kick it from old age, and Jason would go the exact same night.

CHAR: Sounds like a movie.

STEPH: What are we going to do? I mean, the LORD must really hate us.

CHAR: There's literally no way he's even real.

STEPH: Why would you say something like that?

CHAR: Well if he is real, then he's trying to kill us!

They stand in silence for a minute.

STEPH: In case I don't say it enough, I'm really grateful for our friendship...

CHAR (*overcome with emotion*): I—

Right then, MOSES *stretches out his arms before the wild and spraying sea. An eastern wind rushes past them, causing the water to open up, leaving a path of dry ground on which for them to walk. A wall of water on their right, a wall of water on their left.* CHAR *and* STEPH *have barely recovered from the wind whipping through their hair when they look up to see what's transpired before them.*

CHAR: You've got to be kidding me.

STEPH (*in awe*): He's made a way for us...

CHAR: Girl, no, I'm building a raft.

STEPH: We already went over this—we're in a DESERT.

They look at each other with expressions of abject horror and also a barely perceptible dose of relief. The walls of water are several stories high and the moisture is thick, with droplets sprinkling over the Israelites like a spring shower. While it is obvious that they can walk through it, the nearness of the sea—its deafening sound (almost protesting its weight and strength having to be held back)—doesn't exactly make the Israelites keen to forge ahead. The girls turn to look at each other again, weighing their prospects: Egyptians behind, walls of water on either side, a pathway through the walls ahead, and a sea that could swallow them at any moment should God choose. Rather than moving excitedly forward down the path, the group consensus seems to be a slow, fearful, begrudging amble through the imposing walls. STEPH *and* CHAR *tremble every long step of the way. They are certain that this is where their stories end.* STEPH *makes a show of kissing each of her children goodbye.* CHAR *grips tight to the hands of her beloved husband and children. But the path doesn't give until every last Israelite has crossed the sea, inexplicably dry, improbably safe.*

THE NEXT DAY, CHAR *and* STEPH *use the ladies room together behind a dead bush.*

STEPH: Okay, so we need to talk about what happened last night.

CHAR: Yeah.

STEPH: This is getting WEIRD.

CHAR: To say the least.

STEPH: Israelites are not "beach people." And then God goes and tells Moses—APPARENTLY—that's the exact route we have to take to stay under his protection? So God takes us on a journey he knows will terrify us?!

CHAR: I mean, logically, I feel like this so-called "God" would be a touch more generous, you know? "My people are enslaved? Poof, go free!" "My people are being chased by an army? Poof, go free!"

STEPH: I mean, that's kind of exactly what he did...

CHAR: Yeah, but in a super roundabout way...

STEPH: It's almost like God knows what we're most afraid of, where we trust him the least, and then he goes in for the kill—

CHAR: The kill?

STEPH: —straight to that place in our hearts.

CHAR: Okay, Deepak Chopra.

STEPH: Well, you saw it—HE MADE A PATH WHERE THERE WASN'T ONE. Right through the middle of the sea! God's been super unpredictable lately.

CHAR: Totally moody.

STEPH: So what if he decided to just let go or whatever? And that water came gushing down like it did on the Egyptians? We would've been goners instantly. Watery graves and all that. I shook the whole damn time we were walking.

CHAR: You're right. I know you're right. It was like nothing I've ever seen.

STEPH: The path on the one hand, and the water, loud as hell on the other. And just enough room for us and our baggage—and I'm not just talking about suitcases, ya heard? Seemed like our relief AND terror walked through it with us.

CHAR: You should write a book.

STEPH (*pondering the idea*): I have always felt I possessed an abundant knowledge of things like pop culture and brisket...

CHAR: Steph, I'm pretty overwhelmed by all this.

STEPH: Me too, but I'm also in awe. And a little scared. I feel very confused.

CHAR: I literally can't even talk about it.

STEPH: Hey, can you pass me a leaf?

STEPHANIE'S
GRATITUDE
JOURNAL
SYDNEY EDITION

JANUARY 2017.

Sydney, here we are.

The last time I was on the ground in Sydney, I spent a lot of time in a hotel room wondering what the hell we were doing. Particularly after one morning meeting at a potential school for James, when the registrar, after we discussed our child's challenges, acted as though we'd just told her we were carrying the plague. I don't remember what she actually said, just how I heard it: "You're not welcome here."

I only knew Sydney then from a couple of unfruitful school visits, a run along the harbour, a trip to the Opera House to see *My Fair Lady* (Jason and I both fell asleep), and the Marriott.

That is not the city we've landed in. Now, north of the bridge, we have a house. As of this morning, we have a gym. And the ladies there who run childcare, when I told them about James's challenges before committing to the membership I desperately need to feel sane, didn't act as though we had the plague. They actually *shrugged*. "No worries," they said.

THEY SAID *NO WORRIES* Y'ALL. And just like that, I felt welcome here.

If only there weren't any worries, though. If only I could push the boys in this stroller all over our suburb and, with every metre covered and every millilitre of sweat dripped, wipe away my concerns: James's new school year looming, his therapy centre, twenty minutes away, which I'll have to start driving to next week—on the left side of the road. Finding Will a preschool. Figuring out where to buy decent groceries. Making friends. I can't figure out, most days, if the breathlessness I feel is due more to pushing all their kilos of weight around or my own general anxiety over all that has to happen in the next few weeks.

I am utterly out of control. *Still.*

I currently know the way to a bakery, the liquor store, and an organic market. Oh, and the gym. These are my new landmarks. I need…more.

Days before we left, the boys and I were driving—on the right side of the road—toward James's school. I was worried then, too: about all the stuff that worries me now, plus the goodbyes, plus the flight. All down the street ahead of me, rays of light cast their beams, waves and particles visible only because they were traveling through something– between leaves, around branches, through dusty pollinated air, gray and scattered clouds. William Blake's verse came to mind, the one that never leaves me even when my grocery list and name do: "And we are put on earth a little space/ That we may learn to bear the beams of love."

It's time to ride the waves that lifted us out of the life we knew and into the one we are called to now, the one being written by a love whose beams I am constantly relearning to endure, a love that sends me on a reckless trip halfway across the world and gathers clouds just so I can see its light on a typical Tuesday morning, leaving the path we're on full of so many unknowns even while the road ahead is scattered with illumination.

So today…I'm grateful for that light. Which is here, too, even if I can't see its beams because it's summer and we're near the beach and light is just *everywhere*. I'm grateful for love, even when it hurts. Which it seems to do all the time.

I am being forced not to take the reins. I am being forced into choosing faith. I am being forced to let go…and be loved. How awful. How wonderful.

Sydney, here we are.

FROM THE DIARY OF
CHARLOTTE GETZ

Dear Diary,

Whoa gratitude. I have recently made a dear friend whose kids are the exact same age as Margot and Ford. She's exasperated and broken and almost as funny as Stephanie, which basically makes her the total package. Our kids have become great friends. Our husbands have become great friends. Maybe this place won't swallow us alive. The jury is still out, but the thought is still inspiring.

My mom prayed that California would offer answers to my brewing health woes: acute upper abdominal pain, fatigue, panic, fevers, rashes, joint pain, eye infections, chilled extremities, oh, and "extreme urgency." Just last week, I found this doctor who actually listened to me. She sat with me for an hour, wrote all kinds of things down, and at least appeared to believe that I wasn't over-exaggerating. She's now running all kinds of tests and seems to think it's possible that things like rashes and eye problems might (bizarre as it sounds) be a part of the same root condition as crapping-your-pants. It's the first time a doctor hasn't looked at his watch with a yawn and sent me away with a prescription for something like antacids. I'm afraid to hope—because

I've hoped so many times before. But my fingers are tentatively crossed, Diary. But unless he reads this I won't even tell Alex about the crossed fingers. He's heard it before, too. And we're both tired.

Even more exciting is that Ford's heart murmur is "non-worrisome," as in, we never have to go back to a pediatric cardiologist again. Super glad I engaged in all that highly productive worrying. But here's the thing…the relief that washed over me after our appointment was embarrassingly minimal even though God actually answered my prayer in the *exact way I wanted him to*: a non-worrisome heart murmur. It almost sounds cute, like a whisper. Maybe that's how I'll describe it to Ford one day—both God and his murmur—*a whisper*.

I hear you, Jesus.

CHAR AND STEPH
WANDER THE DESERT

ACT III

ABOUT A WEEK *after the* LORD *parts the Red Sea, deep in the desert, the Israelites have been without water for three days.*

STEPH (*wipes her brow*): I'm so damn thirsty.

CHAR: My tongue feels like leather.

STEPH: God must really hate us.

CHAR: He literally doesn't even exist.

STEPH: Were there not enough graves in Egypt? So God brought us here to die?!

CHAR: I'm not breathing very well.

STEPH: Do you think this is it? As in...*the end?*

CHAR: We're for sure all going to die this morning. If not this morning, then later this afternoon.

LATER THAT AFTERNOON, *the Israelites find water in a place called Marah.*

CHAR (*on her hands and knees, takes a sip and then immediately spits it out*): Tastes like shit.

STEPH (*follows suit*): Literally, like clear, liquid shit.

CHAR (*still spitting*): What are the symptoms of cholera again?

STEPH (*still spitting*): If you had it, *you'd know.*

CHAR: As in?

STEPH: Lots of butt stuff.

CHAR: If God can turn this around, I will never doubt him again.

Right then MOSES, *who they now realize is just a short distance away from them, throws a piece of wood into the water.*

RANDOM HEBREW: HE SAYS WE'RE GOOD TO GO WITH THE WATER!

The girls take a hesitant sip to find that it tastes...well...like water! They give bowls of it to their children and then gulp it down themselves to their hearts' content.

LATER THAT DAY, *lounging amongst springs and palm trees...*

STEPH: I drank that water like it was my JOB.

CHAR: I'm starving.

STEPH: Sidenote: why does it seem like every good thing is either preceded or followed by something super hard?

CHAR: That's what she said.

A MONTH AND A HALF *after the Israelites' departure from Egypt, they arrive in the Desert of Sin. The girls are lagging.*

STEPH: Are we there yet?

CHAR: The kids are starting to look like two-legged ribeyes.

STEPH: Just looking at them is making my mouth water.

CHAR: Throw in a little salt, maybe some ketchup...

They glance at each other with expressions of concern. This is an alarming level of rock bottom.

STEPH (*changing the subject*): This is so lame. Let's just go back to Egypt.

CHAR: You say that like you know the way.

STEPH *turns around, trying to identify the way they had come.*

STEPH: Well...it's just over...how *did* we get here?

CHAR: Why won't someone up front just stop and ASK FOR DIRECTIONS?!

STEPH: I think we really are goners this time.

CHAR: Belly up. Cold in the grave.

STEPH: God has CLEARLY abandoned us.

THAT EVENING, CHAR *peeks out of her tent after a fitful afternoon nap...*

CHAR (*à la Clark Griswold's dad from* Christmas Vacation): QUUUUUUUAAAIIIILLL!!!!

Everyone fights to gather their share.

RANDOM HEBREW: TAKE ONLY ENOUGH FOR TODAY! FOR THE LORD ALMIGHTY WILL PROVIDE FOR US TOMORROW!

STEPH (*tearily to the heavens*): I get it now, Yahweh! You are with me always. I trust you...

A FEW DAYS LATER, STEPH's *tent begins to smell of something rotten.* CHAR *comes knocking.*

CHAR: Girl, what's going on in there? Haven't seen you in a few days.

STEPH (*whispering*): Uhh, don't come in!

CHAR: What, are you naked?

STEPH: Hold on, I'll be out in a sec.

CHAR: Seriously, you're starting to worry me.

CHAR *forces open the canvas flap of the tent to see piles of moldy, rotten manna, and young* JAMES *and* WILL *looking more than a touch overfed.* STEPH's *cheeks turn a ripe vermilion.*

CHAR (*hands on hips*): Hoarding the manna? Really?

STEPH *shrugs as she continues to chew, ashamed.*

CHAR (*cont'd*): Yo, let me in on that.

After leaving the Desert of Sin, the Israelites wander (seemingly haphazardly) as God leads them from one place to the next. The people are thirsty.

STEPH (*wipes her brow*): Does breathing dust count as eating?

CHAR: We are all going to die.

STEPH: God must hate us.

CHAR: Or he doesn't even exist.

STEPH: I'm almost ready to stone Moses.

MOSES *goes ahead of the Israelites, strikes a rock with his staff, and water gushes forth.*

CHAR: THE LORD IS TRULY AMONG US!

The Amalekites, a tribal people living in Canaan, want to destroy God's people. Unprovoked, they travel deep into the desert to attack the Israelites. MOSES instructs JOSHUA to take a group of men to go to war with them. STEPH and CHAR nibble on some manna with the kids back at the campsite.

STEPH: Where's Alex today?

CHAR: Joshua picked him to help fight the Amalekites. I'm a little nervous. I hope he's okay.

STEPH: Wow, that's really intense.

CHAR: Yeah. I mean he's pretty strappy. You should see his thighs. But it's always a little scary not knowing if he's going to come back this time.

STEPH: Man, I can't imagine.

CHAR: Where's Jason?

STEPH *(a little embarrassed):* He's...he's helping hold Moses' arms up.

CHAR: He's—

STEPH: I know it sounds weird.

CHAR *(in a high-pitched voice):* No!! It really doesn't...

STEPH: I mean it's not "war" or anything.

CHAR: No, no, it sounds really important.

STEPH: You think it's weird.

CHAR: No, seriously, it sounds really cool. I mean, it's *Mo-*

ses. Wow. I'd wax that guy's legs if he asked me to!

STEPH: Yeah, I guess.

THREE MONTHS AFTER *leaving Egypt, the Israelites stand at the base of Mount Sinai looking up, waiting on direction from* MOSES.

STEPH (*whispers*): What are we doing exactly?

CHAR: Moses is up there trying to talk to God.

STEPH: Right, but why are we all standing around watching? It's not like God's going to actually show up.

Thunder and lightning and smoke and trumpet sounds fill the air around where MOSES *stands on the mountain. The voice of God rises above the fanfare and He announces ten commandments by which His people must abide. The Israelites, instead of moved and awed, are left terrified and trembling.*

CHAR *holds her children back behind her.* STEPH *is cold to the touch.*

CHAR: God isn't going to come out of that cloud, is He?

STEPH: No...He wouldn't...would He?

CHAR: WE WILL LITERALLY DIE IF GOD SPEAKS DIRECTLY TO US. I KNOW IT.

STEPH: That's kind of a leap.

MOSES *disappears into the smoke and has a more private convo with God.*

CHAR (*relieved*): Oh thank God.

STEPH: Did you even hear what God said to us up there? Kind of a disappointment. Just seemed like a lot of rules, if

I'm being honest.

CHAR: A *LOT* of rules.

STEPH: Can't we just sort of agree to be decent people and leave it at that?

CHAR: You are *such* a decent person.

STEPH: Ugh, so are *you!* I feel like God is asking an awful lot of us these days.

CHAR: Right? I mean, the no killing thing I get. Unless someone's being a real dick and then it seems appropriate?

STEPH: Definitely.

CHAR: But what about the whole honoring the Sabbath thing? Doesn't He get that parenting is a seven-days-a-week gig??

STEPH: Clearly he has no idea what it's like to be a parent.

CHAR: I feel tired just thinking about it.

STEPH: Haven't we already put in our time back in Egypt? Hey God, maybe a vacation is in order.

CHAR: What were we actually thinking when we decided to follow this chump into the desert?

STEPH: No idea. I thought we were doing pretty well in Egypt!

CHAR: That's how I remember it!

STEPH: Egypt was the best!

TWO WEEKS LATER...

STEPH: What has Moses possibly been doing up there for *two weeks*?

CHAR: Get your head out of your ass, Steph. *Moses is dead.*

STEPH: *Shhhh*, not in front of the kids!!

CHAR: Sorry. You know how I get.

STEPH: I mean, it feels like God has really abandoned us this time. What has He done with our leader??

CHAR: God really could work on the whole transparency thing.

STEPH: And timeliness. Whew. Get a watch, dude. A two-week meeting is too long.

CHAR (*with a shard of rabid hysteria in her eyes*): Okay, hear me out... If God probably doesn't exist, and Moses is obviously dead...maybe we should make a new god...

STEPH: ...Stands to reason.

CHAR: SOMEBODY GET AARON!

The girls tell AARON *their plan.*

AARON: ...Stands to reason.

STEPH: Here, take my gold earrings...

CHAR: Your best hoops!

STEPH: I know...

CHAR: You're so righteous.

AARON *gathers the gold jewelry from all the women and children. After fiddling for a few minutes with his back to the crowd, he turns around and lifts their new god high into the air.*

CHAR (*unimpressed*): Seriously?

STEPH: A baby cow?

CHAR: Did not see that coming.

STEPH: Not even a lion? Or a wolf?

CHAR: Still...the thing has to be more reliable than this God who brought us out here for literally no reason at all but to abandon us.

FORTY DAYS *after* MOSES' *ascent up Mount Sinai, he finally returns to the camp to find the Israelites singing in revelry, worshiping their new little god.*

CHAR *and* STEPH *are in the front row of people dancing violently, as if in a trance, worshipping the small golden calf. Their hair is wild and their faces have been smeared with something resembling dirt or blood. Their four children are in a similar state of phony transcendence.*

STEPH *(to the calf)*: Praise be to our lord who brought us out of Egypt!

CHAR: Surely he is our god!

MOSES, *furious, hurls down two tablets—written by and with the hand of God—before the feverish Israelites. The noise and gesture seems to break the hysteria.*

STEPH *(to* CHAR): He's alive...

CHAR: And he brought something with him...

STEPH: Looks like it's from God?

CHAR: So...I guess God *is* real?

STEPH: I guess he doesn't hate us after all?

CHAR: Now I feel a little silly.

The girls look at each other in all their cultish mess, and then to their tiny, bovine, false god.

STEPH: In the light of day, the calf does seem like a bit of a stretch.

CHAR: Was worth a shot?

STEPH: Totally worth it.

The people arrive outside Canaan, and MOSES *sends twelve spies—each one a leader from a tribe of Israel—to explore the land and report back.*

CHAR: Milk and honey sounds ridiculously good right now.

STEPH: Imagine the recipe possibilities!

CHAR: The quail is getting a little old.

STEPH: I literally cannot change another manna diaper.

AFTER FORTY DAYS, *the spies return.*

ISRAELITE #1: THE PEOPLE ARE TALLER AND STRONGER THAN WE ARE!

ISRAELITE #2: THIS LAND WILL DEVOUR US!

CHAR: THE LORD HAS BROUGHT US OUT HERE TO DIE!

STEPH: CAN WE PLEASE GO BACK TO EGYPT ALREADY?!

MOSES *and* AARON *beg the people to trust God, to not be afraid. They promise that God will lead them safely into this new land.*

CHAR: Oh fuck that.

MESSAGE IN A BOTTLE

DEAR ANXIETY SUFFERER,

We've got it all figured out, so we're literally sending our newfound wisdom out into the world via this empty bottle of chardonnay. LISTEN UP. And congratulations on taking your first step toward achieving mental health.

Anxiety isn't just a more clinical-sounding title for being high-strung, or a badge of honor for people who want you to know they're *super, super busy and emotional*. Rest assured, it's an actual condition, independent of circumstances. You don't have to live in a war-torn country or with a domestic abuser to be anxious. No, here is how you get anxiety: *you have it.* That's it.

So once you realize *you have it*, and that it is affecting the way you parent and interact and *live*, you might decide to do something about it. Yoga? Meds? A two-week meditation retreat? Your husband might refuse to sign off on the last one. You may be tempted to exhaust other options before taking on a daily pill (like you need one more thing to remember). So when once-a-week restorative yoga doesn't work (you even dodge big-city traffic to get to that class: Move out of my f#$%ing way, people! I'VE GOT TO RE-LAX!), you find a counselor and ask for a cure.

Ugh. Turns out there isn't a Ten-Step Plan to Getting Rid of Anxiety Forever, regardless of what you've read on Refinery29. But there are techniques. Chief among them is the idea of mindfulness, or living in the present moment. Anxiety is, after all, a future-focused form of worry (so said the cutout from that magazine you kept by your bed for five years... "Pay attention to the water flowing over your hands as you wash the dishes" and that kind of thing. IT DIDN'T CURE YOU? We're shocked). You could go even deeper, like stepping outside yourself and watching as you get all anxious and seeing what it does to you. And you can get into some really psychological-sounding voodoo like talking to your inner child, which isn't exactly staying in the present moment, but that inner child is *affecting how you respond* to the present moment so, you know, attention must be paid to that chick. So talk to her, right?

We aren't knocking these techniques. All of them can be helpful, to varying degrees of success. But when there's an explosion outside your window in said big city (turned out to be a water main, but tell that to your restless leg), or your kid has locked you out of the car AGAIN and the only thing standing between you and a prison sentence is a pane of glass and a shard of sanity...then you might need a more reliable form of rescue. Here is our scientifically tested prescription:

- Drink wine, but not too much wine
- Drink beer, but not too much beer
- Chew peppermint gum
- Splash cold water on face
- Tell somebody how you're feeling!
- Write about it!

- Take deep yoga breaths
- Snap rubber band on wrist
- Desperation-text your husband
- Take your meds
- Chew your damn gum
- Oh yeah, pray

AND/OR:

- DIE.

Now, you might be wanting to call us 'Willis' and ask what we're talking 'bout. Let us explain. It's all well and good to have strategies; strategies can work! Techniques can help! SYNERGY! Wait, what? What we're trying to say is that lists will only get you so far. The real secret (lean in close) is this:

THE GOSPEL!!!

Oops. Didn't mean to yell. Now don't get your whities in a wad. We aren't calling God a genie or a luck dragon or anything. We're just saying that the Good News really is good. And when your meds are off and you think the edge might literally cut through you, it's the one thing to cling to that (in the ultimate sense) cannot disappoint. The edge might stay with you, the pain might stay with you, but God stays with you, too. Not a bad set-up. The gospel gets a bad rap sometimes because it says you have to die before you can live. Which is a hard pill to swallow when you didn't even want to take a pill in the first place.

Here's how it goes: girl has anxiety. Girl gets tools to deal with it. Tools help. (Occasionally.) But girl ends up in a situation (usually involving failure, humiliation, menstruation, her children, all of these things, or NONE OF THEM) in which she ends up feeling totally defeated by her anxiety; we mean, *crushed*. All hope appears lost. She thinks she will never get better. She can't bear to think about the looks she will get when everyone sees she's STILL a mess. She thinks she will actually die. None of the techniques help. She is drowning, and she cannot breathe. She is sinking, sinking, sinking…and everything goes dark.

Awful, right? Like, Shakespearean tragedy-awful. Except there's this other thing—death—and it relies not at all on the sinking girl, but on her being miraculously and improbably revived by something [Someone] entirely separate from herself. No strategy, no implementation, just plain being lifted up out of the depth of despair and placed atop some blessed rock. Death, but then…resurrection. See what we're getting at here?

We know it's not as simple as a granted wish. We know there's a whole lot of fist shaking, swearing into the sky, and *despair*. But it took Jesus himself three days, people. Settle in: this may take a while. Chances are, we're probably going to be staring that bastard (mental dysfunction) in the face off-and-on our whole lives until we arrive at that beautiful buffet in the sky, where there's endless white bread and the bill is already paid. But God is right with us. The ultimate hope—for us, for our kids when we fail them, for our friends when we hurt them, for our marriages when we flounder, for our jobs when we blow it—is in the throes of death that transform into the pangs of new life.

Drown, resuscitate, repeat. Fail, get forgiven, go again. Despair, hope, defeat, redemption, over and over, until one day you wake up and you realize you're still anxious, but you see it more clearly, for the cloudy lens it is, and you know—even though you're not there yet, because TODAY IS A DOOZY—you *know* that you're going to be okay. Ultimately, you will be whole. And you're headed there. So you breathe, and you put one foot in front of the other while recognizing that you're actually being carried. And your anxiety hasn't disappeared; nope, it's still following you around like a hot, wet rag someone keeps chucking at your face, but you're no longer a table for two. You've got company, and it looks strangely like a lifeboat with all the provisions onboard (see what we did there?). You settle in, and soon other passengers come aboard your lifeboat, so you open a bottle of wine and hold hands and breathe together, everyone facing the same direction.

Love,

Stephanie and Charlotte

PART FOUR

AVOID EATING THE OTHER DUDES IN THE BOAT

RECOVERED TRANSCRIPTS FROM LIFEBOAT 815

EXTERIOR: DAY—SOMEWHERE IN THE PACIFIC.

STEPHANIE *and* CHARLOTTE *recline side-by-side in their lifeboat—which flails around in the wild and unpredictable waves, somewhere between east and west. Their husbands,* JASON *and* ALEX *(who have been in the boat the whole time, behind the scenes, doing the heavy lifting and other "important" ish) finally get a chance to really talk while they take over rowing for a bit.*

JASON *is a 38-year-old financial wizard in the body of a weightlifter who's been on break for a couple of months. His pecs and calves, however, have NOT suffered. He has kind eyes, a sincere laugh, and looks to be constantly assessing the situation.*

ALEX *is a 28-year-old, who you might mistake for a 45-year-old. He has the torso of a firefighter and the heart of a cranky, loner, cabin-in-the-woods grandpa or creative-type. A restless caretaker at his core, he's been plotting their hypothetical rescue this whole time.*

JASON: So, seems like our wives are friends.

ALEX (*out of breath from all the rowing*): Yeah. Charlotte really loves Stephanie.

JASON: Yeah, Stephanie is pretty taken with Charlotte too.

ALEX: Wanna get a beer some time?

JASON: That'd be good.

Obviously, they are BFFs.

SCENE.

RECOVERED TRANSCRIPTS
FROM LIFEBOAT 815

EXTERIOR: DAY—SOMEWHERE IN THE PACIFIC.

MEANWHILE, *as their husbands row and also appear to be engaged in a deep, highly intelligent conversation,* CHARLOTTE *and* STEPHANIE *relax and whisper over happy hour at the bow of the boat.*

STEPHANIE: Are men born stupid when it comes to anything involving domestic life, or do they just become that way when they get married?

CHARLOTTE: I see you're working on your next women's Bible study there, Steph.

STEPHANIE: Only if it meets at a bar and profanity figures in heavily to the mix.

CHARLOTTE: Shit yeah. (*They clink glasses.*)

STEPHANIE: Well my sister has a theory that men *can't* be as dumb as they act at home and also hold down actual jobs. So she thinks they just fake ignorance around the house to get out of helping us. Like, "Durr, I don't know how to put a fitted sheet on a bed" or "Blerg, I've lived here for ten years but still don't know where the Tupperware containers go so

I'll just leave them stacked on the counter here after I've halfway-emptied the dishwasher."

CHARLOTTE: These examples sound very specific.

STEPHANIE: Please tell me I'm not the only one who deals with this.

CHARLOTTE: Oh no girl, I feel you. I'll be honest, Alex is pretty good around the house, but he has ruined every single one of our headboards.

STEPHANIE: Wha...you mean, like, sexually? Ew.

CHARLOTTE: Yes... NO. I mean, with his greasy hair when he lies against it. Like when he's *reading* at night. The guy showers every morning and it still stains! Like, something is seriously up with his scalp. And he will not position his body in any other way but to rest his head against the headboard! This grease even stains wood, dude.

STEPHANIE: NO!

CHARLOTTE: He's such a financial drain on our family.

STEPHANIE: You poor thing.

CHARLOTTE: I've tried everything. Today, I attempted to buff off the stain using only soap suds... ??? because some internet blogger said so... ??? ...didn't work.

STEPHANIE: I mean, "get a pillow," "close the drawer." *These are not missile codes.*

CHARLOTTE: What the hair stain is really saying is: "I do not care about you or love you enough to respond to even the tiniest of requests. We will not make it to our 10th anniversary because, *hot secretary.*"

STEPHANIE: YES. Jason apparently has some disorder? Where he is unable to close a cabinet door after he's opened it? And the open cabinet message is: "You are in this alone, dude. I've got my own crap to deal with and you can take care of all the rest."

CHARLOTTE: I know, just say what you're trying to say, rather than leaving these obscure hints all around the house.

STEPHANIE: Marriage.

CHARLOTTE: Marriage indeed.

STEPHANIE: I wouldn't trade him, though.

They gaze lovingly over at their men.

CHARLOTTE: Oh me neither. He's my best friend!

I PROMISE NOTHING, AND EVERYTHING

Stephanie

I HEARD THAT when Brad Pitt and Jennifer Aniston got married (RIP), they wrote their own wedding vows that included such cuteness as "making banana milkshakes" for each other and "splitting the difference on the thermostat." Fat lot of good *that* did them.

But I'm stealing the idea anyway. I'M REVOLUTION-IZING THE VOW INDUSTRY, PEOPLE.

And I'm not the only one! In 2015, *The New York Times'* column *Modern Love* featured a piece about how vows would actually read if full disclosure were to occur. Short answer: no mention of milkshakes. Author Ada Calhoun writes about what she'd like proclaimed at weddings:

> I want to say that one day you and your husband will fight about missed flights, and you'll find yourself wistful for the days when you had to pay for only your own mistakes. I want to say that at various points in your

marriage, may it last forever, you will look at this person and feel only rage. You will gaze at this man you once adored and think, "It sure would be nice to have this whole place to myself" ("The Wedding Toast I'll Never Give").

It is February 2017, and were it not for the fact that I haven't yet learned to drive on the left side of the road and don't have a job in Sydney to cover the rent, I'd be scouring the local paper for studio apartments to hide in for some alone time. THERE IS A LOT OF TOGETHERNESS HERE—between me and the kids while Jason is at work, and between me and Jason since we don't have any friends here yet. We sit out by the pool and contemplate this life of ours, which has been suddenly and radically transplanted, and it turns out that this move has heightened my awareness of tiny issues that, back when we were on familiar ground, were just slight annoyances. And yet, where can I go? Yep, it's not enough that my husband dragged me to a beautiful poolside in Australia...he also had to contribute half the genetic material to two beautiful boys who drive me insane, give my life meaning, and bind Jason and me together forever.

Ball and chain indeed.

I found the minister who officiated my wedding by receiving seven years of counseling from him first. The fact that he was even willing to perform my ceremony gives me hope in redemption. One thing that he talked about, outside of and within marriage, is giving ourselves space for feelings, particularly grief: grief as an acknowledgment of another space, the space between how things are and how things should be.

I went to a wedding recently that was officiated by a friend of the couple and featured homespun vows. Despite the generous open bar I knew was awaiting me at the reception, I wanted to halt the ceremony with a loud farting sound followed by some yelling and well-placed f-bombs. Overkill? Maybe, but there is nothing more ridiculous to a married person than hearing commitments of eternal, uninterrupted love between two people who have never brokered an in-law visitation schedule or argued over who changed the last diaper. (Wait, yes there is: it's when a parent gets parenting advice from a non-parent.) Some weddings leave me feeling like the worst kind of cynic: the kind who offers unsolicited advice with an air of superiority before yelling at everyone to get off my lawn.

I can only approach any discussion of marriage from a wife's angle because (a) I am a wife, and (b) my husband doesn't complain as much as I do so I'm not as privy to his ideas of the downsides. I do know this, though: a 2010 study by Harvard Medical School revealed that married men live longer than single men[1]; five years later a University College London/London School of Economics/London School of Hygiene and Tropical Medicine (yep, they *all* got in there) study was like, hold up, there's also this: single women don't face the same disadvantages as single men[2] (i.e. not having a laundress or cook on hand, I guess). So let's unpack that with an air of superiority before I tell you to get off my lawn.

I often wonder whether my husband washed his sheets like, ever, before we were married. Same goes for replacing toilet paper rolls and throwing out the empty milk container.

1. "Marriage and men's health." *Harvard Men's Health Watch.*
2. Knapton, Sarah. "Marriage is more beneficial for men than women, study shows." *The Telegraph.* 2015.

Married men are cared for by another person in ways single men aren't. In turn, single women sleep later and go to spin class more often. Does that explain the study?

I know that this caretaking is mutual; at least, I choose to believe it is. Maybe our husbands are too busy to pick up their own socks because they're buying us birthday presents or sorting out our 401k's. But this is what so much of marriage can feel like: a comparisons game between the partners, or between life now and life pre-wedding. This is anathema, of course, to a healthy relationship. It's also impossible to avoid.

Though marital discord is inevitable, some of it can be avoided in practical ways that won't land you in prison or on the nightly news. And if there's anything I am (besides flawed, occasionally sanctimonious, and often bitter), it's practical! So I've put together this handy list of topics to cover in your vows if you decide to go rogue and ignore the traditional "honor and cherish" route.

1. DISPOSAL: You're going to need to have a nice, long sit-down about waste management. No, it's not sexy, but it has to happen unless you want Trash Day every week to leave you searching for that studio apartment.

> "I promise to empty the diaper genie twice a
> week if you promise to take the trash cans to
> the street every Wednesday."

2. RENEWAL: How many M&Ms can be left in the bag before a new one is purchased? Is an empty soap bottle in the shower a sign of aggression, or did he just forget to replace it?

> "I promise not to steal and eat the cookie
> dough you hid in the freezer and WHEN I
> DO, I will buy more immediately."

This brings us to...

3. COMMUNICATION: I have a friend who requires her husband to look into her eyes when she's telling him something important. This sounds ridiculous to single people, but to married people it is as essential as court reporters during a murder trial. We all (men) have a way of "forgetting" key information when our feet are to the fire. We all make an ass out of you and me by assuming too much. The unspoken words that flow between two people can be more damning, or more redemptive, than those uttered aloud.

> "I promise to actually tell you out loud when
> information passes through my brain that is
> relevant to our daily life and/or well-being."

4. CONFLICT RESOLUTION: They say when you marry someone, you marry their family. This is terrifying, and true. So prepare, before the in-laws arrive for their first visit, for their departure. As in, discuss how long you allow visitors to remain in your home. As well as other boundaries, like whether your father-in-law is allowed into the room when you're nursing a baby (NO) or whether any of your parents have a say in your children's names.

> "I promise to bodyslam my mother if she attempts to take the baby away from you without permission."

Later on in her *Modern Love* piece, Calhoun writes this:

You can be bad at a religion and still be 100 percent that religion. Just because you take the Lord's name in vain doesn't make you suddenly a non-Christian. You can be a sinner. In fact, I think it's good theology that no matter how hard you try, you are sure to be a sinner, just as you are sure to be lousy, at least sometimes, at being married. There is perfection only in death.

If the choices come down to these two—married or dead—well…yeah, I choose married. Because even if it's like holding a full-body mirror an inch away from your naked self after you've carb-loaded in a cave for three months, there's this: someone's standing next to you and, by not leaving, is saying "Yes" to you all over again. Which may, in the end, be the best vow anyway: YES. I take you, period.

U2 sings that "there's no end to grief, that's how I know… there's no end to love." Along with our families, our wardrobes, and our wedding china, we all bring our own set of expectations into marriage with us. They will undoubtedly be some combination of unfair and untenable. There will be space between them and reality, and grief should be allowed to settle into that space. We grieve the death of our expectations, the death of our independence, death, PERIOD. But the great thing about the greatest love is that it keeps the promises we can't, and specializes in the business of resurrections. So although "Say YES to death—get married!" may not catch on as a slogan anytime soon, maybe it's the sort of promise we actually can make. Then we watch as we are brought back to a new kind of life. A life full of socks left on the floor, and each other, always there.

OH THERE YOU ARE!

Charlotte

ALEX GRADUATED FROM GRAD SCHOOL at the top of his class (literally...he won "Graduate Student of the Year"). So I shouldn't have been surprised that he would land an impressive job demanding extremely unimpressive amounts of time and effort on his part; as in, young millennial slavery; as in, he's never home. These missing hours have brought out the worst in me, especially as we continue to assimilate. I spend my days walking, exploring, meeting new moms at the playground, and raising our children. Alex must leave well before we wake up and he returns, at best, just as the kids are getting ready for bed. Is this becoming my place and not *our* place? Exasperated, I say to him, "*I can't do this all on my own.*" Is this a reality we have to settle for? Does Alex want to succeed at work and provide for us, or does he want to be *away* from us? Am I losing him? Am I losing myself?

These questions and their answers seem insultingly obvious to him. But that doesn't leave my feet any less stuck to the ground in all the awful gravity a marriage can generate.

We have these conversations constantly, as if they were penciled into our schedules. The day I blow, typically a Thursday, means that I have reached my threshold of strength and goodwill (which on a good day looks a lot like a banshee with Botox, i.e., not fooling anyone). Alex has usually claimed he'd be able to get home earlier than he actually does. I pout until he pours me a glass of wine and then I go nuclear on his ass, almost always starting with "*I can't do this...*"

When we are finally all out of words—in both the basic and the emotional sense—we reach for each other's hands. This has always been our way. And in California, our hands often say far more than our mouths.

I tend to take my hands for granted. They carry things, they type, they brush my teeth, scratch things, rub things, move things, etc. But hands are so much more than that. They serve as a sort of map, for better or worse, of our lives. They remember things more than our minds ever could. They connect us to people, to events. They pray. When our eyes, words, minds, and memories fail (or refuse) to be our guide, our hands do the job instead. We feel our way through time and space.

Tough hands are a genetic gift from my mom. She used to be a hand model. As a kid, this was one of my go-to bragging rights—a distinguishing legacy of my DNA that meant I, too, might have hands held in high-esteem by people like advertising executives. But it turns out that the story I *heard* her say was slightly over-glorified. My mom wasn't actually a career hand model. She only did it once while working at an advertising agency in Chicago. While working on a print ad for a furniture polish, it occurred to my mom that the hands of the model they had hired were too perfect—they looked brand new, store bought, elegant, un-blemished, unused—not the storied hands of a woman who would actually polish furniture. She brought this to the at-tention of her boss.

"Why don't we use *yours* instead?" he suggested.

My mom probably looked down at her own hands, which were appropriately sized for her thin frame. Staring back at her were weathered, worn, scarred palms—even at age twenty-seven because she was, and still is, a doer. Her hands had a slight leathery-ness from her propensity to over-ti-dy. Or from countless days passed slaloming under the hot Minnesota sun, where she and her three sisters spent their summers. They were nearly an imprint of the years gone be-fore her. She took the job and has, to this day, remained a hero to me on the level of Xena.

I have my mom's hands, strong and sure on the surface. Maybe I don't yet really know what's beneath their weary exterior.

IN THE MOVIE *Hook*, when Peter Pan returns to Neverland as an adult, none of the Lost Boys recognize this man, this *lawyer*. He used to fly, used to fight, used to crow. Grown Peter, slightly overweight and wearing glasses and a busi-ness suit, looks like he could do none of those things. Even *he* didn't remember who he really was. But Pockets, one of the younger Lost Boys, doesn't trust what he sees with his eyes—and so he steps forward and touches Peter's face, squishing it every which way under the feel of his more trustworthy hands. Suddenly a smile spreads over his face: "Oh there you are, Peter!" The rest of the Lost Boys rush forward to touch Peter's face—and under their hands, rather than before their eyes, is the man they had known so well. The man they had been missing.

THE NIGHT I FIRST REALIZED I might have a crush on Alex, I beat him in a Hand-Holding Competition. Now, you may not have heard of a Hand-Holding Competition, so here are the lengthy and complex instructions: you hold hands with a person until someone lets go.[3] My winning strategy that night was simple—I out-sweated him to victory.

I had met Alex several weeks prior as we began the MFA Photography program at the Savannah College of Art and Design. I was twenty-six. When Alex walked through the classroom door on our first morning of class wearing tight jeans, a navy hoodie with emo lyrics printed on the front, messy hair, big brown nerd glasses, and what can best be described as black jazz shoes, I thought he was either the most cliché male artist I'd ever seen, or gay[4]...definitely *not* the future father of my children.

What I learned about Alex in the following weeks:

- He was not gay
- If he could be a tree, he would be an Ent (a talking, walking, wise race of trees) from *Lord of the Rings*
- He was from middleofnowhere Illinois (but claimed [lied] that he was from Chicago)
- He had decent taste in music
- He was interested in girls much younger than

---

3. Wusses out.

4. Two safe assumptions, given what I knew from my experience of SCAD's cliché fem-hipster counterculture. Pedophile mustaches and the like.

    myself
- Because he himself was much younger than myself (by five years)
- We would never ever be more than friends

But obviously, something changed along the way that made me decide to marry him and have his babies.

A week after the Hand-Holding Competition, a good friend of mine came to town and a group of us went to a swanky rooftop bar at the Bohemian Hotel in Savannah. Evan, the Hot Waiter from the Pink House (and the guy I had been going on dates with), joined us after he got off work. He arrived right as Alex and I were reaching the peak of a heated debate.

"Falcor, the dragon from *The Neverending Story*, is definitely a dog," Alex argued coolly, not letting the disagreement get to him.

"Do you even hear yourself? You just described him as a dragon in *your own argument*." I was not as cool.

"Doesn't matter, he's a dog."

"Good comeback. NOT. He calls himself a Luck Dragon in the movie! He's a dragon!" I was furious [I was correct].

"He looks like a dog."

"Just because you *think* he looks like a dog does not make him a dog. How can you not just admit that I'm right?"[5]

Evan pulled up a seat between us.

"Evan, Falcor from *The Neverending Story*, is he a dragon or a dog?" I asked.

"What's *The Neverending Story*?"

Crickets.

---

5. Don't cross me on *The Neverending Story* or I'll go all Gmork on your ass.

That was the night I realized how much more fun I had arguing with Alex than I did doing anything at all with Evan the Hot Waiter.

Right around the time of this realization, Alex had attracted the attentions of Sadie the Awkward Roller Skater.

Sadie was the type of girl I had actually imagined Alex would end up with. She was tiny, cute, artistic, played roller derby, and she never wore a bra (never needed to). Ideal. By all appearances, she was a free spirit—she looked like she just woke up cool. When I think about it now, I imagine it took a great deal of effort on her part to play such a specific role in life. Contrasting Sadie, I was bigger (in boobs and stature), irrevocably neurotic, lacking any badass recreational hobbies, and not remotely elfish.

If I sound a little bitter, it's because Sadie was also just kind of mean.[6] She was the type of person[7] who would say something like, "Well maybe it's because you're so ugly!" to a person she barely knew. And then she'd laugh maniacally, eventually throwing in a "just kidding" for good measure. Everyone around her would get awkward and quiet and whisper encouraging things to the person like, "You're so pretty, don't even think about it, I'm sure she's just drunk!" I never saw this particular exchange occur but trust me, somewhere, with someone, it happened.[8]

So Alex and Sadie began to hang out very casually. And all of a sudden, with a bit of lively competition in the ring, I wanted him so badly that my skin hurt.

A month or so into whatever they were doing, a group

6. And also hogging my man to herself.

7. Bish.

8. Sadie dressed up as JonBenét Ramsey for Halloween. I believe this to be an important character detail.

of us went to the beach at Tybee Island one night, sans Sadie. It was mid-November, and the air was the kind of crisp that feels exciting, like it's almost Christmas. Alex and I lay next to each other on the sand and watched the stars, our buddies doing the same close by. By now, Alex and I were great friends. By now he was doodling funny pictures of me during class, dressing up like Andy Warhol at Halloween because he knew I was obsessed, and stopping by my apartment unannounced just because I had a bad day. We were dancing to The Cure on his front porch, staying up all hours of the night laughing at YouTube videos, making each other mix CDs, sitting next to each other in every class, and bantering back and forth to everyone else's great annoyance.

"Charlotte?" he said quietly as we looked out over the broad expanse of stars.

"Alex?"

"In the case of a nuclear apocalypse, if I could choose anyone else to survive along with me, it would be you." He reached over and held my hand, and I let him. This time, he didn't let go. And we held hands all the way back into town, with "Heads Will Roll" by the Yeah Yeah Yeahs blaring over the radio.

As far as I am aware, Alex and I invented the Hand-Holding Competition. During his toast at our rehearsal dinner, he would refer to this game as a form of relationship chicken, some warped metaphor for how he and I have challenged each other from the beginning. And here we are still, challenging each other—albeit in a far less flirty way. When we are overwhelmed with love, we hold hands. And when we are overwhelmed by all these questions that do not have answers, problems we know will be problems for years to come—feet meeting gravity—we also hold hands.

We (as a civilization) put our hands together to pray—assuming that some desperate message of thanks, exasperation, or unbelief will be transferred from the mere gesture. We press them, palm to palm, and communicate something.

Alex and I seemed to find each other in this way, as if we desperately needed to hold on to someone and were nearly incapable of holding on to anyone else. And when we held hands, in a way, we were home.

In the beginning of *Hook*, Granny Wendy presses her wrinkled hand to lawyer Peter's face and laments, "Peter, don't you know who you are?" He had forgotten. It's easy to lose both yourself and your spouse in marriage. I had for so long hedged my bets on a husband being the great gap-filler of my life, thinking that once I had one, then I'd be content or complete. I'd finally feel beautiful. Marriage, played out, has instead opened wide so very many of the gaps that were already there, poured fuel onto my raging sin and shortcomings. And like adult Peter, I keep forgetting who I am at the heart of things: boundlessly, beautifully in need of rescue. "Oh there you are, Charlotte!"

Unlike my pre-wedding visions, my marriage is not out of a summer box office hit, with unceasing talk of *The Neverending Story* and nuclear apocalypse and whatnot. It is not a constant montage of bare skin and smooth jazz. Sometimes it is all of these things, but most of the time we just watch great TV, dream about buying a boat one day, and grind through the difficult weekdays until the eve of blessed Friday.

My Perfect Male ~

- Brownish Blondish Hair
- Brown / Blue eyes
- Has to have good eyes (sparkle)
- Kind of messed up hair
- good smile
- Funny
- not necessarily nice
- skinny but jacked
- same interests as me
- Any arts
- Doesn't mind PDA
- Not to attatched, but doesn't ditch me.
- Tan -- but not too tan
- Deep deep voice
- Play with my hair
- likes to hug
- Nice stomach
- likes the beach
- Roses
- likes music - good @ complementing
- once again. Funny

Actual excerpt from Charlotte's actual 9th grade diary

The rescue we both need, we are incapable of providing one another. Alex having more vacation days will not satisfy it; not even (dare I admit) our capacity to choose East Coast over West. And there is a great freedom in this realization, because we remember the One who is so infinitely more capable than either of us, the One who satisfies needs we didn't even realize we had. When I look at my hands from the foot of the cross, I see that they are markedly weak, incapable even. My knuckles and wrists are sore from all the doing. And I suddenly remember that I'm *not* doing this all on my own, regardless of how early (or late) Alex makes it home from work.

Marriage reminds us that we were once chosen, and continue to be chosen day in and day out, on Earth (if I don't blow it) and more importantly, in heaven (even if I do). I'm not calling Alex Jesus, but many years ago he first held my hand despite *(or maybe because of)* my age, my quirky neuroses, and my lack of roller prowess. And I chose him, sarcastic artsy bravado et al.[9] In all of his flaws, Alex seems to urge despite all of mine, "Charlotte, don't you know who you are?"

On our best days, he gives me the boost to resemble someone like my hero-self—which is really just a thin whisper of an Eden-self or a heaven-self. And it makes just being *me* seem bearable. When I've got to use the bathroom in the middle of the night, I don't have to hold it, because he is close by and that makes me a weird sort of brave. If I start to sink into a suffocating depression, Alex recognizes it because I say vague things like "I don't feel good" and then he makes me get out of the house, or talk to him, or

9. But only after making him burn the black jazz shoes in a bonfire. I have my limits.

call my doctor, or stay busy, which has a wonderful way of making that Fat Man of a feeling get up off of my chest and walk away. When I got fired from an important job, Alex said and meant things like, "This was the best thing that could have happened," and "You have the opportunity now to come back to the drawing board and see who you really want to be." And when we found out about California and I carelessly blurted things like, "*I can't do this on my own,*" Alex reached out for my hand and said, "No you can't, but at least there will be water, at least there will be sun."

In *Hook*, Toodles rambles nervously to a police officer, "I've forgotten how to fly!" The officer replies dully, "One does." On our worst days, long and ambling because Alex's work is unrelenting—which makes my work unrelenting— marriage reminds me who I really am, of my severe needs *that neither I nor my spouse are capable of meeting.* "I can't do this all on my own," I urge to God instead of Alex this time. With this redirected outcry, there is hope. And my feet begin to wobble and shake and loosen and defy, inexplicably wanting to leave the ground. I can run, but when I grow weary, I am carried. I can walk, and when I become faint, there is rest.

Every evening, when Alex still isn't home and my blood starts to actually boil, I do my best to remember that he is not my savior. What strange relief it must be for Alex to not have to carry that weight.

As both our best selves and our worst selves, he and I hold the power to be this horribly imperfect reminder to each other of the Love that surpasses all understanding— the un-human, impossible Love that is patient and kind, and does not envy or boast. The Love that chooses us, that lifts us with ease from the mire and the mud and the long, long-ass days and reminds us we don't have to do the flying at all.

Bangarang.

THE SEVEN-YEAR BITCH

Stephanie

THIS YEAR MY HUSBAND AND I will celebrate our seven-year anniversary. Which is in August. Which is in the winter. Because we live in Australia. Which was never in the plan. Which is an apt description of almost everything that happens once the "happily ever after" part of the credits roll. Which is *marriage*.

I am counting those seven years, to be clear, not via the method celebrity couples do when announcing the end of their unions: "They were together seven years, five of them married." Um…*no*. You don't get to tack on the years you were dating to add to your final tally. Those were child's play compared to The Big Game, The Real Show. To be honest, maybe we shouldn't even count the wedding day or the honeymoon in the total of our time together because who *can't* get through a champagne-soaked party followed by a week on the beach? No, reality sets in once you cross the threshold of your home together, file away that piece of paper recognizing your legal partnership, unpack your suitcases, and, as the old adage goes, "stop being polite and start getting real."

Marriage *is* the real world.

Some exposition: my husband was not supposed to be The One. He was an unavailable friend I'd met when he returned to New York after a job abroad. I had recently given up on the idea of getting married: I'd even asked my parents for my "wedding fund" to be redistributed in the form of a fabulous thirtieth birthday party, preferably on a boat with an open bar. In response, they laughed and asked, "What wedding fund?" Ah, memories. It wasn't that I didn't want to get married, it was just that I lived in the Singles Capital of the World and had recently run out of people to date, so I thought I was done. I had even made a tentative peace with the idea. I would be such a cool aunt! Then Jason showed up and we became fast friends, which was so convenient because he wouldn't be one of those creeps who might hit on me later. Too bad he was straight!

Then I inconveniently fell in love with him. Which took awhile for me to figure out, as it had never happened to me before. And the rest, as they say…is history.

Or the present, as it were. As it *is*.

I should have known there would be trouble when, contrary to previous men in my life, Jason refused to let me pick fights with him. Annoyingly unflappable, he even referred to my recurring ire (which had, in past relationships, been given a name rhyming with *itchiness*) as though it were cute: I sure did get fired up a lot! Then there was the issue with his constant refusal to see the worst in people, a talent I had perfected. *Why couldn't he play along?!* And, dear God, what was *with* his kindness? It was almost as though he walked through the world unafraid of being manipulated and mistreated!

Our first date, after a year of friendship, which included

my drunken confession of love a few months in and some healing afterward, occurred at a tapas restaurant. We ordered multiple plates and bottles of wine, and the next week I walked past the establishment and noticed signs that announced it had been shut down by the health department. Perhaps this should have been a red flag as well, in addition to the kindness and all. But we forged ahead anyway, getting engaged a year later and married eight months after that. And marriage, it was easy! I had married my best friend! We had fun together! And, not too infrequently, sex! Then we had kids.

Has anyone started a Facebook group yet for those couples who have kids to save their marriage? Because I'd like to know how that went for them. I'm only five years into this parenthood thing, but so far it has challenged every facet of my being: physical, mental, emotional, spiritual. Jason and I were such a great couple before we had kids; some referred to us as a real-life Jim and Pam.[10] We had the kind of connection that pissed me off when I was single because I wanted it and couldn't find it. We laughed at the same jokes, loved the same movies, wore the same clothes.[11] Then James and Will came along and, suddenly, it wasn't just about us. Our Saturday morning sleep-ins were cancelled. Our movie nights disappeared. We began to eat at chain restaurants and say things like, "This fried ravioli is pretty good!" We became unrecognizable versions of ourselves: sleep-deprived, irritable, sniping, score-keeping.

He used to leave his socks on the counter and I'd think it was cute. Someone even gave him the nickname "Socks"

---

10. I'm the only one who has referred to us that way. But I think it could catch on.

11. Kidding. *Or am I?* (I am.)

one summer at my family's vacation rental! Now when he leaves his socks lying around *I want to kill him.* And there's this thing he does with the lights, I think it's called LEAVING THEM ON ALL THE TIME? And with each of my huffy swats at the switch to turn them off, I am reminded of my dad complaining about how I wasted electricity when I was growing up and instead of seeing this echo across time as something to smile about, I want to turn Jason in for crimes against the environment.

I guess every couple faces the end of the honeymoon sometime; for us, it happened the day we began welcoming beautiful children into the world and our home. The equation seems to work out this way: dream your dreams + watch your dreams come true = turn into the worst version of yourself. Because here's the kicker: I thought I'd be so good at marriage and parenting, you know, before I entered these institutions. They looked easy! It's not rocket science, is it, being nice to your husband, or keeping kids alive? Then it turns out that the joke is on me because it's harder than I ever imagined. I mean, I should be able to handle this. I should not think sarcastic thoughts every time I do a favor for my husband along the lines of "Glad I went to grad school for six years so I could take all those classes on HOW TO PICK UP DRY CLEANING FOR A MAN."

The other night I was cleaning my jewelry (because sometimes my priority is that the externals look clean rather than my cold, black heart) and dropped my wedding band down the bathroom sink drain. Naturally, this unleashed a torrent of emotions: anger that it happened; regret at such a mistake; fear over whether accidents really exist or if this was my subconscious sending me a message. But mostly, annoyance over the inconvenience after another hard day of living in the first world. So I texted Jason what happened, along with some sweet sentiment at the end like, "I hate everything." Within twenty-four hours he had gone underneath my vanity, opened the pipe, and retrieved the ring. And the first thing I said? "Did you clean it?"

It didn't help that my beloved had upset the delicate balance of my cabinet when retrieving the ring and failed to put every item back into its rightful place—*the nerve!*—thereby rendering me akin to the victim whose life is saved by a Good Samaritan's CPR, who then sues that hero because he cracked her rib.

Marriage is a mirror, and I do not like what it reveals. I am forever astounded by my capacity to be a nasty person, and most of all by my capacity to be such toward the people I love most: Jason and the kids. I think there's something in the knowledge that they won't leave, a beautiful certainty that I pervert by testing it. But mostly, I know, what's really going on here is what's always gone on in every human heart but for one: I am sinful. I need not a crutch or even someone to carry me across the sand so there is only one set of footprints. I need life support—and so does my marriage—if we're all going to survive.

Why does this keep surprising—and offending—me?

Louis CK did a bit about the marriage tip of going on a date with your spouse. His response? "I already took her on a date...and I don't wanna call her back." They divorced shortly after that bit.

Jason and I groan about this thought all the time because (1) We're not allowed to laugh at CK anymore, and (2) there's truth in it. Then I imagine what our first date, all those years ago over tapas (and rat feces, apparently) would have looked like had all our cards been out on the unsanitized table. Had we stopped being polite and started getting real, from the very beginning. There would have been more tense silences, less laughter. I probably would have found a way to work in some snide comments about the amount of time he spends on his phone. Then we would have gone to one of our apartments and read our books on separate ends of the couch, farting silently into the night while my mud mask dried.

Oh, God. What have we become?!

Well…we've become us, it seems. We are still becoming us, the two of us bound by our own weak and completely assailable promises, along with our progeny, in this four-sided family unit that struggles daily. And it turns out that we are not isolated in having dark sides. Brennan Manning writes:

> Only in a relationship of the deepest intimacy can we allow a person to know us as we truly are. It is difficult enough to live with the awareness of our stinginess and shallowness, our anxieties and infidelities, but to disclose our dark secrets to another is intolerably risky. The impostor does not want to come out of hiding. He will grab for the cosmetic kit and put on his pretty face to make himself 'presentable.' Whom can I level with? To whom can I bare my soul? I cannot admit that I have done wrong. I cannot admit that I have made a huge mistake, except to someone who I know accepts me (*Abba's Child: The Cry of the Heart for Intimate Belonging*).

I find them incredibly painful, these daily deaths to self brought on by marriage and parenthood—not the least of which involves being forced to see my own darkest places and worst inclinations. And y'all, I'm talking about *much* worse than wasted electricity. This sacred covenant we've entered appears constantly threatened by the desecrating forces of my own sin and inadequacies. But it's not. The union holds; the institution remains; the vows are intact—and none of it is made less beautiful in the end, only more real. This is a battleground where the distinction between my efforts to "get it right" and the "it is finished already" truth of the Gospel are writ large and daily. There are failures; oh so many. There are wounds. At the end of every day, there are two people lying in a home that often doubles as a battlefield, casualties of our own characters.

But there's also this: the waking to each other, still here. Nobody disappeared in the night. (*Yet.*) This gift we give each other, so much more than jewelry and topical t-shirts: the *staying*.

Which echoes the gift given to us on the cross, at Christmas, and throughout the history of grace: *He stays.*

We have a magnet on our fridge that I brought with us across the world. It quotes the book *The Fault in Our Stars*: "Maybe okay will be our always." We walk by it, together and separately, and laugh ruefully at its edgy elements of truth—together and separately. We walk by it day in and day out, on good days when we each still think the other is our favorite person and on bad days when we…don't. We walk by it because it is in our house, our home that we share, the place we always come back to. The place where we are held by promises greater than ours, unassailable even, that carry the both of us, the four of us, through what looks just okay now, but is becoming so much more.

directions to each other

...I love you...

one year later.

PART FIVE

HOW TO
FIND YOURSELF
(YOUR REAL SELF)

.

RECOVERED TRANSCRIPTS
FROM LIFEBOAT 815

EXTERIOR: DAY—SOMEWHERE IN THE PACIFIC.

It is day 127 that CHARLOTTE *and* STEPHANIE *have been "out to sea."* STEPHANIE *is dealing with a resurgence of her clinical anxiety.* CHARLOTTE *comes face-to-face with a diagnosis.*

CHARLOTTE *and* STEPHANIE *have jerry-rigged a crude tent for shade using old grocery bags and soiled clothing. They huddle underneath as the sun blazes down on their already torched skin.*

STEPHANIE: What if we just quit?

CHARLOTTE (*distracted*): Quit what?

STEPHANIE: Quit parenthood. Quit life. Quit everything.

CHARLOTTE: So dramatic.

STEPHANIE: Okay, are you going to let me vent or what?

CHARLOTTE: Sorry, I'm in a mood. Go ahead.

STEPHANIE: So last week was great: my increased dosage of meds left me feeling nearly blissful. I felt like I had my life back. Or my sanity, at least. I was patient with the kids,

I had my shit together on the home and school administrative fronts—as in, not forgetting any lunchbox essentials, therapy folders, major holiday acknowledgement cards, i.e. our anniversary.

CHARLOTTE: I'm missing the problem...

STEPHANIE: Okay why are you rushing me?

CHARLOTTE: This just seems like a really long story.

STEPHANIE: Oh I'm sorry, are you in a rush to get somewhere?? (*She gestures out to the wide expanse of ocean that surrounds them.*)

CHARLOTTE: Point taken.

STEPHANIE: So last week was great, and then *this week*, everything seemed to fall apart. It all started when I decided to do this "cleanse" a friend recommended. Basically give up alcohol and red meat, cut back on sugar and eat a truckload of vegetables.

CHARLOTTE: Yikes.

STEPHANIE: I did fine for the first day. The lack of sugar-crashes made me feel superb!

CHARLOTTE: Well that sounds encouraging!

STEPHANIE: I feel like you're patronizing me.

CHARLOTTE: Sorry.

STEPHANIE: So the first day was fine. Then the second day...

CHARLOTTE: Uh oh.

STEPHANIE: I got really hungry. And irritable. And Will

dropped a chair on my foot, right after I broke our blinds—don't ask; I wouldn't even know the answer. My big toe puffed up like a lobster and started bleeding underneath the nail. (*She slides off her ragged sock and shows* CHARLOTTE *the black and blue toe.* CHARLOTTE *curls her nose in disgust.*) I screamed...let's just say, something other than *fudge,* at the top of my lungs. Our neighbors have surely reported us to the police by now. Now I'm just waiting for my toenail to fall off as I doctor it daily and anxiously try to keep it away from tiny feet that always seem magnetized to step on it.

CHARLOTTE: I mean, you really went through all this with no wine?

STEPHANIE: Well, cue the breaking of the alcohol ban. The next day I was driving with Will asleep in the back, and I hit a curb—they spell it *k-e-r-b* in Australia; I can't decide if that makes sense or is the dumbest thing ever—and popped a tire. The upsides are that I was a block from our house and was able to make it back, Will didn't wake up, and I didn't have to use the car again that day.

CHARLOTTE: And the downsides?

STEPHANIE: I POPPED OUR EFFING TIRE BECAUSE I DIDN'T SEE A CURB/KERB. What the fresh hell? I tried to do some yoga this morning to recenter or whatever, and put my mat on the floor. Went into the bathroom for a second, came back to the mat, and it wasn't there. My children had thrown it down the stairs. How cute. Oh, and James had a meltdown on the elevator (lift), which resulted in a snide comment from an older woman and a confrontation between me and her. Cue the rising blood pressure. And more alcohol. Between my children mocking my attempts to stay calm, and injuring me with furniture, and my own boneheaded mistakes, I feel like a prize-winning idiot right now. And you know what?

CHARLOTTE: What?

STEPHANIE: There's a part of me that's always felt like a screw-up—like everyone's going to figure out eventually that I'm a total mess. I felt that way even as a kid. I felt that way when I moved to New York, and especially when I got FIRED there—remind me to tell you that story. I feel that way as an American transplant here in Australia. Sorry, that was long and super negative. But do you know what I mean?

CHARLOTTE: Yeah, I know what you mean.

STEPHANIE *waits for* CHARLOTTE *to elaborate as the boat bobs gently.*

STEPHANIE: ...that's it?

CHARLOTTE: What?

STEPHANIE: I just gave you my Declaration of Independence of rants. Aren't you going to match me?

CHARLOTTE: Sorry, it's been a hard week. I'm all out of sorts.

STEPHANIE: Go on...

CHARLOTTE: Well, you know I had that doctor's appointment last week?

STEPHANIE: Oh I totally forgot!

CHARLOTTE: I don't know what I was even expecting. I mean, I've had like 600 doctor's appointments over the last few years. Everyone has a new hypothesis for what's going on, but nothing is ever conclusive.

STEPHANIE: The worst.

CHARLOTTE: Well, turns out my rheumatologist finally reached a conclusion.

STEPHANIE: SERIOUSLY?!

CHARLOTTE: I guess I just thought this appointment would be more of the same. "Yeah it looks like an autoimmune disease, but we aren't sure." They're always "not sure." But now I guess he's sure. I have Lupus.

STEPHANIE *nearly knocks over their tent in surprise.*

CHARLOTTE *(cont'd)*: Yep.

STEPHANIE: You let me go on and on with all that curb/kerb nonsense when you have LUPUS?!

CHARLOTTE: Well that's not all...

STEPHANIE *reaches over the edge of the boat and splashes some cold water on her face.*

CHARLOTTE: I found this weird bump on my chest. Went to the doc, and it looks like it might be the Big C.

STEPHANIE: I'm guessing by Big C you aren't talking about your bra size?

CHARLOTTE: Nope.

STEPHANIE *gets quiet and her eyes start to well up with tears. She gazes out over the water and takes a deep breath.*

CHARLOTTE (*cont'd*): DON'T CRY! You'll waste your fluids!

STEPHANIE (*now sobbing*): Are you dying? Just tell me now. I swear I can handle it.

CHARLOTTE: Steph, it's like a tiny skin cancer, *if that*. They're cutting it off next week.

STEPHANIE (*sobs slowing*): Oh...but what about the Lupus? How...how long do you have?

CHARLOTTE: You don't know what Lupus is, do you?

STEPHANIE: If it's not in the mouth, I didn't learn it. But it sounds bad.

CHARLOTTE: It's totally manageable, in my case. For now, at least. I take medicine and need to stay out of the sun.

The girls both pause, recognizing their invasively bright and sunny surroundings.

CHARLOTTE (*cont'd*): I just need to wear long sleeves and sunscreen. Should be fine. (*But she isn't sure.*)

STEPHANIE (*slaps* CHARLOTTE *on the shoulder, annoyed*): Why have you been all doomsday today if everything is going to be fine?! I literally thought you were dying.

CHARLOTTE: Sorry but it's just been sort of shocking! I mean, even though I've known something wasn't right with my body for a long time, hearing that it's actually true was a blow. I thought finally getting a diagnosis would be a relief. And don't get me wrong, it is. But it also hits home to what you were talking about before—I can't measure up, not even in my body, the thing I need most for survival. I just sort of feel like a failure. Like my weaknesses and my inability to cure myself are totally exposed now—I mean *literally* exposed. (*She points to the basal cell on her chest.*)

STEPHANIE: Will you get some sunscreen on that thing already?! (*She hands* CHARLOTTE *an empty-ish bottle.*) Here, you can use my ration for today.

CHARLOTTE (*rubbing lotion on her chest*): I guess I also just feel untethered or something.

STEPHANIE: As in a tetherball?

CHARLOTTE: Yeah, only like a tetherball that flies off the string and knocks out an elderly person or something.

STEPHANIE: Dude, we get each other.

CHARLOTTE: It's like I know God is here and deeply in all this and whatever, but at the same time I'm also pretty sure he brought me out here to die.

STEPHANIE: YOU SAID YOU WEREN'T DYING.

CHARLOTTE *rolls her eyes.*

STEPHANIE (*cont'd*): If Amazon delivered to Sydney, which apparently *it does not*, I'd buy you the cutest rash guard ever. With a picture of One Direction or something.

CHARLOTTE: They broke up.

STEPHANIE: So it would be retro. Get off my back.

The girls are lost in thought for a few minutes.

CHARLOTTE: I just hate feeling so exposed.

STEPHANIE: But we're all exposed, technically speaking. That's what life and parenthood *does*. It's what happens when we stop pretending to be strong!

CHARLOTTE: Or when we're *forced* to stop pretending we're strong...

STEPHANIE: Yes! By diagnoses and rashguards and just life.

CHARLOTTE: By our kids' poor behavior at malls and in church.

STEPHANIE: By your husband seeing you without your makeup on, and smelling your farts, and knowing you aren't that good of a cook even though you own all of Ina Garten's cookbooks and DVR every episode of *The Barefoot Contessa*.

CHARLOTTE: By our children saying things like, "Mommy has a nice voice in public around other people, but in private, she's a step away from Joan Crawford with a wire hanger."

STEPHANIE: By the guests you allow into your home for a visit, knowing they're gonna see that floater in the toilet and how you shut down emotionally when you don't get enough alone time.

CHARLOTTE: Or by the *FedEx guy!*

STEPHANIE: You lost me.

CHARLOTTE: If he didn't want to see me with my bathrobe open then maybe he should've just left the package on the front stoop and walked away *without ringing the doorbell that woke up my kid.*

STEPHANIE (*long pause*): Dude...I think that one's on you.

CHARLOTTE (*sheepish*): Yeah. Still, I think we're onto

something here.

STEPHANIE *notices that* CHARLOTTE's *body has crept ever so slightly back into the sunlight. She adjusts the tent so it covers and shades her friend again.*

CHARLOTTE: Thanks.

STEPHANIE: I got you, girl.

THE INNER CHILD
RETURNS...
AND FLASHES BACK

Stephanie

FEBRUARY 2017
Sydney, Private Residence. 3AM.

STEPHANIE *sits on the toilet with her eyes half-open.*

STEPHANIE *(to herself):* I am *so tired.* Must...sleep...

LIL STEPH *peers around the doorway, silently watching, eyes wide in fear.*

STEPHANIE *starts to snore lightly, then awakens with a jerk and remembers where she is: inside her bathroom, hiding from her family.*

STEPHANIE: Maybe I'll just leave. DO YOU HEAR THAT, SLEEPING MALES? Maybe I'll just *leave.* (*Silently considers this.*) Dammit. No. I'm too tired. I'd have to pack. And my best t-shirt is in the dryer. I'd have to go to the ATM. Probably get a bunch of cash out so they couldn't trace me by my credit cards. And I so don't know Sydney's public transportation. I'd run through taxi money so fast. DAMMIT! Why does everything have to have so many STEPS?!

STEPHANIE *flushes the toilet and heads toward the sink, near-ly stumbling over* LIL STEPH *in the process.* LIL STEPH *backs away quickly, raising her palms in surrender.*

LIL STEPH: Sorry, sorry! I didn't mean to run into you! Or eavesdrop! It's just…I haven't seen you in awhile, and I was worried…that you didn't need me? So I thought I'd check in? And it seems like maybe…things are a little crazy?

STEPHANIE *sighs heavily and washes her hands.*

STEPHANIE: Have you just been standing there like a creeper the whole time I was peeing? You know, I don't get a lot of privacy these days. Maybe you can let me know when you're here? Or shoot a text first? A text, not a phone call, to be clear.

LIL STEPH*'s eyes fill with tears and her lip quivers.*

STEPHANIE: Oh damn. I'm sorry. That was harsh. It's just… it's been a night, okay? We've only been here a month and James just woke up barfing. I had to throw a bunch of clothes in the wash, and now he and Jason are dominating the bed and…it's just too much. I was hoping we had es-caped…well, this kind of stuff. I know that's stupid. I know you can get sick in Australia. It's just…never-ending, this parenting thing. They need me *all the time.*

LIL STEPH: So…that's a problem? I mean, everything sounds really messy, but…you have to do it! You have to do all that stuff. If you don't, then maybe…Jason and the kids won't know you love them. Then *they* won't love *you*! And if any guests come over and see the place like this, they'll think you don't know how to take care of your house and family. Horrible things could happen! Okay. I can help. I'll make a list. First, the laundry. We've got to get that laundry done. Then we can take James's temperature, and give him medicine…

STEPHANIE *looks at her warily.*

STEPHANIE: Oh, yeah? And how would that "we" work? You don't know how to do laundry. You won't even learn that until college. And you're not a doctor, last time I checked. So how exactly would you help, other than by making lists? *I already know what's on the list.* It's staring me in the face all day and all night. It's actually doing what's on it that's the problem.

LIL STEPH (*eyes darting around*): Um…well, I could…put more clothes in the washing machine? If I can reach it, I mean. You'd have to do the soap stuff. But come on, if we start now it'll be done before the morning, and no one will notice that everything was so crazy!

STEPHANIE (*yawns*): The only way you can help me right now is by turning into a sleeping pill. I'm going to bed. To my sliver of it, at least. And praying for no puke or diarrhea the rest of the night. Peace.

LIL STEPH *watches* STEPHANIE *head to bed and her eyes fill again.*

LIL STEPH (*whispers through tears*): I know I can help. I *know* I can be useful! Maybe I'll start cleaning up. Except I don't know where anything goes… (*She wanders around, looking lost.*)

JULY 2007
New York City

STEPHANIE *walks down 3rd Avenue, her upper lip glistening with sweat and her armpits downright soaking in it through her white t-shirt.* LIL STEPH *hustles behind her, practically running to keep up.* STEPHANIE *seems to be trying to avoid* LIL STEPH, *even picking up her speed.*

STEPHANIE *(to herself):* Dammit. This was a misguided wardrobe choice. What was I thinking, a white t-shirt and lime pants to my first day on the job during the heat of summer? Not only does it all scream *GAP* on the Upper East Side, where they don't even *know* that store, but I look like I just stepped out of my serving position at Margaritaville. I'm so not cut out for this. Plus, I'm running late, and I'm going to smell like the inside of a gym locker when I get there.

LIL STEPH *(runs to catch up and listen):* Hey! Hey, I'm here! Just…so you know. If you need any help? I think you look great! Just smile a lot and remember everything you learned over six years of dental school, and don't mess up, and—

STEPHANIE *(seething):* Look, can you just…do something else today? Like, maybe walk around the city? This is my first day, my first real job out of school, and I'm FREAK-ING NERVOUS. I don't need a voice in my head telling me what to do. Go on, go!

LIL STEPH *(still running, but starting to tear up):* But I can help! I can whisper things in your ear, like encouragement and stuff! You *never* let me help!

STEPHANIE: That's because you're *not* a help. Sorry, but it's true. You drag me down. You make me more nervous because deep down under all those tips and rules, you're scared too. Dude, I think I'm growing out of you. I've done two years of counseling now. Don't you think it's time we took a break?

LIL STEPH: That's…that's not nice. You don't mean it. You need me. Besides, it's not safe for me to be walking around the city by myself. I don't know why you came here. This place is not good for us.

STEPHANIE: That's *why* I came. Because you were too scared to, and I knew that if I listened to you, I'd never grow. I'm going to make it here, okay? You can't talk me out of it, and you can't help me by giving me tips either. So go over to Lex and grab the 6 and head downtown. Visit the West Village or something. Those Magnolia Cupcakes are good—go try one. I'm on my own now.

STEPHANIE *rushes ahead as the crowd thickens and* LIL STEPH *loses sight of her.*

TWO YEARS LATER
New York City

STEPHANIE *stands outside one of several doorways within a dental office. Light strains to peek through the basement-level windows surrounding her, and children cry inside several of the rooms off the hallway where she waits.* LIL STEPH *appears around the corner, hesitant. She finally walks up to* STEPHANIE, *who jumps upon seeing her.*

STEPHANIE (*whispering*): What are you doing here?!

LIL STEPH: I came to help.

STEPHANIE: Help? I've been fine for the last two years, and

you show up to help *now*? Why?

LIL STEPH: It just seems like something bad is about to happen. You look nervous. I feel scared.

STEPHANIE (*sighs*): Sometimes I think you *want* me to be scared. Gives you an excuse to show up. Listen, I'm about to go in there to meet with the office manager. So you need to go.

LIL STEPH (*uncertainly*): Okay...maybe I'll just wait outside?

The door opens and OFFICE MANAGER *beckons* STEPHANIE *inside.* STEPHANIE *casts a warning glare back at* LIL STEPH, *who hangs back for a second before hurriedly dashing inside just as the door closes.* STEPHANIE *rolls her eyes.*

OFFICE MANAGER: Sit down, please.

STEPHANIE *obliges, taking a seat and ignoring* LIL STEPH, *who stands by the door, biting her nails.*

OFFICE MANAGER: Well...there's no easy way to say this. But...the deal is, we no longer require your services.

LIL STEPH *and* STEPHANIE *draw the same sharp intake of breath.* LIL STEPH'S *mouth hangs open as she stares first at* OFFICE MANAGER, *then at* STEPHANIE, *then back and forth between them. Tears fill her eyes.* STEPHANIE *begins to sweat, first from her upper lip, then her armpits, then the back of her knees. Her face turns the same crimson as* LIL STEPH'S. LIL STEPH *draws near to her until they are both in the chair, almost indistinguishable from each other, they are so close.*

STEPHANIE: Wh-what?

OFFICE MANAGER (*patting her helmet of hair, adjusting her*

glasses, and pursing her red-stained lips): Didn't the bosses drop some hints to you? They told me this wouldn't be coming out of left field. Dammit, they always do this to me. They didn't warn you?

STEPHANIE: I-I-I don't remember anything... I mean, if they did I don't remember...

LIL STEPH (*whispers so only* STEPHANIE *can hear*): They never did that! At least, I don't think... I mean, I don't remember either... I was usually hiding in the hallway...

STEPHANIE *and* LIL STEPH *speak in unison*: Why? Why is this happening?

OFFICE MANAGER (*sighs*): Look, you know the bosses aren't getting along, and the thing is, they're probably going to split up. And they think you could probably fit in better here if they could train you, you know, help with your confidence, but there's no time for that because they're getting lawyers involved and this whole thing is about to get messy. And you did a few fillings that fell out, and people here, they expect perfection, you know? So...it's just not working out. Okay? (*She shuffles papers and slaps them onto her desk, appearing ready to move on.*)

LIL STEPH (*quietly*): I knew this was going to happen. Nothing ever works out. We always mess up. Tell her you'll do better! Tell her you'll be more confident! Tell her they need you here!

STEPHANIE: I...I mean...okay? When do I leave?

LIL STEPH: Tell her that you deserve to be here! MAKE HER SEE YOU!

OFFICE MANAGER: We're giving you two months.

STEPHANIE: So…right before Christmas?

OFFICE MANAGER (*nods*): Yep.

LIL STEPH: Tell her you'll do better!

STEPHANIE (*looks down at her hands; just wants to get out of here*): Okay. I…I guess that's it then?

LIL STEPH: NO!

OFFICE MANAGER: Yes, we'll discuss more later, but that's it for now. And don't take it too hard, okay? They're impossible to please. I'm sure you'll find something else.

STEPHANIE *exits the office and grabs her things, leaving the building with* LIL STEPH *trailing behind her.*

LIL STEPH: Well…what are we going to do?!

STEPHANIE (*defeated and sarcastic*): *We?*

LIL STEPH: Well, yeah! You need me now. How are you going to pay rent? Who's going to be hiring at the end of the year? What's your next step? This is *so hurtful.* I knew this place wasn't good for us. What if people back home find out you lost your job here? They'll think you couldn't handle this life! They'll make fun of you behind your back!

STEPHANIE (*turns to her angrily while the rest of the people on 75th Street walk by, oblivious*): SHUT UP! Just shut up, okay? You're not helping! We can't strategize our way out of this! Not right now, anyway. It's exhausting. Clearly I'm a screw-up—in your eyes for sure. Maybe just period. Now please give me some space.

LIL STEPH (*tearful*): But I'm afraid of being alone! We should go back to Alabama, where it's safe. You can find a job there and make money and show everyone you've got it together and—

STEPHANIE: I don't want to go back. I'm not done here.

LIL STEPH: But New York is too big! And you probably won't find another job. Let's just go back. I'll help you pack! We can—wait, aren't we taking the subway?

STEPHANIE: I need to walk. And I want to do it alone. Just go. I'll figure this out on my own.

STEPHANIE *rushes ahead down the sidewalk while* LIL STEPH *watches her go.*

PRESENT DAY
Sydney, Private Residence, 4AM

STEPHANIE *emerges from her sons' room and heads toward the master bedroom.* LIL STEPH *is standing in the doorway. They both look a bit ashamed.*

LIL STEPH: Are they asleep?

STEPHANIE: Yeah. I guess James is feeling better now that he's emptied his entire stomach, and the retching is no longer keeping Will awake.

LIL STEPH *giggles and looks at* STEPHANIE *as if wondering whether this is the appropriate response.*

STEPHANIE: Look—

LIL STEPH: So—

They both laugh.

LIL STEPH: You go.

STEPHANIE: Okay. So…here's the thing. I know we've been through a lot together. And I know you want to be helpful.

I remember how that felt…just wanting to be needed, and seen. And when you show up, it just reminds me of all that…that *need*. Sometimes to the point that, even when you're not around, I act like you are. I practically parent my children as if *they* are you, because…well, you're all so damn needy. And you probably look at me and think it's amazing that I'm finally in this part of life where I'm needed so much, but really? It's hard. It's so, so hard. I get climbed on, and kicked, and screamed for, and it's wonderful and awful at the same time. It doesn't validate my existence like you always thought it would. It…it drains me. And I feel like I'm not enough. That I'm messing up. I've just got a lot on me right now, you know?

LIL STEPH (*looking down*): I know, I just…a long time ago, you would've given anything to be needed like that, and now you act like it just bothers you.

STEPHANIE: Yeah, I know. And I feel guilty about that. Like, *all the time*. On top of the irritation. Believe me, it's complicated. The grass is always greener, I guess. I just…I need you to know that I'm okay. That *we're* okay. That you're going to be okay. Life is messy and hard but…it's good. There's enough good, anyway, to make the hard worth it. Most days. So you don't have to be so worried all the time. You don't have to arrange everything so it will all work out. This is just what life looks like right now. Feeling at home and lost at the same time. I think it's just going to…*be* that way for awhile. And we both have to get comfortable with that, or we'll go crazy trying to change it.

LIL STEPH: It's just that if things could run more smooth-ly…

STEPHANIE: Then what? You'd feel better? So would I. But

I think we're doing the best we can here. Some days that will look good and some days, it'll look like shit—

LIL STEPH (*eyes wide, whispers*): You shouldn't say that word.

STEPHANIE: Oh honey, we are so far past that. Now come downstairs with me and I'll give you a taste of wine before I pass out from exhaustion.

LIL STEPH: No, no I can't have that. Can I?

STEPHANIE: Live a little. Come on.

LIL STEPH: Okay…but do you think you might yell a little less tomorrow, maybe? And get dinner ready on time?

STEPHANIE: Maybe. Probably not, though. But spoiler alert? It'll be okay anyway.

LIL STEPH: How do you know?

STEPHANIE: Past precedent, kid. Let's go.

CAST OUT BUT NOT
FORGOTTEN

Charlotte

SOMETIMES—IN MOTHERHOOD, IN MARRIAGE, and in this flopped body of mine—I wish there were an eject button, like that scene from *Top Gun*, only Goose lives. Other times, some invisible finger rudely presses 'eject' when all you want to do is stay put, cruising through the pillowy clouds like Superman. Either way, I have found it a challenge to exist for too long in the exact space or welfare I think I should be: in the South, married without children, healthy, or employed.

I'M *REALLY REALLY NOT* OBSESSED with cockroaches. But I think it's important to point out that scientists say they[1] can withstand a nuclear apocalypse—something about a nearly supernatural ability to adapt in any situation, and that their cells divide extremely slowly. They're basically immortal.

In the fall of 2012, after two and a half months of surviving my first teaching job in Savannah, GA, my otherwise spotless car became infested with the hideous creatures.

1. Roaches, not scientists.

Okay so there were only three or four of them over the course of those terrifying days, but in the moment it felt like a Biblical plague. The first time I saw one, I was driving down I-80 towards the school, watching a fall orange sunrise over the lowcountry marshes, the *How to Train Your Dragon* soundtrack blasting through my speakers. The windows were down, so my hair was doing this once-in-a-decade perfect supermodel/industrial fan thing. Then, with no warning at all, the brown, antlered, and armored pest scuttled across my dashboard all entitled, like it was *his* dashboard.[2] I swerved violently. My vision went white, as if someone had just hurled a baseball right at my face. Then, before I could even pull over to scream, the thing disappeared to find a new hiding spot within my vehicle. I was visited by this winged harbinger three more times over the next few days, precipitating unparalleled levels of paranoia, perspiration, and near-death driving incidents.

I should have known something unsavory was afoot.

But maybe, in a good-natured way, the cockroaches were like an omen—not only of the difficult time to come, but that I, like them, might withstand it.

IN THE SPRING OF 2012, I applied to PTS[3], a startup classical school in Savannah, to teach high school English.

However, several weeks after my first interview, I received a call from Pam, the principal, asking if I would instead consider teaching a combined fifth and sixth grade class.

"There are only three fifth graders enrolled in the school," she explained. So why not just have them skip a grade and

---

2. Proportionally, cockroaches run at a rate three times as fast as a cheetah. This is possibly the worst news ever.

3. Fabricated acronym.

join the twelve-year-olds!

"And you want me to teach all subjects to them?" I asked nervously.

"Yes, all subjects. You'll learn as you go."

From your perspective, this is not sound reasoning, but Pam was the type of leader who spoke with the perfect dose of moxie and intelligence. She was both physically beautiful and emotionally compelling. People listened to her and they wanted what she was selling; I was no exception. After Pam wooed me, both over the phone and in a second interview, my ego got the best of me.

"This has been the hardest teaching spot to fill, and we just see something special in you… Charlotte…you are our only hope…"[4]

Perhaps this was my destiny, my *raison d'être*. There seemed to be an impossibly precise teacher/hero-shaped hole in this burgeoning school and I, the perfect piece to fill it.

Is there anything quite so seductive as feeling needed?

Parents would meet me, their eyes glossy with tears of hope, as if they were shaking hands with Susan B. Anthony, Beatrix Potter, or Cyndi Lauper. "Thank you for what you have done for our children," they'd manage through their weepy admiration. Maybe this was Who I Was. Charlotte Botsford [Getz, two months later]: Fifth and Sixth Grade Savior. Give me a week, and I'd revolutionize the place. My students would be literary and pop-culture geniuses, calculating fractions in their sleep, and reciting Homer and Jay-Z over their Eggos and OJ at six in the morning.

"This is your big break!" encouraged Alex, my fiancé at that time.

---

4. Minor embellishment.

Did I like the challenge Pam was presenting, or was I falling prey to her need for me?

Either way, it worked, and I accepted the position. I hadn't completed my graduate work in photography with the Savannah College of Art and Design yet; I naively figured I'd have plenty of time to toil away at my thesis on nights and weekends. I was also deep into wedding planning, the big day already scheduled to occur two and a half months into the school year.

But how could I say no? What more capable person could possibly fill this role?

CUT TO:

INTERIOR: FIRST DAY OF SCHOOL AT "PTS"—MORNING.

"Hey guys, so I'm your teacher this year, 'Ms. Botsford'" (although I have already written my name, as all first-rate teachers do, in large whimsical letters on the whiteboard). "But I'm getting married in a few months, so don't get too used to that name!" The kids chuckle, nervous on their first day of school. I look around our classroom, also anxious. Can I at all live up to everyone's expectations of me? Parents, students, principal—can I possibly measure up? Time will tell. Our room looks shrunk from my position standing beside the whiteboard. Was it always this small? I start to sweat and so dab my glistening forehead with the lesson plan in my hands. The eleven- and twelve-year-olds staring back at me look comically humongous and squashed together around their makeshift table, as if circled up for teatime in a doll's house. As the day progresses, any time they are asked to retrieve a book for our next subject or to line up for lunch, we're so cramped up in this little bunker that I feel the walls shaking. Kids trip over backpacks and jackets and pencils and I CAN'T BREATHE IN HERE. There are no windows in the room, which is ideal in the case of a tornado or a Soviet threat, but leaves us all feeling like we've just walked out of a movie matinee any time we leave the classroom. Everyone shields their eyes dramatically. I worry what this will mean for our vitamin D levels and things like Seasonal Affective Disorder. Nonetheless, I press on.

"Let's open our grammar books to the first chapter, where we'll review diagramming sentences. Y'all should have learned this last year, I believe." Half the kids nod and turn to their books, the other half raise their hands timidly with blank, terrified expressions washed over their faces.

"Ms. Botsford, I don't know what that is," says Jane, a little embarrassed. The kids with their hands up nod in agreement.

I write on the board: "The cat ran."

"I think you'll remember this once we get into it. Okay Jane, what's the subject of this sentence?" She stares at me, bewildered. "Anyone else have a guess?" I ask. The other—older—half of the class eagerly shoot their hands into the air.

This is going to be a problem.

The knowledge gap between my sweet fifth and sixth graders becomes clearer and clearer throughout the school day (or murkier and murkier depending on your side of the puddle). At any given moment, half the class seems either totally puzzled by the unfamiliar material, or bored with their heads on the table because this is old information.

At 3PM everyone's bags are packed and ready to return home. "I'm so honored to be your teacher this year, guys. Today was great! We're going to learn a ton and hopefully have some fun in the process!"

THE END OF DAY ONE.

After a few weeks, I gained some amount of celebrity status among the faculty as the only teacher who would dare take on this social/educational-carnage-of-a-class.

"You're doing great!" encouraged Pam on a near daily basis. Although I was highly suspect, and although she'd never actually sat in on one of my classes, I took her word for it.

For the sake of adequate preparation, I had to teach myself roughly 10 out of the 13 subjects I was asked to instruct. So almost any free moment was spent with my face buried in something like a History of Medicine textbook. This was not how I imagined the Fifth and Sixth Grade Savior going about her school day: tight in the bladder and scrambling to stay a few days ahead of the curriculum. But as the only teacher at PTS who was new to teaching, I felt I had something to prove. And I have to be honest, I think I was at least earning my keep. By all appearances, I had everything under control.

The Reality: Most [all] of my evenings were spent lesson planning, grading, and fielding emails and phone calls from parents. I never saw my friends. My relationship with Alex consisted mostly of him cooking dinner for me and desperately laboring to keep me psychologically afloat. My house was a mess. I was stress-shedding weight like hair in the winter. In the proverbial swimming pool of life, I had about a quarter of a nostril out of the water. And although I would never have admitted it to myself, I knew very early on that teaching a combined fifth and sixth grade class at PTS was not my destiny. Rather, for a year or maybe two, it would be just a chapter in my story [or book, as it were]. But that doesn't mean I didn't invest every ounce of effort and energy and fiber into Making It Work.

The week of our wedding came and went without a hitch. I hustled to prepare lesson plans for my substitute in time, but ultimately, I had survived my first two and a half months as a teacher. In front of all of my family and friends, I married the man of my dreams.[5]

Then, just three days after returning from our honeymoon, my life erupted into flaming confetti.

CUT TO:

INTERIOR: 5TH AND 6TH GRADE CLASSROOM AT PTS— MORNING.

It is an average school day, and my fifth and sixth graders work quietly in their seats on a thesaurus exercise—an exercise laid out in our curriculum. We first read an article on Helen Keller, and now the students are looking up synonyms for the word "feel," as in, "Helen *felt* relieved that she finally found a way to communicate."

"Mrs. Getz, does 'embrace' work?" asks Sarah.

"Not quite, Sarah. You're on the right track. To embrace someone is physical, like to touch them. But we're looking for synonyms that are emotional, like to *feel* sad. This is a tough one, guys!"[6]

"What about 'perceive?'" Sarah says right away.

"That works!"

Justin looks up from his thesaurus, deep in thought.

"Justin, you look confused. What's up?" I say.

---

5. False. Alex is nearly 100% different than the man I *thought* I'd marry. But thank God. The dream guy was a real douche.

6. I know, I know, I was the best teacher, right?

"Well, what does 'grope' mean? Does that work?" I am totally caught off guard. My mind goes completely blank. Despite my best efforts, a few of the kids smell a rat.

"*What does it mean*, Mrs. Getz?" asks another student curiously.

"Well…"—total panic—"I guess to grope would be like if Justin slapped Sarah in the butt." Some of the kids giggle to themselves. "Alright, alright, let's get back to work!"

THE END.

I THOUGHT MY RESPONSE had been smart, clever. I'd even prided myself later that day on how I'd been honest in my explanation but also added a much-needed flair of light-heartedness to the situation. This incident was so insignificant in my mind that I didn't even think to tell Alex about it later that evening.

Around midnight, when I received a very solemn email from Pam asking me into her office the next morning, I had no idea why. I nervously went through the past couple of days and considered events that could potentially incriminate me:

- I had left the kids alone for a few minutes during a restroom emergency.
- I noticed yesterday that the top button of my shirt had accidentally come undone. Maybe it had been that way for longer than I realized?
- Earlier that week, I'd been corrected by the Lower School Lead Teacher for being too detailed in my mid-semester student evaluations.
- I had referenced The Hunger Games in a discussion on plot. Was that bad? The kids were all

reading it anyway.
- Could this be about the "Grope" Incident from the day before? Nah!

BUT WHEN I SAW PAM in the halls before school the following morning, I knew the situation had to be worse than I imagined. She was completely deadpan.

"What's this about, Pam?" I said, trying to stay cheery in case I had over-thought the tone of the email.

"We'll talk about it when you come to my office."

I had not over-thought her tone. The polite smile dropped from my face. "Okay, when should I come by?"

"I'll send someone to get you." Vague.

The school/church building started to feel even smaller.

I tried not to cry. I felt so ashamed but still wasn't sure why. Pam's assistant pulled me out of first period, "Pam wants to see you now."

As I walked into the office, Pam and the Lead Teacher of the Lower School looked up at me grimly from their chairs. The air felt still.

"What's going on?" I said.

"Sit down, Charlotte," said Pam.

I sat.

"We got a call from a parent about something you said in class yesterday. Do you know what I'm referring to?"

I mentally went through the list of potentially incriminating things. "Was it about the word 'grope'?" I asked. That *did* happen yesterday.

"Yes it was."

Although I distinctly sensed that I was being lured into a trap, a part of me felt relieved, thinking that when they heard the story, they'd laugh. "Good move!" they'd joke, and pat me on the back. "Close call!"

I told the story simply, just as it had happened. But they did not look to be in as good of humor as I had hoped.

"We take this very seriously, Charlotte. This is the kind of thing you should have told us about immediately afterwards."

"I'm so sorry! To be honest, it seemed so insignificant that it didn't even occur to me to tell you."

"We are going to have to talk this over and we'll get back to you about our decision." *Decision?* Decision about what?

"I'm so sorry, y'all," I said. "I totally panicked. Should I call the parents to explain and apologize?"

"No, we'll let you know about our decision later in the day."

After being dismissed, I walked out the door, down the hall to the faculty bathroom, and cried for exactly seven minutes. Something you should know about me is that I break out in hives when I both eat and cry. So all the while in the bathroom I desperately tried to calm myself down, to stop the tears and the forthcoming rash, because I had to return to class and teach. These people had placed such hope in me. I had so desperately wanted to be pleasing to them.

I prayed.

Hey God, remember last May when we talked about this? We talked A LOT. I said, "If this isn't the right job for me, please don't let them offer it to me." I know I didn't FULLY mean it, but still...DO YOU REMEMBER THAT? What is this? Have I built this house on sand? Is this my story? Did you lead me out here just to have me die on the vine a few months in? Please don't leave me now. Please. Please. Please.

I managed to squelch my fear and humiliation. I returned to the classroom and did what I had to do. During my lunch break, I called my dad from the parking lot to explain what happened. By now, I was angry. Anger felt easier to sit with than total terror and humiliation. Alex and I had gotten married only a week ago. We had just moved into a house with a rent that depended on *two* salaries. But, more so, a teacher is something you *are* (and also something I'd only just begun to accept about myself). To have my very identity called into question was unraveling me like a thin spool of thread. I felt[7] cut off. Separate.

Six and a half hours later, the assistant called me out of the last class of the day: "Pam wants to see you in her office, Mrs. Getz."

I walked into the now familiar scene of two very sinister and disappointed women staring up at me, the hooded executioners wielding the axe. "Charlotte, we take a situation like this very seriously, and we're going to have to let you go," said Pam—my mentor until yesterday. Just like that. She spoke with a sense of resolve.

"Oh-*kay*," I said quietly, as if the word would extract some sort of clarity.

"We had expectations of you when we hired you, and you did not meet those expectations." In sixteen words, Pam had verbally confirmed the thing I had feared most my entire life. This statement still lingers over me while I'm brushing my teeth in the morning, during commercial breaks, or when waiting idle at a stop sign. "*You have not lived up to my expectations.*"

I had failed.

I was exposed.

What is the opposite of hero? *Villain*?

Tears rolled down my face, hives be damned, as I quietly

---

7. The emotional sense of the word 'feel.'

listened to Pam explain all of the reasons why I was not a good fit for PTS. "We think you just haven't picked up the classical model of teaching as quickly as we had hoped. We threw you into the ring without enough experience… You bring too much of your youth minister background into the classroom… The fact that you don't think that what happened yesterday was a big deal is exactly why this isn't going to work… That will have been some of the most sexual language any of these kids has ever heard…" I doubted that. But the basic insinuation was that I had single-handedly opened my students' eyes to the world of sex, and also I was not teaching to their liking.

This is where I might have said something like, "How would *you* have responded?" or, "You have never observed my classes, so where are you getting your information? How do you know *anything at all* about my teaching? Do you have a *nanny cam* stashed somewhere in my room? Is one of the children *a spy/informant*?" But I didn't say any of this. Because I still wanted to please them.

Instead, a strange calm washed over me.

"Do you have anything you want to say?" Pam asked, finally.

"You know?" I said. "I almost feel relieved." I really did. Pam told me I could come back and student-teach in a while, if I wanted to, which was ridiculous if you think about it. It was a Thursday. I asked if they wanted me to finish out the week. They said no. I asked what my students would be told. They said I could write a letter to them if I wanted. When I tried to get in touch with Pam about writing said letter, I never heard back. I do not know what my kids were told about my whereabouts. I hope they understood how sad I was to leave them.

THIS IS HOW the mighty fall. And the walls I had worked so hard to keep standing all came tumbling down.

MY TEACHING CAREER was brought down by the word "grope."[8]

To be fired for it felt unjust and personal. Upon receiving the news, it took everything in me to restrain my Inner Child from blurting something like Chevy Chase's rant from *Christmas Vacation*: "I want to look [Pam] straight in the eye and I want to tell [her] what a cheap, lying, no good, rotten, fart-flushing, low-life, snake-licking, dirt-eating, inbred, overstuffed, ignorant, blood-sucking, dog-kissing, brainless, hopeless, heartless, bug-eyed, stiff-legged, spotty-lipped, worm-headed, sack of monkey shit [she] is! Hallelujah! Holy shit! Where's the Tylenol?!"

AFTER LOSING MY JOB, I became a fear-biter[9] and a recluse—almost as if I had been diagnosed with a disease that made me photosensitive.[10]

Alex compared our lifestyles then to those of the grandparents from *Charlie and the Chocolate Factory*. We rarely left the bed, and not in a sexy way. You see, a few weeks before we were married, we happened to rent a house in a neighborhood where many of my now ex-students and their overly involved parents owned homes. That, of course, was at a time in my teaching career when it would have been a delight to happen upon a student of mine in the streets

8. I'll permit you now to think this is sort of funny.

9. Think sad alley mutt.

10. See what I did there? LUPUS.

playing hopscotch or double dutch.

In the first few weeks after being asked to clear my desk, my life looked like this:

7AM—Wake up (because I am used to waking up even earlier to get to school on time).

7:15—Pour some coffee, watch the *Today Show*.

8—(Because I know parents will be away dropping their kids off at school) I sneak outside, wearing a cap and sunglasses and a thick scarf (you never know...), to collect firewood. I light a fire in the fireplace and hold myself. Cozy.

11—*Today Show* ends, I turn on *Gilmore Girls* reruns.

2:45—(Because I know parents will be away picking their kids up from school) I get out of my pajamas and bathrobe and go for a light walk with Hercules, my beloved puggle.

6:30—Have dinner with Alex at the seediest bar in town...smoking permitted indoors...overly-involved-parents heavily discriminated against.

This is how you very quickly become unglued. Silly putty instead of kneecaps. Macaroni where there once were bones and organs. I feared I'd split all the way from my sinews to my epidermis; finally and utterly, disconnected from who I was. Knuckle from finger from hand from wrist, like a spacecraft separating after entering deep space, I'd completely fall apart. Fractured. Because now I was a newlywed, newly unemployed, who was also about to find out she was accidentally pregnant.

EVEN EIGHT MONTHS after being fired, my routine looked surprisingly similar (excluding the early wake up time and the mid-morning fire). I avoided things like toy stores, triple-A baseball games, ice cream parlors, anything beach related, early dinners out, any event where buns or quilts or fireworks may be involved, pet stores, newly paved side-walks, parks, grocery stores within a 35-mile radius of my bunker (home), Halloween, G and PG-rated movies, and any establishment that offers free miniature toys or color-ing books with a meal. The only difference was that where the school building used to be a half-hour drive away, they bought a new building just four short blocks from my home, my haven, my hideout. I think this is what being smoked out of your foxhole feels like.

The most disparaging part of everything is that I was the dumpee, yet I was also the one who darted from shadows to alleyways—lest someone spot my red A—in order to ac-complish the most basic tasks throughout my day. At least when it's a real breakup you can drop twenty pounds, glue on some fake eyelashes, and feign the "Yes, But I'm Hot-ter Now" card. But at eight months post-teaching I was fat [pregnant] and getting fatter [pregnanter]. And because of that I was also virtually unemployable. The upside is because Alex and I were very poor, it meant fewer trips to places like ice cream parlors and baseball games.

THIS, I THINK, IS HOW paparazzi-stalked celebrities must feel—laid painfully bare before people such as ogling tweens (or helicopter parents, or something so basic as the sun). I earned my undergraduate degree from a university in Mali-bu so, you see, I have a basis of knowledge when it comes to the rich and famous, especially since I *was* said ogling tween at the time. In 2002, Malibu was primarily just a college town on the weekdays (excluding the ever-present Jeremy Piven). But on a warm and sunny weekend the place might be overrun with famous folks [Denise Richards] out for a pristine [pre-contracted] walk with their children, flanked by ten or so thirsty men with cameras. You could always tell when someone wanted [was getting paid] to be photographed, and when they didn't.

One rainy Wednesday in December, I headed into town to grab some coffee at my favorite spot, the Coffee Bean. Malibu Country Mart was all but abandoned due to the poor weather. But as I scurried through the rain back to my car, I noticed a horde of paparazzi outside of the pet store across the parking lot. Naturally, I walked up and casually tapped one of them on the shoulder. "Who's in there?" The guy, Serbian I would guess, exhibited in his eyes the hysterical glint of a rabid hunter. "Britney, Britney," he said in a harsh whisper, as if I were a halfwit not to have known. Just a few moments later, Britney Spears emerged from the pet store dressed in ordinary civilian attire and carrying a small bag of dog food. She wore sunglasses even though it was dim and overcast. She looked to the ground as she walked. I felt sad for her. The poor girl needed some dog food and could hardly leave her house without a team of flashing shutters waiting to exploit the toilet paper stuck to her shoe, or the mascara smudge under her left eyelid, or the pair of purple bedazzled Crocs she dared to wear outside on her own balcony. That evening, my roommates and I were throwing a Christmas party. As Britney walked stoically past me, I was overcome with the urge to invite her.

"Hey Brit, I know we don't really know each other…although 'Lucky' really spoke to me in middle school. Truth be told, I stopped listening to your music a while ago…but I'm a southern girl too. And maybe you'd like to have just a normal night out with normal people. We're having a party tonight! You should totes drop by. Bring some dip."

But, of course, I let her go. I said nothing. She slid coolly into the front seat of her black Range Rover and disappeared into the thick layer of winter rain and fog. It was just a year or so later that she became unglued and shaved her head and had to be forcefully dispossessed from her own home and children. I can't help but blame myself.

What I would say to B if I knew then what I know now: "I know what it's like to be anxious and self-conscious every time you leave your home. As if you're being followed…a government drone always lurking just around the next corner. I know what it's like to calculate your every move in hopes of avoiding certain people…the sense that you are surrounded, and yet thoroughly alone. I know what it's like to be a disappointment. And Britney, I forgive you for driving your car with your baby in your lap. But if you'd like to be seen and heard, I've got a group of good people coming over to my dump of an apartment tonight to celebrate the birth of tiny baby Jesus. I'd be happy to collect their cellular devices as they come through the door, although I don't think that will be necessary. There will be cocktails. You like cocktails! There will be food. Who doesn't like food?! You could bring your dog. You could take off your sunglasses. And girl, you've got some toilet paper stuck to your shoe…"

SOMETIMES, WHEN I FELT soaked through with my own blithering humanity, deranged with anger and self-pity, here's how I imagined the "Let's Fire Her Meeting" playing out:

SETTING: Clandestine meeting. Small, smoke-filled room. Wednesday evening before the firing.

Pam, Lower School Lead Teacher, and six overly involved parents sit with arms crossed around an oversized poker table.

"We told you before we even met her, this girl isn't *experienced* enough," gruffs one mom as she takes a delicate puff of her cherry flavored cigarillo. "She's too creative, too... interesting..."

"We're paying for this damn school to run as it is, and we expect it to be *as stale and uninspiring as promised*," agrees her husband as he twirls a corner of his waxy black mustache.

"Shouldn't we get a say in who stands in front of our kids every day? In her lesson plans? Her attire? The color palette of her dry-erase markers?"

Pam furrows her brow—she's in a tough spot. She, after all, did convince me to take the job. "Well, I suppose I see your point. She...she does seem to be overly invested in the education of your children..."

The parents, like a frenzied band of pirates, all "Aye!" in savage agreement and clink their pewter goblets together.

"She gave my kid a C for doing poorly on a test! That's not what I hoped all of our hard-earned, long-awaited inheritance money would go towards!"

"Yeah! My kid really doesn't *enjoy* homework! Does that mean he should *suffer* for it?!"

"No!" they all chime in together.

"I mean, is this what's important to PTS? If it is, I'll pull my kid and my funding right out of here, and we'll go somewhere that APPRECIATES MEDIOCRITY!"

Pam is nervous now. "No! No! I assure you that valuable and challenging education is ABSOLUTELY NOT what PTS is all about..."

"Don't forget the whole 'grope' thing! She's a pervert! She's purposefully trying to disturb our kids!"

And, perhaps high due to the fragrant fumes of their stogies, giving in to the frenzy of the mob, the group begins to chant wildly, "SHE'S A PER-VERT! WE WANT A's! SHE'S A PER-VERT! WE WANT A's!"

"Burn her at the stake!"

"Well…I've never observed her class, but I suppose she *does* seem to care too much for the welfare of her students," offers Pam after a while. "She *is* a bit of an overachiever…" and they all snigger in revelry, gold chains and pinky rings clanking merrily with the hardy convivial shakes of their opulent, overstuffed bellies.

Sometimes I frighten myself.[11]

As I PROCESSED the actual cause of my unemployment, I knew I did my best; I also couldn't help but wonder if I really did scar these kids for life. I was asked to leave without so much as a word of explanation or apology. And so I was left to hypothesize what my students knew about my sudden disappearance. Was this a Lindbergh baby type of missing persons situation? Did they cry at night when they were trying to sleep, missing their dear Mrs. Getz? Or would they throw stones at me if we happened upon each other at the local well or while strolling about the marketplace? "Perv!"

This kind of public embarrassment, or a mass betrayal of who you really are—*one who unwittingly sexualizes children*—is not all that dissimilar to a medical diagnosis like, say, Lupus. I didn't mean for either thing to happen, but I

---

11. I think it's important to make an aside that, in spite of what may come off as mutinous hostility, I am profoundly grateful to have been let out of this job. It's the hows and whys and whats of it that are so disruptive to the very foundation of what I know about who I am. Of course I understand by now that I, like the quality of education at PTS, was also just a casualty of the school's first year of operation. But thank God, right? I hear the school is doing really well, and that makes me happy I think.

feel utterly unprotected all the same.

Since being diagnosed with Lupus, I cannot leave the house without full-body sunscreen application. It's thick and sticky and a pain in my pale ass, but it is the base to my necessary armor. Then, I must put on long pants and a long-sleeved shirt (usually with UVF protection, which means my average outfit is about as stylish as a hazmat suit), and the sort of sporty, wide-brimmed hat that won't blow off in an ocean breeze. I'm like the superhero you would pay *not* to read about: *"Indoors, she looks just like your average mom. Outdoors, you might mistake her for an Asian person during the 2003 SARS scare."* It may not be pretty but, like the cockroaches, I am basically a shield.[12]

After being fired, though, I had very little to cover myself with.

Both Lupus and involuntary unemployment have rendered me a missing person unto myself—translucent, invisible in some way, like one of those sad jellyfish that washes too far up onto the shore. It just sits there, frying in the sun day after day, slightly dismembered, with people like overly involved parents wandering by and asking each other jovially what the hell it is—the chemical innards of some sort of cooling device? Lemon jelly? A prude clearish vomit? Could it have been a real living being with a pulse and everything? Nah. What do I, a phantom, the indistinct trace of a real person with putty for knees have to offer to the world now? This is how you become unglued. This is how you lose yourself. Once, you had a purpose, a charge. But now, you've been deemed unworthy, unqualified, *not fit to exist in daylight.* And suddenly your hands seem too tiny to really do anything, and your legs too flimsy to carry yourself,

12. Upside?

and your insides too empty to function. This is where the cockroaches really won out in the whole evolution thing. They should make a cast for this sort of break.

THIS DIAGNOSIS HAS thrown me into new depths of a Very Dark Season. I know it's not like gangrene or anything, but you can never assume what will or will not sever a person.

Sometimes I struggle to pray at all. Other times, I manage to eke out short, dramatic barbs like "What now?" or "Why me?" or "*What did I do to make you hate me??*" This is not what I expected from my life. Sometimes I lean feebly on the hope that God is big enough to fill in on His own the unspoken real-talk of the human heart, however off-color it might be; maybe just directing my gaze toward him is all he wanted in the first place. And every morning so far, I have been able to get out of bed in spite of hard, debilitating symptoms of my disease.[13] This in itself is a victory, one that I—a real, in the flesh non-hero—can't take a shard of credit for.

And sometimes from the trenches, buried beneath my SPF and the shadowy folds of my wide-brimmed hat, I crack open my eyes and find myself overwhelmed by a calming sense that life may be just a series of Very Dark Seasons—but hopefully followed by a spring, when everything that was hidden and broken grows back full.

---

13. PAIN. RASH. PANIC. FATIGUE. *THERE IS NOT ENOUGH SLEEP IN THE WORLD.*

MESSAGE IN A BOTTLE

When Martha Stewart Becomes Annie Wilkes

Dear Therapist,

Thank God for podcasts. When we need some "quiet time" on the boat, we peruse our downloads and zone out together to some informative entertainment. We both like *Invisibilia* a lot because it's easy on the ears and makes us feel smart. Like being able to quote this little nugget: "Apparently locusts are just grasshoppers that got mad!"

The episode was called "True You" and discussed whether there is an essential, unchangeable "self" within us all, or if personality is more of a fluid thing, changing with growth and circumstances. The example of locusts was mentioned because, apparently, scientists recently discovered that grasshoppers—docile, solitary, quiet, harmless creatures—turn into locusts when a drought occurs. The grasshoppers all have to crowd onto the same area of grass and start rubbing their legs together, you know—*like they do*—and this makes them kind of crazy. They release a chemical that transforms them into the locusts of biblical plagues and your nightmares, destroying civilization with their packed swarms.

This, naturally, led us to a conversation about hosting and houseguests.

Here's the deal: we are *such* grasshoppers, man (me more than Charlotte who just naturally exudes a bit more locust on the daily). Did you know that when one grasshopper sees another grasshopper, they run away from each other? Totally me at parties! And when I see my neighbors! But when the both of us have people staying in our homes, we go straight locust: surrounded by others (not by choice, usually), we go *batshit crazy*. This is what we've coined a "First World Drought."

The process takes about three days.

Which is how long they say it takes for both fish and houseguests to go bad. Coincidence? "They" being "wise people who know what they're talking about." (Look, Therapist, we don't make the rules—we just quote them when they support what we already believe.)

This is why we're writing you: because we're tired of being locusts, but we don't really see any way around it. Living across the country and world from so many of our family and friends, and so close to the beach, we are the Destination *du Jour* for, like…all of them (last we counted). And we are so not fans of having our space invaded. I mean, you should have seen what happened when Charlotte thought I stole a set of earplugs from her side of the boat the other day. *Drama.* You'd actually be proud of how well we've handled being in each other's space. Two fellow locusts in an inflatable boat is a doable scenario: write that down.

But for the sake of our loved ones (who don't necessarily need to know about our propensity toward this unsightly transformation), is there a technique—like a chant
or visualization or something quick—that we could do to
fix this about ourselves? Because being exposed like that
is…dicey. And by *dicey* we mean: not everyone will make
it out alive.

I mean, if someone takes a magazine into a bathroom
adjacent to the living room and doesn't even try to hide
it—basically waving a banner that reads "I'm about to
desecrate this and all surrounding areas with my smelly
dump"—shouldn't the immediate penalty be banishment
to a hotel at their own expense?

We can already imagine what you're going to say, of
course. We were actually just talking about it, because
you're so inside our heads. We basically uttered your pre-
dictable response in unison a second ago: "What do you
think this frustration with exposure is really about?" The
way you'd slide that word in there—*exposure*—as if we
wouldn't notice, because it allows you to totally reframe
the situation while letting us feel like we reached our own
epiphany. Because yeah, we know that's what is really going on here: sure, we're annoyed at sharing our space, but
even more than that, we're afraid. Afraid of being seen for
the jerks and messes we really are. Those skid marks in
the toilet may as well be on our *souls*, because the toilet is
actually a lot cleaner than we are. And when someone—
anyone—stumbles off a plane and into our homes, they
are likely going to figure all that out. If there's one thing
we both hate—okay, two, because the first would be trite
wall hangings concerning the idea of dancing like no one's

watching—the other would be people seeing us as we really are.

SOS, Therapist. It's going to take a whole other bottle to unpack *that* one.

Cue the locusts.
Please write back.

Swarmly yours,
Stephanie and Charlotte

MOTHERHOOD AND THE MARIS CRANE IN ME

Charlotte

I LOVE BEING A MOM. Motherhood, however, has also savagely birthed a hideous new version of myself into the world.

SCENE: I pull up to preschool, tenderly remove my kids from their car seats, and immediately transform into the cheeriest, most in-control yet carefree version of "mom" since Carol Brady. I don my overpriced (now sun protective) activewear (the official jersey of mothers everywhere). I offer excessive hugs and kisses, the likes of which my kids pretty much only witness at preschool drop-off. I say things like: "Be kind to your friends, sweetie!" (manners), "Make sure you eat all of your lunch!" (diet), and "I love you!" (that one's from the heart). Then I tell their teachers to let me know if there's *anything at all I can do to help* (selfless as hell). Most importantly, I make sure that all of these affections and gestures are public, as if to say, "See, my kids aren't being beaten at home. The love I have for them is *unquantifiable*. And oh, and by the way, I just won this drop-off" [drops mic].

I return to my car and I think something like, *Nailed it!* And the thought alone brings my tail between my legs. Away from the gaze of my fellow competitors, I morph like nutty melted chocolate back into this unsightly new version of my real self—both exhausted and restless, selfish but always required to give, wrought with self-loathing and yet impossibly entitled. Don't misunderstand me, the love I have for my babies really is unquantifiable. But from the moment I became a mother, I also became someone I didn't like all that much.

Mary Karr says in her book, *The Art of Memoir*, that the real self "… growls like a beast and stinks of something rotten." I've come to see that this Other Growling, Stinking Charlotte—the whining, diseased, fire-able, performance junky Charlotte—bears an unfortunate likeness to Maris Crane from one of my favorite TV sitcoms, *Frasier* (1993-2004).

Frasier follows the two eccentric Crane brothers (Niles and Frasier), their ex-cop father (Martin), and Martin's quirky British caretaker (Daphne). Maris is Niles' fragile, domineering, and nearly sociopathic wife. Mrs. Crane, as it were, has no children and (in all eleven years of the show's running) the audience never actually *sees her*.

> FRASIER: By the way, where's Maris? I haven't seen her all night.
>
> NILES: She's on your bed.
>
> FRASIER: My bed?
>
> NILES: Yes, she's asleep under the guests' coats. She exhausts easily under the pressure to be interesting.

Maris is the worst. She's absurd. And in my current season of life, *I get her.* She would rather recline in her bed than stand and do anything else. She prefers darkness to light, recoils at the idea of anyone needing her, has her "public self" perfectly rehearsed, and is always looking for the next quick fix (be it elbow transplants or horseback riding) to heal whatever it is that ails her.

I used to be interesting. Now, I google things like "CoolSculpting" and "vegan sunscreens." Thrust into just about any social situation, Maris-me (overcome from the anxiety of "it all") tends to accidentally drink excessively (from the nerves) and prattles endlessly about things like her *incredible* children and the most effective sleep training methods (the nerves provoke her Inner Child).

> FRASIER: I thought Maris was joining us?
>
> NILES: Oh, no. I'm afraid Maris is having one of her episodes. In the middle of dressing for the evening, she suddenly slumped down on the edge of the bed in her half-slip and sighed. Of course, I knew then and there that dinner was not to be.

Motherhood is a role that's been played since the dawn of time. It's been depicted in art, music, film, and religion as one of the most revered positions a woman could endeavor. Billions of women embody this role at any given moment. So why do I so often feel like I am playing a part I'm unsuited for? I don't think I'm alone in this. Mothers today are overwhelmed, dissatisfied, guilty, pulled in every direction— we are not enough. And we live out most of these feelings and fears (like Maris Crane) alone and unseen. The issue is not that I don't love being a mom. Rather, I don't love the mom (or the person) *I actually am*. Since childhood and throughout pregnancy I had a different, more patient and graceful vision for how I'd play the part.

God warned Eve in Genesis 3 that because of her betrayal, "…with painful labor you will give birth to children." I wonder if He wasn't also talking about the painful work of making babies into children—a relentless undertaking which asks that we (much like the labor in childbirth) completely surrender our own comfort and desires.

Maris-me makes this beautiful act of submission look more like the medical force-feeding Actual-Maris had to undergo as a child.

The typical day-to-day happenings I *don't* share over social media (or in my calculated preschool interactions) go something like this: frustrated, defeated, and worried texts exchanged with my husband; Cookie Crisps for dinner; hours of watching Disney Jr. What you don't see on Instagram is my incessant and self-bullying inner-dialogue: "We should be outside right now," "But the sun is too strong at this hour," "I should have them making more art."

In short, my new self would like on staff a maid, a masseuse, someone to answer her texts and emails, a therapist, a priest, a psychiatrist for her 'scrips, a nanny to make art with her kids[14], someone to chat with her husband when he requires social interaction, and Gwyneth Paltrow's personal chef.

Oh, poor dear Maris.

> NILES: Dad doesn't get along with Maris.
>
> FRASIER: Who does?
>
> NILES: I thought you liked my Maris!

14. Something like macaroni necklaces or Matisse studies.

FRASIER: I do. I—I like her from a distance. You know, the way you like the sun. Maris is like the sun. Except without the warmth.

Like Florence + the Machine sings, "It's hard to dance with a devil on your back." The devil in this metaphor is obviously not me, it's *Maris.*

NILES: Maris found a grey hair!

FRASIER: Daphne, get Niles a brandy.

NILES: It was right at the apex of her widow's peak.

FRASIER: Better bring the bottle!

NILES: She blames me, Dad. She said it's from the stress I caused her last night when I thoughtlessly turned on the light while she was getting undressed.

I fear Alex will look back on our marriage and think something like this:

NILES: Life with Maris wasn't so bad. It was my fault, after all! I was too rigid, I was always making demands!

FRASIER: No, Niles!

NILES: "Eat something!" "Unlock this door!" "Don't throw that!"

The Maris eyeing me in the mirror whispers that the key to relieving both my actual and my metaphysical angst comes down to things that can be fixed by a strict Paleo diet and hot Pilates classes.

NILES (*on the phone*): Yes, yes, Maris, I'm sure.
No, no, you can't gain weight from a
glucose I.V. No, no, my little worry wart,
there's no such thing as a NutraSweet
drip.

But none of these things ease the sacred weight of raising children. And so I prefer—as so many mothers do—to either wearily play the part or to hide, to deal with my devil behind closed doors, *unseen* by any gawking audience.[15]

ROZ: I don't see her; maybe she went back out.
Oh, wait, I see her coat on a hat rack.

NILES: Look closer. Is the hat rack moving?

ROZ: Oh my *God!*

Motherhood is blessed, and motherhood is hard. One truth doesn't negate the other.

If I'm being honest, maybe becoming a mother didn't birth Maris-me from scratch, but rather handed a microphone and an amp to this beast who was always there, snarling and gnashing and biding her time to come out in full force. By the end of *Frasier*, it's not hard to see that Maris (in all of her insane glory) is actually no more self-serving, entitled, cold, or ridiculous than any of the show's protagonists. It is more comfortable to villainize her, however, than to acknowledge that there might be a little bit of Maris Crane in us all.

Perhaps this is why mothers would rather compete, or retreat—because both activities place us safely on the other side of having a problem. In wagging my finger at Maris, at

15. The upside of having to avoid sunlight.

moms who feed their kids refined sugar, in hiding behind the filters on my Instagram account, I avoid having to confront my own inevitable Maris-self. Doing so might be too dark, too painful; I might incinerate faced with the growling, rotting truth of who I really am.

Like Hagar running from the oppressive Sarai (Genesis 16), I think I can find freedom in solitude and these false personas. But when the angel of God meets Hagar in the wilderness He says, "Go back to your mistress and submit to her…I will so increase your descendants that they will be too numerous to count" (this was apparently a good thing). God is going to bless her *right where it hurts;* not while she's masked, hidden, alone. Hagar responds, "You are the God who sees me."

Often times, the idea that God might truly know me—fragile yet domineering, loving and sociopathic—is terrifying.

> NILES: Maris is unable to have pets. She
> distrusts anything that loves her uncondi-
> tionally.

To Hagar though, God's intimate knowledge of her real self is a *relief.* And it is relief to me as well. It means that God sees me (Maris et al.), and He loves me all the same. This doesn't necessarily mean that the Maris on my back, the Maris in my heart, has fully flown the coop. But remembering God's immeasurable love for me opens my eyes to His manna in the small things: baby kisses, Saturday morning snuggles, and the bizarre hilarity of toddler-thoughts. It means I can give grace to myself during these severely gorgeous yet painful years of childbearing and child rearing.

As a mother, I sacrifice my needs, my wants, my sleep, my sanity, and I must even carry around the extra weight of a tiny but toxic lady named Maris Crane. God looks through the thick armor of all my UVF attire. He sees me. He knows every word of my shallow and self-serving inner-dialogue. He loves me. And although "Maris dislikes public displays of rhythm," he gives me the strength and sustenance to clumsily tango with my Maris-self.

SHATTERED
INTO PLACE

Stephanie

I DON'T REMEMBER A SINGLE moment, but a series of them: tiny differences that began to add up over the months and years. "Red flags" that sent me to the internet for quizzes: "Is Your Child on the Spectrum?" "Warning Signs for Autism." I asked speech therapists and pediatricians what they thought, bracing myself for what turned out to be ambiguous responses. Meanwhile, my firstborn son, the boy who had made me a flailing and uncertain mother, persisted in the behaviors that made him both different from the rest of the world and, often, similar to me: a tendency to remain on the outskirts of social settings. A quiet intensity and focus on preferred activities. A bent toward methodical organization, revealed most frequently in his lining up of toys, a series of cars, for example, stretching out across the room in a multicolored and perfectly straight queue. The world called them warning signs and red flags, and so my anxiety grew, even as I wondered if there might be more to it than that. If there might, rather than a list, be a story here.

I HAVE A CONFESSION to make: I believe that I caused all of my son's challenges.

Back when Jason and I first moved to Atlanta, life appeared to *finally* be on my chosen track. Career? Check. Husband? Check. Happy ending? Almost definitely check. I found myself pregnant nearly the day after we started trying. Score! A deep part of me had always feared God would punk me with infertility issues like so many women I know. I mean, I certainly hadn't spent my twenties as a paragon of sexual virtue. My inner child—the one raised on washboard-abs, flowing-locks, and angry-temple Jesus—harbored notions of karmic payback from a God who *should* move in acts of grace but *really* just wanted to teach me a lesson. I lived in a perpetual state of "waiting for the other shoe to drop," which I think rhymes with "functional atheism."

Just three days after I found out I was pregnant, putting me at about five weeks along, the staff of five women at the office in Atlanta where I worked as a dentist approached me. They had suspected for weeks that another staffer was embezzling money from the practice, and now they had proof. I immediately called my boss and left her a message. She called back quickly, listened to the evidence from one of the women directly, then asked to speak to me again privately. She instructed me on how to fire this individual, as she would not be back in town soon enough to do it herself.

When I hung up the phone, I started shaking.

I had fired exactly one other person in my life, and I hadn't slept at all the night before doing it. Thoughts of an office duel hurtled through my mind alongside my own memories of being fired and how devastating it was. When I'd done the first firing, it had gone smoothly; I was able to make the reason sound impersonal, and we parted ways amicably. But this time? This time was more akin to an act of war. The staffers warned me that the embezzler sometimes carried a gun in her car and I almost threw up. My heart pounded like a drum gone wild. I sat alone in my office, alternately planning my script and struggling for breath. All the while, my son's tiny nervous system was just beginning to form. I was in the initial weeks of growing another person within my own body and already I was getting it wrong.

James was born early, seven months after that day. At two months, his pediatrician noticed his tilted head, diagnosed him with torticollis, and referred us to a physical therapist. From six to twelve months, he wore an orthotic helmet to correct a flat spot in his skull. At twelve months, he underwent unsuccessful neck surgery to fix the head tilt. At eighteen months, he had an MRI, and the doctors discovered that his first vertebra was askew, which was causing the head tilt that PT and muscle surgery hadn't fixed. Just after that, a coworker told me about her daughter, a month younger than James, who was babbling her head off, and that was when I realized my son wasn't speaking a word, and this could be a problem. So in he went for speech therapy. At two years, he had spinal surgery to fix his wonky vertebra. A year later, he still wasn't speaking, and we were referred to a developmental pediatrician who, after thirty minutes' observation and about five hundred questions, diagnosed my son on the autism spectrum.

Does that sound like a list? Because it feels like one, writing it. My life felt like a sheet of bullet points, *bullet* being the operative word: each event piercing my heart and soul, leaving me marinating in a cocktail. And not the good kind, but one of resentment (toward God, for letting this happen), panic (knowing I wasn't enough for this and none of the books I'd read on sleep training offered a plan for this particular path), and the special kind of fear that arises when you sense that all the horrible things you know about yourself are (a) coming back to haunt you and (b) about to be on display for the world to see.

Will was four months old at this point, and I was unwittingly about to doubly descend into postpartum depression on his behalf and a cocoon of guilt on James's.

After three months of descent, I finally checked in with Therapist and told her through hacking sobs that I was reasonably certain I had caused James's diagnosis. And that while I realized it sounded crazy, I had evidence: there was that whole firing incident and the temporary though monumental stress it had inflicted upon me. There was the fact that when he was an infant, I would often put James in his swing facing the window in the family room and then go to the kitchen to make dinner, leaving him alone while I cooked twenty feet away. There was the one[16] time when, at about a month old, he had been crying so hard I had hissed at him to "just shut the hell up already." In my mind, my record as a mother pointed to glaring insufficiencies and consistent mistakes, which clearly had landed us all where we were now: navigating the waters referred to so kindly (and often condescendingly) by the world as "Special Needs."

Therapist was gentle as always but firm in her response. "That's not how this works. And the thing is, you *know* that." She was right—I did—but also…*I didn't.* Because, in

16. (under)estimate

my experience, this *is* how motherhood works: every day is a damn roller coaster full of extreme joys and horrid lows, but the one thing that remains consistent is the guilt, the pervasive feeling that I could always be doing better. And, come to think of it? That pervasive feeling has followed me around my whole life.

WHEN I WENT BACK to work after Will was born, I left him at home with a nanny in my attempted re-do of another source of my firstborn-related guilt—daycare—and James ensconced in his special class in a suburban Atlanta public school. I sobbed gutturally from the driver's seat as I backed out of the driveway and headed east toward my office. I cued up the podcast I had pre-chosen for the occasion upon a friend's recommendation: the aptly-named *The Longest Shortest Time*, which was helping me put off *Serial* and its discussions of murder until I was in a better mental state. I listened for the next few minutes, rapt and eyes dry as I hurtled along Highway 400, and a woman talked about her lifelong struggles with anxiety that had peaked—in insurmountable fashion—since she had become a mother. Before I knew it, I was sobbing again, but these weren't sad or guilty tears as much as fragments of recognition: I heard my own story in hers. I had always thought of anxiety as a sin to counter or a weakness to be overcome, but now I was hearing it as a legitimate condition, and the exposure of this condition within myself was setting me free. *Un-shaming me.* There was a name for all the difficulty I battled on a moment-by-moment basis, and I was far from alone. The shame slowly ebbed.

Once I began to see what an inborn and lifelong plague anxiety could be, memories from my past and observations from my present popped up all over my mind. I saw my child self tying and re-tying her shoelaces until they were just right; that same girl rotely saying prayers for her family out of fear that if she didn't, they would all get into a horrible accident; teenage me dealing with the red-faced, sweaty-pitted onset of constant social awkwardness; and adult me, still mired in all of it but finding coping mechanisms to hide behind. Like avoiding social events—a difficult thing to do when you're in a new country and need to meet people so that your family isn't its own lonely island in foreign waters. So...drinking too much alcohol at social events. And on the couch, alone.

When James was three, I could see his own anxiety, in lining up toys rather than interacting, or scanning the perimeter when placed in new environments. *You and I are so much alike*, I thought. And you know what? Maybe that did mean it came from me. Just not in the way I had thought. The shame began to take the shape of something more beautiful.

A FEW MONTHS BEFORE we left Atlanta, my husband and I went to a meeting at James's school with his teacher, occupational therapist, and the special ed supervisor. A team that sat on the opposite side of the table from us and felt more like a firing squad. We listened to their reports and looked at a screen of multiple grids reflecting his progress, strengths, and weaknesses splayed all out there for the room to see: a quantitative measurement of my boy.

I hated it.

Sitting in a chair inside an office inside a school was like returning to myself as a child—to that unsure, insecure, fearful version of me that lives for approval and dreads disappointing. (Yes, present tense. She's still in there.) I began to wonder how my unseen neuroses might rub off on James and Will and pop up later as their own issues. I was constantly reminded of my own shortcomings, of my own unsettled spots. I felt like I was getting graded on my parenting. Like I might get fired from *this* job, too. UNFIT MOTHER, the headline would read. I wasn't even meeting my own maternal requirements, as reflected by my child's development and the charts that purported to summarize him.

Then I thought back to the rules I used to have for parenting, and how, when I think of them now, they sound like a list. Like bullet points. I knew everything about parenting *before* I had kids. Now I find myself breaking all those rules. Cut to at least one kid ending up in our bed each night despite a fervent commitment against such nonsense after reading the sleep books. I constantly judge and assess whether this rule-breaking is a net good or bad thing and have come to the conclusion that my life—*our* life—just doesn't fit inside those simple black-and-white parameters anymore. We're living in, on, around, through, and off of mystery.[17] Plus, the harbour view from our room is pretty spectacular. And I've made a grudging peace with this state of affairs. Most of the time. I mean, at least…10% of it?[18]

---

17. Psalm 78:25 says, "Man ate the bread of the angels; he sent them food in abundance." The psalmist is referring to manna. The word *manna* means, *"What is it?"* As in, this bread is a mystery. Which means mystery is the food of the angels. Which means God has us on the same diet.

18. (over)estimate

JAMES IS IN KINDERGARTEN. Because Australia runs on a different calendar with different seasons—which feels strangely appropriate for our family and its ever-surprising trajectory—he qualified to start school eight months earlier than he would have in the States. IRONY! And, possibly, foreshadowing.

When we go to his school for meetings now, it's an informal affair around a kid-sized table while he and his brother play in the background. We're surrounded by his team, who don't pick a side of the table opposing us and feel less like a firing squad and more like his advocates. And there's another big change—James. He's been unearthed more and more since we've relocated homes; not unmoored, as I was afraid he would be. In moving here, we've discovered him. He's embraced by his classmates. His teacher says he's a gift to the class. He changes the people he meets. He's changed *me*. I needed it.

As I look back, though, I realize it didn't happen overnight, this coming into his own. The memories that once looked like a list now take on the form of a narrative, melded so closely with my own that the two are almost inextricable. There are his doctor visits, waiting rooms, hospital stays; his teachers and therapists in the U.S.; the uncertainty that enveloped us all in the early days. There is my own childhood anxiety and fear, my early misunderstanding of God and grace, my personal crises that led me to New York which led me to Jason which led me to this life we now have in Sydney. The shattering of what was expected giving way to the beauty of what was meant to be, what is still becoming.

This grace-driven story is made up of a hard healing. I can't tell you how many nights I've spent crying in a hot bath over regrets from the day, or the grief that lies between what is and what should be. But this is not a barren grief; it's a promise-filled, hope-held grief. And it points to *more*. It makes room for more: more joy, more pain. More of James. More of Will. More of everything.

So there are still occasional tears, but they're the kind that are impossible to divide between grief and joy, which I know now are so linked that it's as pointless trying to separate them as it would be to try and untangle the Claire's Boutique gold-plated necklaces from 1989 at the bottom of my jewelry drawer. This is life, real life, full life: this down-to-the-grain, side-by-side mixture of *all* the feelings, *all* the experiences, without one of which I wouldn't be who I'm becoming, and James wouldn't be who he is. I don't want to trade our story for another one—I want to live this one, because it's only in this one that we're all being painfully, constantly saved and exposed into who we're meant to be. And as I write this, my now-six-year-old—the one who simply won't stop talking—burrows into me, knocking my fingers from the keyboard. "Tell me a story," he says as he does every day now. And with a mixture of irritation and indulgence, joy and frustration, *all* of it, I think, *I'm working on it.*

PART SIX

HOW TO
LOSE YOURSELF

LOST...AND FOUND, EVENTUALLY

Stephanie

LOST:

adjective

    1. no longer possessed or retained: lost friends.

    2. no longer able to be found: lost articles.

    3. having gone astray; bewildered as to place, direction, etc.: lost children.

    4. not used for good purpose, as opportunities, time, or labor; wasted: a lost advantage.

    5. being something that someone has failed to win: a lost prize.

    6. ending in or attended with defeat: a lost battle.

    7. destroyed or ruined: lost ships.

verb (used with or without object)

    8. simple past tense and past participle of lose.

THE FIRST TIME I EVER met with Therapist, I opened by telling her I felt like a loser. As always, she asked me to elaborate. So I went into detail, explaining how three of my roommates in a row had gotten engaged and left me for a man; how my younger sister was getting married and I couldn't even get a date for the wedding; how I was nearly finished with my career as a student and, embarking on the search for a place in the real world, felt that I would have to evacuate my home in the South to find it. The description, I felt, screamed "*Loser!*"

She sat silently for a moment, in that way of hers that only heightened my already-monumental anxiety, choosing her next words carefully while I rued my own. "I'd like to word that differently," she finally said. "Instead of saying *loser*, would you agree that maybe you're feeling a profound *loss*?"

Angry at being corrected and forced to think rather than being given easy answers, my first urge was to roll my eyes, shrug, and pout. Then I considered the possibility and all it meant: how unkind I was being to myself, how I *had* endured my own form of loss over the years. Loss of the dreams I'd had to marry young and have kids by now. Loss of friendships over time—or at least the former closeness in them. Loss of hope that there was a good man out there for me. Loss of comfort as I prepared to leave home for New York.

The idea that, rather than being a loser, I was a traveler undergoing grief? It sort of changed everything. Making space for grief, like Therapist used to say, is now a familiar practice.

Space to live in Sydney is a high-priced, fast-moving commodity. Space for grief was, at the beginning of our time here, just as elusive. With beautiful water surrounding me on all sides, and men as well—in the form of Jason and the boys—our first few weeks here didn't feel primed to give much space or permission to grieve what we lost by coming here. Instead, the time was spent familiarizing ourselves with our new home in order to avoid being, quite literally, *lost* in the conventional "how the hell do I get back to our street" way. So what I did instead of mourning was what we all do: I stayed busy. I attacked the streets of our suburb the way I attacked those of New York, but this time armed with a stroller loaded with two young boys' worth of pounds[1]—in January, no less, which is the height of summer here. Cut to a middle-aged lady drenched in sweat heaving her kids up and down hills and into and out of shops (mostly bakeries and liquor stores) before ending up in an unfamiliar house and feeling I should be more grateful for its views even as grief gnawed at my heart. I was determined to make this place familiar, to know the streets and the landmarks and make them our own. I put the weight of this endeavor on my shoulders (not just for my sake, but for theirs), and eventually my knees buckled under the pressure.

So I embarked on another journey of loss, this one in the losing of myself for a time. Those bakery and liquor store receipts added up financially, but that didn't compare to the work they were doing on my soul. It's my firm belief that cupcakes and wine are gifts from God meant to bring us joy, but just like anything good—and this is where it can get confusing—they can be abused. Buttercream icing as a drug? You better believe it. I came home with boxes of those sweet angels multiple times a week, burying my face in their sugary goodness and stuffing my aching feelings down with them. And then, when 5 o'clock came around, I handed each of the boys a screen and poured myself my first glass of wine for the evening, heading with it to our beautiful outdoor deck with the gorgeous view and losing myself in rosé and

1. kilos

episodes of *This is Us*, which generated tears for fictional lives rather than my own.

It wasn't the best look, but it wasn't *dire*. I mean, it's not like I was shooting up in an abandoned building and forgetting to pick up my kids from school. Not for nothing, I was *devoted* to those offspring of mine. In fact, their well-being drove me to distraction, which was convenient, as I wanted to be distracted—from the painful but necessary work of grief. I set about compiling a list of babysitters, therapists, part-time preschools for Will, and kindergarten preparations for James. I readied myself for the fresh separation anxiety (for them and me) in a new place; for the process of settling in they (and I) would endure. Then it happened, and they were fine.

I wasn't.

But I also wasn't done with avoidance yet. My plate cleared of all the non-daily kid-related duties, I set about making our house a home. I found a local bed and bath shop and perused it whenever I wasn't at the bakery, stuffing shopping bags full of pillows and tea towels to pretty-up the corporate furniture-laden rooms of our house. I picked out bedding with more anxiety than that which plagued me when I was doing our wedding registry, for these accoutrements had to make us comfortable in an unfamiliar place—they had to *make us a home here*. I bought knick-knacks and candles and diffusers and anything that I thought might make our space *ours*, all the while neglecting the truth that nagged me but wouldn't be immediately solved: I had no place yet.

One afternoon it all hit me. I was in IKEA, waiting for Jason to return with a forgotten item and policing the boys, who were fighting in the shopping cart while other patrons stared and my face flamed. Silently, I broke. *I want to leave*, I kept thinking. *I just want to run away.* The boys screamed in my face, and Jason remained inexplicably, annoyingly *away* from it all in the way that he always seems to be when it hits the fan. I know that's not even true, but it feels like it is, which—in heated moments like this one—is pretty much the same thing. With each protest from the kids, my blood pressure spiked and my grip on the cart tightened, until I considered letting it go altogether. But I stayed. I stayed, and that made me even angrier, pulse rising even higher. I felt imprisoned in this moment, adrift and alone in my misery, away from everything familiar except my children, who were way *too* familiar. I looked ahead at the exit to the store and the beckoning light-filled, open spaces of the mall. I wanted to run.

I've only actually run away once in my life, and it was to the backyard of our house when I was about eight. My parents were largely unconcerned—they say now they could see me through the window, but I doubt the veracity of that claim; I think they just enjoyed the break. I came back inside around dinnertime, hungry and disappointed with the lack of drama. That frustrated attempt at cutting the chains to home has followed me ever since, culminating in my move to New York and the utter terror and freedom that came with it.

Now, as a wife and mom, I am tempted by other forms of running away: a silent trip in the night to the bus station or airport, an escape to an undisclosed location full of sun and devoid of responsibility. That afternoon in IKEA was the closest I've come to just walking away, and it wasn't even close—I didn't do so much as take my hands off the cart. But the urgency with which the desire hit me plunged me into an awareness that I was *so not okay*. I was lost. By the time Jason returned, I was tearful with anger. I could barely breathe. I seethed at him and, wisely, he just pushed the cart wordlessly. I don't think I talked the whole way home. It took the full forty-five minutes for my blood pressure to level off to the point where I felt steam wasn't coming out of my ears. I climbed out of the car, feeling both defeated and determined: defeated, because I knew I needed help from outside myself. Determined, because I decided to seek it.

Chemical interventions were at the top of the list: I hurried to a new doctor and asked for a refill of my antidepressant, followed by an increase of the dosage. Then there were the tearful goodbyes to the bakery owner and wine-store cashier, which did not actually occur in person but in my mind, and not completely—just in terms of frequency. Waking with dry-mouth and sugar cravings, I realized, was not the culprit, but definitely wasn't helping matters.

These practical steps were all well and good, but what I really needed was soul care. This is different from self-care, you see, in that someone beyond myself and Oprah are involved. Namely, the persistent deity who brought me here in the first place. I had it out with him, on beaches and decks, in our house and on the street. Through these confrontations, I was brought face-to-face with all the losses I had not grieved: the physical closeness to family, and watching firsthand as my nieces grew bigger each day. The church that was like family—except non-judgmental and totally inclusive. A network of true friends. Power outlets that make sense. My kitchen stand mixer. A familiar system for determining temperature, distances, and weight. A steering wheel on the left side of the car. Super Target. All of these things had to be—and continue to be—grieved and mourned, their absence a constant reality as long as we live in Sydney.

But life in Sydney, once faced for what it isn't, has shown all that it *is*. All that I've gained alongside the loss: friends, beaches, cases of Australian wine. And thus begins the process of my being found. Or, as I like to think of it…coming home.

I GOT ONE FOOT ON
THE PLATFORM,
ANOTHER FOOT ON
THE TRAIN

Charlotte

WE'VE OFFICIALLY BEEN "CHURCH-SHOPPING"[2] FOR six months. Most of the churches in our area are extremely passionate about things like social justice, evangelism, and dimly-lit worship concerts. I'm definitely in favor of justice and worshipping God, but I'm not very good or consistent at either. Most of the pastors we hear from are super smart and inspirational on the skin surface of things: talk abounds of Christ-likeness and sanctification and *all that we can do for Jesus*. I'm initially encouraged by the exhortation to be like Christ. I think giddily to myself, "Is that possible?" and then froth from the mouth at visions of my surefire greatness and *all that I could do for God's kingdom*.

After I take a step back and my vision clears, everything

2. The arduous process of bouncing from one church to another, looking for the elusive "right fit."

starts to feel like kind of an awful load. I start to feel sleepy and want to take a nap.

Sanctification has always been a real head-scratcher to me in that way, especially as it relates to the deadness I feel in my own sin and fragility. This deadness is so real to me that it nearly has a life, breathing and stinking and ever threatening to burst too plainly into sight. Sanctification, if I gloss over it without asking questions, feels a lot like law: *be a better person already—stronger, faster, kinder, MOVE!*

When I think things like this, my living deadness stretches its lazy, sun-starved arms behind its head. It kicks up its bare feet, strikes a match, lights a cigarette, and says with an encumbered exhale, "NOT TODAY, DUDE."

But sanctification, as a word, isn't quite so onerous. It means "set apart."

And sanctification as a practice means something like "being made, or becoming holy."

I like those descriptions. "Being made" and "becoming" both have very little to do with my own efforts. *To be made* seems to place the burden on something external; if I am to be made, there must be a maker. *This* sanctification seems much easier for my poor living deadness to cope with. And I'm already halfway there. For I am nothing if not over and again, acutely, literally, *set apart.*

As a kid, when I was set apart from my siblings and parents every night (the psychologically punishing event of *bedtime*), I had my routine of encroaching doom. This routine, if you'll recall, began by arranging everything exactly in its place, and ended with the happy parts of Psalm 23. *The Lord is my shepherd, the Lord is my shepherd, the Lord is my shepherd.*

This was less of a repeated assurance and more of a plea or a threat.

Hey Lord, you better lead me beside still waters, GUY.
And for the love, REFRESH MY SOUL.

Come to think of it, my prayers as a "mature" woman don't sound too dissimilar...

MAKE ME LIE DOWN IN GREEN PASTURES, K?

But I was alone. Where was this shephard? Sometimes, I worry I'm still looking.

Be it a bedroom in Alabama, a dorm room in Rhode Island, or a bungalow in Long Beach, I have always done my best wrestling with Jesus separate, away, *apart*. Exile and adventure ride a precariously thin line.

Why did I expect this California displacement to be any different?

It wasn't until I went away to boarding school (adventure or exile?) as a high school sophomore that my paralyzing nighttime anxieties finally, sort of inexplicably, went on leave. Away at boarding school is also where I lost myself—which, of course, is almost always the gnarly precursor to finding yourself.

In Birmingham, you generally did not go to boarding school unless you'd developed a nasty coke habit or stabbed a guy. Boarding school was for weirdos. Very rarely did a person go voluntarily. You "got sent." Every time I came home for a holiday or vacation, some well-meaning parent of a friend would approach me with sad eyes and lay a sympathetic hand gently on my shoulder: "Do you get to come back yet, sweetie?"

"Nope, nope. Like I told you last Christmas, Mrs. Campbell, not until I either graduate or stop tagging underpasses."

So, in case your town has similar apprehensions on the practice, I should explain that it is *tradition* in both my immediate and extended family to go away to boarding school starting in the tenth grade. We aren't bad people. At least not in the sense that you're thinking (as it generally applies to kids who get sent to boarding school).

Finding the right school was pretty much the exact same process as finding the right college. In the ninth grade instead of the twelfth, my parents and I spent a long weekend trekking around New England to check out several different spots.

The stakes of this trip were high—my parents had precisely four days to convince me how great the boarding school experience would be. At the time, I was not into the idea of leaving Birmingham. Not even a little. Beyond my obvious fear problem, I had crushed the ninth grade. I lost a little weight that year, got pretty good at tennis, and I was thriving in the most fun group of friends like ever. That very month I had been heading up a venture to travel cross-country via golf cart, with the sole purpose of stalking Leonardo DiCaprio. What *boarding school* could possibly shape me into a more entrepreneurial and goal-oriented person than I already was?

Mom and Dad rolled out the red carpet. We stayed at some charming New England inns, ate at nice restaurants, and really made a vacation of our Tour de Prep Schools, 1998.

But every school we visited seemed to be even less of a fit than the last.

My parents had almost lost hope until we visited our final spot on the tour—St. George's in Newport, Rhode Island.

Driving through the front gates of St. George's, one felt like Marie Antoinette (pre-revolution of course) in a horse-drawn carriage upon entering the lush grounds of Versailles. The front drive was grand, with towering leafy trees arching perfectly over its new arrivals. The three of us were silent as we made our way to the front circle, in awe. Our puny white rental sedan seemed too inconsequential to be a part of this sumptuous backdrop. To our left were beautiful old brick dorms and a quad with both male and female students in khakis and pastels playing Frisbee and giggling on quilts. To our right, and just a five-minute walk away, the vast Atlantic Ocean roared as it crashed onto an idyllic New England beach. The whole scene looked like something out of a Tommy Hilfiger ad. We walked into the main building, where the admissions office was located, and craned our necks like gawking tourists. The space felt like the hull of an old ship—dark wooden walls and rich crimson carpeting covered the place. The smell of salt was in the air, and so was the scent of adventure and the unknown.

But none of this seemed all that impressive (at least not compared to my sweet social setup back home) until envisioning it on the arm of Tom Biggs.

I met Tom later that morning while observing a History of the Middle East class alongside a girl named Sabrina, my tour guide for the day. Sabrina was cute and bouncy and I could picture myself being friends with her. In fact, I could picture being friends with most of the kids in this class. But from a single glance at Tom Biggs, I knew that I would attend St. George's next year, and we would fall in love. Everything went in slow motion, and I heard music when our eyes first met.[3] He had baby blue eyes and sported a pair of Oakley sunglasses held on by croakies in his shaggy, sunkissed brown hair. Tom was cool, charismatic, and wearing the school's dress code—a blazer, tie, and khakis. He looked like a lifeguard in off-season or that his name could have

3. Something like Manfred Mann's "Blinded by the Light."

been something like Brad or Chaz. After the class was let out, he caught up with Sabrina and me.

"Hey, so are you going to come here next year?" his voice rang like a perfect riff.

I thought I would throw up. "I dunno," I said shyly. "Maybe!"

"Where are you from?"

"Alabama."

"You should go here. SG is the best!"

"Yeah?" I said breathlessly. God he made that acronym sound cool.

"Yeah," he said.

Did he just ask me out?? "Maybe I will."

In that blissful moment, I had made up my mind. Fear? What fear? I'd make it work. Maybe boarding school wouldn't be so bad. If I had to go into the unknown, to leave my friends and the nighttime security of my parents, it would be to this place, to Tom Biggs—to my destiny. *Away.*

PLAYED OUT, my "destiny" ended up looking a lot more like a compass that had been stomped on by a stiletto. In all of the hormonal, away-from-home teen chaos, I lost myself. Things went fine in my first months at St. George's. Survival Mode and the like. But by the time I started school that fall, Tom had moved on to another girl. Go figure. In better news, I had stopped being afraid at night…at least, not in the obsessive way I had been before. And if you don't believe me, my sophomore dorm was actually an old war infirmary—a breeding ground for the paranormal—and still, I got by. Did I attribute this miracle to God? No. I just chalked it up to something I must have finally done right, karma if you will, and went on surviving.

By and large, the student body of St. George's was made up of wealthy kids from fancy places like Connecticut or Manhattan. These were deep and fast waters, and although I was an expert at the free-style, I was unprepared for the strains of trying to fit in. People up here thought it was weird that I talked with an accent and bought my clothes from the Limited.

I don't have an accent, YOU HAVE AN ACCENT.

On one of my first afternoons of JV soccer practice that fall, a teammate asked me, "Why do you wear tube socks pulled straight up your shins like that?" Her nose was curled in disapproval. I had only been at St. George's for a few weeks. Looking around, I realized with a pit in my stomach that all the other girls wore ankle socks. For shame.

"I don't know, that's how I like to wear them," I said as if this were something I had ever remotely thought about. Why *did* I wear tube socks pulled up like that? That's how everyone wore socks back home. I was just swimming with the current!

But the current had changed. And the temp was frigid, y'all.

The girl continued to look me up and down. "And why do you part your hair on the side like that?"

Good God, I *did* part my hair on the side like that, didn't I? I'm pretty sure that was just how my hair naturally fell, but obviously it was time to intervene.

I began to look at myself in the mirror each morning with a new, Yankee sort of scrutiny. Was I too chubby? Too outrageous? What were the right clothes? The right hairstyles? Who is Lily Pulitzer, and how can I convince her to be my friend? What were the right bad habits? Should I suggest [lie] that I'd been sort of slutty back home? It seemed like everyone was sort of slutty here…

What do they think of me?

As I walked through the hallways those first few months, I became paranoid of the judging gazes of my peers. The questions I imagined pouring through their stares:

"Why are her pants so short?"

"Do you think she lives on a farm?"

"Can you understand a single thing coming out of her mouth?"

"What does she think she's doing here?"

I spent more time questioning myself in those first few months than I did just actually *being* myself. But what did it even mean to be myself? Who was I anyway?

Worm food.

Lost.

Nowadays I can think about boarding school with a bit of prudent hindsight. And while I'm sure some people likely did ask themselves at least some of these questions, their biggest question probably looked a lot like mine:

"What does *she* think of *me*?"

ALL THREE YEARS at St. George's, I fancied myself the master of my own fate. I would probably have defended the existence of a God, but not with any conviction. I asked Him for things[4] from time to time but never really expected to get them. One way or another I dug in my heels, gripped life's strings white-knuckled, and everything was under control. I'd find my own way through this new territory.

And I did, in a manner of speaking. High school is high school, whether you board there or not.

After a few years of being settled at St. George's (or as

4. Boys.

settled as I was ever going to be), during my senior year, the road got bumpy again, and my legs lost their footing; the strings were cut. It began in September with 9/11. Many of my classmates were either from Manhattan, or their parents worked there. In the days following the attack, we'd stare outside over the acres of sloping grass surrounding campus, and my male classmates would wonder out loud if soon enough they'd be drafted, training for war on those very fields. This fear might seem far fetched so many years out from the tragedy, but at the time, any horrible thing appeared possible. Just a few weeks after that, a friend and old crush died in his first year of college. He was goofing off with some buddies and slid down what he thought was a laundry chute, into what was actually a trash compactor. In November, my roommate's mother had a rare and violent recurrence of breast cancer and passed away within weeks. And then about two weeks after that my cousin, Johnson, who was my friend and the same age as me, died in a car accident.

This season of loss was and continues to be incredibly surreal to me. You might wonder at my lack of detail about the whole thing, but that's just how it felt—like a quick, nondescript, but excruciating snap.

I couldn't pray at all anymore, not even for the little things[5] that I wanted, not even in desperate wordless pleas. I didn't even have the energy to be angry with God. The truth of life's brittleness sat on my chest like a heavy antique sideboard. All of my worst fears had taken form. And so I lost whatever grip had previously kept me from coming completely unraveled. I felt nothing, adrift in space like a forgotten birthday balloon.

5. Boys.

I didn't want to think about anything, much less God. So I didn't. The first time I smoked pot was in a bush behind the mailbox of a house that bordered the campus. A guy named Greg Nielson enthusiastically agreed to introduce me to the stuff. After my first blessed inhalations, I knew I'd found a cure. Greg said he'd throw me a bone and we could totally hook up if I wanted; nobody had to know. I said I'd just take the pot, thankyouverymuch. Smoking in that bush marked the beginning of an intense and invigorating new diversion.[6]

Everything afterwards is quite a blur.

For the first time, life didn't seem like a certainty. And so I pushed at life's limits a little bit, or at least dealt with my suffering and confusion the best I could with my own human hands. Now, as a 30-something, I still haven't quite figured this out. Faced with uncertainty as an adult, I look to things like essential oils, sleep, spin class, wine, or double-cheese pizza well before I actually look to Jesus.

And as with today, all the distractions in the world couldn't fully dull the pain back then. I found myself swimming around in a pool of darkness—lost—with no real hope to cling to and a barrel full of grief that I never really faced. Nobody had taught me how.

But then something weird happened. I got sent away again. Unbeknownst to me, my mom signed me up to go on a church mission trip to Bolivia the summer after I graduated. I think she was hoping to fill the three-month gap after graduation with wholesome endeavors that might pull me

---

6. The last time I smoked pot was in college. Unawares to me, the stuff was laced and I hallucinated a premonition that I would die in my sleep. It was real. It was terrifying. I did not die in my sleep, but that was the end of the road for me and casual drug usage.

out of the fog and "get me on the right path" before heading out to California for college. But again, there's an almost indiscernible line between adventure and exile. And I didn't have the energy to fight her on it.

On our first full day in Cochabamba, Bolivia, we climbed the steep San Pedro Hill up to the Cristo de la Concordia (the Christ of Peace), which is the largest statue of Jesus in the world if you care to know. The climb up to the base of the statue involved 2,000 stairs at 9,300-ish feet above sea level. Now, you might live this high above the level of the sea, but I did not. Which meant that this hike up to Jesus was a freaking *commitment*. Monotonously making my way up each of the 2,000 stairs, quads screaming and my lungs as tight as a rope, I couldn't help but note glibly to myself how parallel this activity seemed to be with my more personal quest for Jesus—a lot of work, with very little yield. Miraculously, the last one up the steps, I reached the top. And the view from the Christ of Peace—an infinite sky as pure a blue as I had ever seen—was something I'll never forget.

Something inside me began to breathe again.

We saw many different faces of Bolivia in those several weeks—the urban capital of La Paz, the smaller Cochabamba, and the tiny town of Aramasi tucked high away in the Andes Mountains. The common denominator in each of these places was extreme poverty.

I felt totally inspired to fix the problem of Bolivia. After just a few days there, I'd mentally committed myself to returning for a year, wherein I'd donate my precious time (and by then a great deal of money I had somehow acquired), to make it all better. I sat wide-eyed as we drove past cities made entirely of tents. Large blue barrels decorated the entryways of makeshift doors to catch the rainwater for things like baths and dishes. Everywhere we went smelled of something burning. My own battered spirit began to look familiar here. In the same ridiculous way that people are drawn to take poetic photos of rusty door knobs and dead leaves, something about this place began to mesmerize me. It didn't *feel* broken at all. After spending a few days at La Ville d'Amistad, an orphanage in Cochabamba, my plan to return as Bolivia's Great Humanitarian[7] faded into the background. So many people had nothing, yet they were joyful and thriving in a way I had never known.

Amid the awful, infomercial-level poverty in Bolivia, God spoke to me. No, he *literally* spoke to me, y'all. And it came in the form of a quote from *The Lord of the Rings.* "All that is gold does not glitter, not all those who wander are lost." These words began to sing in my head, like a bad song you hate that you know every word to. It had a rhythm and a roll. *Allthatisgolddoesnotglitter / notallthosewhowanderarelost.* Eventually, I told our leader, Gil, what was going on, and that I was pretty sure the Lord was speaking to me by way of the Song of Aragorn.

"Well, maybe that's God trying to tell you something," said Gil. "But maybe it's nothing, who knows. Great book, though." Gil is the type of un-intimidating guy who (in a matter of seconds) could go from saying the most profound thing you've ever heard, to making fart noises with his elbow pit—and it was the most effective form of communication any single person had attempted with me to date.

Later that evening, as I lay in bed, I dared to pray about the Tolkien quote. It was the first time I had prayed in nearly a year. Maybe God was finally going to show.

---

7. Surely this is the name by which they would refer to me in the history books.

I pondered the words again, but this time on purpose.

All that is gold does not glitter, not all those who wander are lost.

The idea of being lost resonated with me in a pit-in-my-tummy kind of way. I had been set apart, wandering since I was a kid—from my bedroom to my parents' room, from my home to summer camp, from school to school, from Alabama to Rhode Island, soon from Rhode Island to California, and then all the myriad personal ways a person wanders to and from, in and around who they really are. But this quote painted the wanderer in a different light. Maybe I wasn't lost after all. Maybe the Lord himself was shepherding me to and through these places and these stories. Maybe I hadn't lost myself, but instead was *becoming*, being made into who I was meant to be.

The full Song of Aragorn goes like this:

> *All that is gold does not glitter,*
> *Not all those who wander are lost;*
> *The old that is strong does not wither,*
> *Deep roots are not reached by the frost.*
> *From the ashes a fire shall be woken,*
> *A light from the shadows shall spring;*
> *Renewed shall be blade that was broken,*
> *The crownless again shall be king*

Aragorn is Jesus, y'all. Everybody knows that.

I began to pray more and more. I wrote my prayers in a journal, starting with something like this: *Help.*

I CAN'T REALLY EXPLAIN why, but in the most twisted, aching, and conflicted part of my spirit, something finally beat, whispered, came alive. Something began to make sense—

even on the very simple level that maybe God, who apparently spoke to me in riddle, wasn't going to operate in the way I had expected him to. Bolivia, like me that summer, was a place beleaguered with ash and destruction—and yet "from the ashes a fire shall be woken." The people I met were joyful, and the place reeked both literally and spiritually of fire. It was as if I had been falling from a cliff, and then some capable arm suddenly reached out and caught me.

Maybe it was that same arm that had pushed me over the edge from the get-go.

This puts a new spin on exile, on boarding school, on loss, on kids, on autoimmune disease, on California *and not Alabama*. Maybe we are cast out, *set apart*, all so we can play this specific part in a great adventure story: the wild improbability of being rescued. It's the subtle difference between exile and adventure; lost or wandering; making or being made.

Exile/Adventure—*Rescue*—Exile/Adventure—*Rescue*.

Inhale / exhale / inhale / exhale. Maybe sanctification is as easy as breathing.

Set apart—being made—becoming—

It isn't always comfortable, *but it is holy*.

RECOVERED TRANSCRIPTS FROM LIFEBOAT 815

EXTERIOR: DAY—SOMEWHERE IN THE PACIFIC.

The girls have been adrift for 270 days—approximately nine months. Their boat has developed a certain order to it. Like a marital bed, they each have a side they prefer to stay on. STEPHANIE *has her most valuable belongings arranged just so, and a tight schedule for the boys starting with urine conservation.* CHARLOTTE *has developed an elaborate system of time-telling, so that she knows exactly where to position her shade (constructed of shreds of toxic hospital waste found floating in the water). They have routines.*

But all this order hasn't fully satisfied their longing to be found. They are losing hope.

CHARLOTTE: We have literally been out here for years.

STEPHANIE: Like five at least.

CHARLOTTE: Nobody is even looking for us.

STEPHANIE: We're going to be stuck out here forever.

CHARLOTTE: Literally, for all of time.

STEPHANIE: And we're coming up on our last rations of

bread and wine.

CHARLOTTE: Yeah, no chance we were going to make *those* last.

STEPHANIE: I don't want to point fingers here, but if we'd gone due north, like I suggested approximately ten years ago, we'd have found some sort of land.

CHARLOTTE *(hurt)*: You *know* I've been beating myself up about that.

STEPHANIE: I know, I know, sorry.

CHARLOTTE: I feel like all this paddling in no specific direction at all is getting super annoying. Especially since I should totally have ripped arms by now and I do NOT feel like that is the case.

STEPHANIE: Um, join the club. *(She waggles her arm flab.)*

CHARLOTTE: Is it time to read to the kids yet? They're begging for *Harry Potter*, the boy who lived.

STEPHANIE: Um, do you mean is it wine o'clock yet? You're just skipping over cocktail hour?

CHARLOTTE: I can't even remember which comes first. Seriously, I think I have sea delirium or something. Is that a thing?

STEPHANIE: You *are* looking a little green.

CHARLOTTE: I am?? *(She grabs a broken shard of mirror and looks at her reflection.)*

STEPHANIE: Maybe you should take a nap.

CHARLOTTE: Meh. It's too bright out. Again, something I've

lost on this journey that I expected to gain: a tan. I should have some sick color by now—we're talking Gisele or Pocahontas on a yacht—and instead I'm buried under a parasol and caftan like an octogenarian on a Led Zepagain cruise, who doesn't know she's about to become a statistic in a large norovirus outbreak.

STEPHANIE: Let's be honest though, does it matter? Ain't nobody looking at our skin tone these days. You know what I just remembered?

CHARLOTTE: To put the pinot grigio on ice?

STEPHANIE: Damn. (*She puts the pinot grigio on ice.*) Well, besides that, I was just thinking of how, when my children were born, I was weirdly unemotional during the whole thing, other than totally afraid, until I heard their cries. It was like, that was the moment they were real to me. And my heart flooded with love at the sound of their voices. But now?

CHARLOTTE: Yeah, now...

STEPHANIE: Not the same.

They gaze at the water together. No escape.

CHARLOTTE: How can the thing that, in a second, completely locates you in the universe...be the same thing that unhinges you?

STEPHANIE: Kind of like this boat. Excuse me, this *fucking* boat.

CHARLOTTE: Whoa. Easy there. How about *I* get the glasses?

STEPHANIE: Whatevs. Sure. But seriously...when are we

getting off this boat? My marriage is not benefitting from the lack of...intimacy due to the setting, know what I mean?

CHARLOTTE: Yeah, I'm actually getting to the point where I'm sort of missing sex.

STEPHANIE: Right?! Usually I'm trying to schedule it around Netflix. But out here, it feels like we've all become roommates. And not in a good way. I mean, I'm learning the smell of Margot's farts.

CHARLOTTE: Well, the stench of Jason's toe cleavage has become pretty recognizable to me. Doesn't exactly make for good romance.

STEPHANIE: But I'll be damned if my kids learn how babies are made by actually *watching* the process. They can learn the way I did: by their mother handing them a book and telling them to come back with questions.

CHARLOTTE: OMG, you got a book too?!

STEPHANIE: So gross. I mean, when you're that age nobody wants to think about their parents—or anyone—*doing it.*

CHARLOTTE: And then *you* do it.

STEPHANIE: Which is usually before you should.

CHARLOTTE: And then you *should*, but you're on a small boat and can't because there is an audience and that is called live porn.

STEPHANIE: Life, am I right?

CHARLOTTE: Speaking of right, by which I mean *writing*...

STEPHANIE (*rolls her eyes*): Really with the puns?

CHARLOTTE: I know. But come on...I think I'm getting carpal tunnel from doing all the documentation of our transcripts. Maybe you could take over for a few days?

STEPHANIE (*sighs heavily*): Okay...so here's the thing. I'm sort of...iffy about the transcripts.

CHARLOTTE: What???

STEPHANIE: Char, nobody's going to want to read that shit.

CHARLOTTE: Why is this only coming up *now*? After we've literally been out here for forty years?

STEPHANIE: Talking about our kids' gas habits? Lack of sex with our husbands? Really??

CHARLOTTE: *I don't know!* I think it's good to have a record! (*Beginning to stew*) I knew something was up. I've been doing all the work lately, what with the—

STEPHANIE: YOU? DOING ALL THE WORK? Do you know how much I have to deal with on a daily basis? Those "husbands" (*she uses air quotes*) over there playing video games, and you and your "transcripts" (*air quotes again*). Meanwhile I'm raising two kids—

CHARLOTTE: Um, HELLO, SAME—

STEPHANIE: And who's been doing MOST of the rowing?!

CHARLOTTE: ME!

STEPHANIE: YOU? YOU? *You've* been giving Alex backrubs!

CHARLOTTE: IT'S CALLED ROWING BY PROXY, K?

STEPHANIE: That is not a thing.

CHARLOTTE: Well, you might at least acknowledge that I'M the one who figured out how to tell time out here...

STEPHANIE (*furious and fed up*): That's it. I need a break. I just need a damn— (*She waves her arms in the air and her oar drops, splashing into the ocean before a current whips it away.*)

STEPHANIE (*cont'd*): Oh shit...

CHARLOTTE: Are you kidding me?

STEPHANIE: That...that's bad, right?

CHARLOTTE (*livid*): I seriously cannot...you know what? Screw it.

She throws her own oar into the ocean, and they watch it float out to sea. After a beat, STEPHANIE *and* CHARLOTTE *turn to each other, eyes wide.*

CHARLOTTE (*cont'd*): Well I guess you'll have more time to help me write now.

STEPHANIE: Pour me some wine. I give up.

CHARLOTTE: God save us.

STEPHANIE: Literally, *God save us.*

CHARLOTTE *pours them each a glass as they sit in silence for a moment.*

STEPHANIE (*cont'd*): We're lost, dude.

CHARLOTTE: Are you really just realizing that now?

Dear Therapist...

Stephanie doesn't know I'm writing to you, and neither does my family—and going behind any of their backs feels wrong somehow. I am not doing well, Therapist. If Alex, Ford, and Margot weren't an extension of me before, I fear the dampness and the salt water have melded us together like an inseparable cluster of moldy barnacles. We are dearly bonded in this crustacean life, but this cement-like attachment in one way leaves me claustrophobic and in another way makes me feel even more vulnerable to loss than I already am. *I love them too much*, Therapist.

But the real reason I'm writing you today is because this is way more than I, than *we*, expected. You didn't prepare us. What I'm saying is, *why are we out here?* Venturing off the grid was a huge mistake, a seventh grade science experiment gone comically wrong—chemicals burning the flesh and whatnot. I feel completely trapped. We write you these desperate letters, and who knows where they actually wash ashore. I mean, the planet is made up of 71% water, and we're sending you notes in old cabernet bottles. So juvenile. Therapist, I am out here drifting while my family back in the South is going through hard times. All I want, like a homesick little kid or something, is to be home with my people. I want to cry with them, tell them how the world is not fair and that because of them, my chronic illness in sunny southern California doesn't seem so bad.

I am exhausted. I want to rest. And yet here I am rowing—rowing—rowing. Or now drifting—drifting—drifting. Poor Stephanie, she really doesn't seem capable of handling all the stresses of the wilderness. I AM DOING ALL THE WORK AND DON'T BELIEVE OTHERWISE. I guess what I'm trying to get to is this: I'm not going to be writing anymore. It's too painful to keep imagining anything but what is clearly the truth: we really are out here alone—untethered, unmoored, in a lifeboat that seems to be doing not much more than just keeping us alive.

I'm not saying I'm giving up. But maybe I am.

In the immortal words of Jeff Buckley, "This is our last goodbye."

Charlotte

Dear Therapist...

I'm worried about Charlotte. She's going through a lot right now—with her family, her health, her inability to work as much as I do...

Scratch that last part. That was mean. Honestly, I'm worried about both of us. Life on this boat feels like we're stuck in survival mode, and whether it's me trying to comfort and accommodate Char, or me trying not to lose my damn mind every time my kids ask for something as soon as I've sat down, it's just tough times. We're tired, and thirsty (and relying on wine more than water to slake that thirst), and irritable.

It's strange being so far away from my country and family and yet not feeling that far away at all. Voice apps and international texting and all that make them feel a bit closer than they are, but then I remember the time difference and the ocean between us and it's all a bit...disorienting. Not far, yet super far. Immediate responses, yet sixteen hours between us. I wake up ahead of everyone I know back home, yet feel like I'm starting off my day at a deficit because there are messages to return, and two little mouths to feed and clothe. It's like being slapped in the face with a soft, warm blanket. Overwhelming just to get out of bed and get started, but also exciting, waking up to that much love on my phone. I don't know. So confusing.

And there's this, boat-wise: I can't stand not knowing where we are. I can't stand feeling lost and, in the darkest moments, feeling like I don't even know *myself* anymore. I've just turned forty, and my hormones seem to be doing battle with my sanity, and to be honest, it doesn't feel like my sanity is going to win this one. Who thought it would be a good idea to move across the world right around the time I could be having a midlife crisis?

Oh yeah…I remember now. Me. Prayers and whatnot. Inescapable answers to those prayers leading us in this direction. In this *direction*, but not fully getting us settled… yet. So now we're on the path we were led to but still adrift, and I'm asking *you* about it. No offense, Therapist—not that you're even likely getting these—but I think maybe I'm directing my questions to the wrong person. I seriously give up.

Stephanie

POCKET LITURGY FOR YOUR TIME AT SEA

When There's Not Enough Food:

Help

When There's Not Enough Time:

Help

When Your Kids Need You Too Much:

Help

When the Storm Won't Cease:

Help

When There's Not Enough Shade:

Help

When You're Exhausted:

Help

When You're Almost There:

Keep helping

When You're There:

Thank You. I still need you. I cannot do this on my own. Please don't stop helping.

KNOCK KNOCK, SPECIAL DELIVERY!

Charlotte

IT'S BEEN ALMOST NINE MONTHS since we moved to this new land: *California*. God seems sort of ridiculous when I see his story for me on paper. My writing hand has whiplash from all the to and fro, the back and forth. At the nine month mark, we finally have a rhythm and something resembling a home. But y'all, it took exactly this long for us to arrive.

A mentor once told me it takes nine months to feel at home in a new city.

It only occurs to me now how suspiciously literary that theory is as it relates to new life.

WHEN I FOUND OUT I was pregnant in 2012, I knew so little about babies that I sent my friend a photo of the pregnancy test to make sure I was reading it right.

I had a hunch something more was going on. My boobs felt like they might explode from my very chest. I was suffering round-the-clock hangover symptoms. And no matter how much sleep I got, I was exhausted—a deteriorating sort of exhaustion I had never known—as if there were *two peo-ple* living off of my already paltry energy.

The probability of pregnancy was not lost on me. Several indications pointed to this possibility. Most notably, December 1st—the night when Alex and I over-served ourselves on our friend's homemade infused liquors, and poor decision-making ensued.

HERE'S HOW OUR "Conversation About Conceiving a Baby" went:

SETTING: December 1st, 2012. Our darkened bedroom. Late, late at night.

Alex and I get a bit animalistic.

"Let's just…see what happens…" Alex says, mischief exuding from every alcohol-drenched pore of his body.

I giggle clumsily like a character from *Beavis and Butthead*: "Huh huh, huh huh huh."

THE END.

This is the reality behind how many [most] babies actually get made. Write that down.

The day I found out I was pregnant, I woke up at 5:30 in the morning to drive several friends to the airport. On the way home, I began to violently obsess over a McDonald's breakfast biscuit. This might not seem that strange to the average person, but I had been on a "life-changing" detox cleanse, willfully eating super-foods like salmon and kale and yadayadayada for the last four months. After I finally succumbed and took a spin through the McDonald's drive-thru, I promptly stopped at the drugstore and purchased a pregnancy test. I drove home, peed on the stick, saw that it was negative, and then laid the thing on the edge of the sink in a breath of relief. I ate my fast food in ignorance, and then returned to the bathroom to wash my hands only to notice that something suspicious had manifested in the petite plastic window of that fateful test: a second negative sign. An *equal* sign? But my eyes must have deceived me. Surely that second line was just a shadow, a phantom. And so I went through the whole process again. And again. Three times.

Equal.

Equal.

Equal.

"Something must be wrong with my pee."

And there you have it—first evidence of my beautiful Ford. Signs of real actual life growing inside of *me*, who just minutes prior had been dead, withered, drifting. At that confusing moment, Ford was tinier than a grain of rice, just a microscopic clump of cells. As I write this now, he is a small child with gifts and opinions and a gap-toothed smile that could literally melt the skin off of a human body.

But this skin-melting swooner was not my plan.

I'd been fired just a month ago and married a week before that. I was lost[8] all over again.

And nine months of waiting is a great deal of time for a person to self-scrutinize. For instance, I never planned on being a stay-at-home mom. The cost of childcare, however, combined with my lack of job Before Baby [B.B.], had rendered me exactly that. My identity seemed at stake in some way. Who was I? Just one year ago I was a bright and creative aspiring photographer—independent, unmarried, with an exciting new career in teaching. Now I was none of those things: only pregnant. In a few months, I would be none of those things either: only a mom. I always imagined I'd be

8. Wandering?

a brilliant artist/teacher *and* a mom. A mom on the side. Like a baked potato or a house salad. Since I lost my career before the baby, did that mean I was locked into the whole stay-at-home thing FOREVER? A lot of women I knew got to "go on leave." But I had nowhere to leave from. I got the boot. While anger-chopping veggies, I'd mentally re-hash the sordid details of my unemployment and start to feel sorry for myself all over again, giving way to an identity crisis of Sybil-esque proportions.

Visualizing my future After Baby [A.B.] was a tough nut to crack as well.

MY BEST GUESS AT THE TIME: I would wake up in the morning (around 9 or 10) to a cooing infant. He'd nurse, and we'd lovingly stare at each other the whole while. I'd lay him in his crib, and he would drift back to sleep like a baby bird. While the baby snoozed, I'd read *US Weekly* and watch *Dawson's Creek* reruns until he woke, and then we'd stare at each other some more…right?[9]

…

Labor was a real head scratcher, too. Alex and I had decided to go the natural birthing route and so engaged in a twelve-week course called the Bradley Method. The Bradley Method basically trained Alex to be a doula, educating us both on the signs and stages of labor and how to cope with each of them. We learned relaxation tactics that, if all went as planned, would help me reach the end without medicinal intervention. We did things like deep tummy breathing and improvised practice contractions, where Alex whispered soothing bullshit in my ear like, "Imagine the baby moving down and out, down and out," or "Visualize this contraction as a beautiful, sparkling, rolling wave that you

9. WRONG: reflux.

must dive through." We also watched outdated live-birth videos reminiscent of the Dharma Initiative tapes from *Lost*. Most of the featured women had long braids running down their hairy backs, extremely "native" lady-parts, and calmly breathed their babies into the world with something sounding like a sigh or a yawn. This, apparently, actually happens. There was no screaming. No bargaining with God. And so we stuck with the Bradley Method in the hopes that I too might defy mainstream perceptions of childbirth and just casually sway the baby down and out, down and out.

Pregnancy is not a state of being that naturally suits me. My second trimester carrying Ford did not, as promised, deliver on that euphoric burst of vitality. I had no energy. For nine months I moved like molasses or a lost tourist.[10] I woke up every morning feeling like Secretariat the day after winning the Belmont. There was no glow. No luscious hair. And until approximately eight months in, my belly appeared severely bloated instead of ripe with new life.

My social life and (by extension) Alex's, fell slowly but surely to its grave. Alex would return home from work around 5:45 where I was, because of the exhaustion, still in bed. Sometimes I would take off my pajama pants and replace them with jeans around 5:30, just to create the illusion that I hadn't been wearing them all day. We would order pizza and eat it, *in bed*. Then we'd catch up on TV shows or watch a movie (also *in bed*) until about ten when we'd both go to sleep. Sometimes friends invited me for coffee during the day or, since it was summer, to swim at the pool, but mostly we became recluses who did little but reminisce on the days when we had it in us to go out until the early hours of the morning. After so many instances of turning

---

10. Wandering?

down nighttime recreational invitations, people eventually just stopped calling.

Being young, pregnant, and newly fired is like being semi-forced to inhabit a new city. You're uncomfortable, lonely, afraid, lost,[11] and usually comfort feeding on things like waffle fries and milkshakes.

It took nine months (as it so often does), but this precious life, Michael Botsford Getz (Ford), arrived on August 22, 2013.

Here's the Rough Schedule (and other dark thoughts and remembrances) regarding labor events:

6:30AM, August 22, 2013: Awaken with most violent urge to "use the ladies room."[12] Alex in shower cleansing before work. I daintily ask [demand] for him to hurry the hell up.

6:34: Use the ladies room.

6:40: Stricken with extremely intense contraction. Labor hath cometh.

I now understand what other women mean when they vaguely assert things like "when you're truly in labor, *you'll know*." This really is the most complete information that one can communicate about those first few pains. "What do contractions feel like?" pregnant women often wonder, in anticipation for the big moment. In my opinion, if forced into more detail on the matter, labor contractions lie somewhere on the scale between heavy period cramps and the imagined physical sensation of something like a grape squeezing itself into and then out the other end of a coffee stirrer. Just imagine the coffee stirrer could feel the whole thing happening, and the grape crying at the end. For that matter, imagine the

11. Wandering?

12. Lower GI "stuff."

coffee stirrer crying at the end too. Hint: you are the coffee stirrer. The baby is the grape. Hope that helps.

Prior to Ford's actual day of birth, Alex and I assumed we would labor at home for a long while, seven maybe eight hours. I hoped to take a nice hot shower, perhaps a bubble bath, shave my legs, and clean up for the Big Event. Alex would walk me through the many visual relaxation exercises we had rehearsed over the past few months. He would stroke my hair and read *Harry Potter* to me while I took deep tummy breaths. Giddiness and excitement would abound over the near arrival of our baby. We would do these sorts of delightful activities at home for eight or so hours (or whenever contractions were coming every four minutes and lasting for one minute) before heading to the hospital right when things got dodgy—so to bypass the window where I could [would most definitely] beg for drugs.

6:45AM: Contractions coming every four minutes, lasting one minute. Abnormal early labor. Panic. Confusion. Hercules knows something is up. Hysterically barking. Alex flipping through Bradley workbook, clumsily seeking answers.

7:15: Alex asking sweetly if I want to take shower. I respond with stink eye.

7:20: Questioning ability to do this. Too late to take it all back?

7:30: Contractions worsening. Alex frantically printing birth plan and throwing last-minute items like massage devices and *Harry Potter* books into hospital bag. We assume there will be time for utilizing such tools.

7:45: Starting to wonder if baby isn't going to come a bit sooner than we thought. Alex still skeptical. Holds me hostage at home until threat of emergency birth on moldy floor of tiny bathroom becomes imminent.

"Alex, I really think we need to go to the hospital now," I say weakly between contractions.

"No, not yet," as he casually eats his pancakes. "It's only been an hour and a half!"

THE FEAR (and what keeps us hesitant about leaving home): That I will arrive at the hospital and be told these soul-crushing words— "You're only two centimeters dilated. Go back home."

Considering how much pain I am already in and with little-to-no time for rest between contractions, I know those words will be the end of my noble attempt to birth without medicine. Pass me a mirror, I will inject the epidural myself thankyouverymuch.

8:30: Run to toilet. Vomiting and contracting at same time. Pushing up and down all at once, extremely perplexing.

8:35: Dog continuing to bark. Wind coming to a still calm. Swarm of locusts approaching. Nature knows, but Alex still needs convincing.

8:36: Use ladies room. There's blood.

Everything's happening too fast.

8:45: Relaxation techniques proving futile as next contraction comes before Bradley exercise can be completed.

8:46: Attempting to imagine myself, as directed by my man-doula, swimming in a deep fertile feminine ocean with a large wave coming towards m—

8:47: Contraction.

9:00: White flag thrown. Leaving for hospital.

9:30: Arrive at hospital after turning what should be a five-minute drive into a half hour. Alex driving snail speed at my demand. Note to self: must draft letter of complaint to City of Savannah Streets Management Department to

FILL THE DAMN POTHOLES.

There is no parking in the emergency parking lot, a deep flaw in the medical emergency system. We refuse to be Mary and Joseph-ed. Alex parks illegally and leaves a scrambled note on our windshield, the script of which resembles a ransom note written by the desperate hostage himself: "Wife in labor. No parking. Sry." Simple. To the point.

By now, I am vaguely aware of strange primal sounds springing forth from my gut. I try to squelch the abominable noise. I cannot. In the trenches of performing the miracle of life, I still find myself embarrassed by the intense, almost sexual moaning, but could no more have stopped it than if someone had asked me at that moment to engage in a krumping battle.[13]

9:40: Limping across parking lot, having contractions all the while, draped on Alex's shoulder. Man unloading a truck staring uncertainly as we stop periodically and I moan in... pleasure? Pain?

9:43: Daft woman strolling through parking lot asking pleasantly if everything is okay, as if she's just eaten a cupcake. We do not respond.

9:45: Alex checks us in. Women at front desk respond too calmly, too slowly (recalling to mind, I'm sure, the lesser women who've wilted through those doors, crying wolf, at just one or two centimeters dilated).

I moan. People waiting in the emergency room exchange worried glances, as if at any moment a small alien in a top hat will violently tear from my abdomen and perform a Broadway routine right before their stunned and tired eyes.

---

13. Also called "clown dancing," krumping is a violent and energetic form of street dance, intended as a nonviolent alternative to gang brutality.

"Who is this ailing Pavarotti?" they wonder nervously at my shaky vibrato, realizing that the toe splinter that brought *them* in that morning would perhaps take care of itself.

The nurses in the emergency room note glibly, pointing to our hospital bag, that we "must be moving in." I feel confused by this, as we packed a pretty small bag. Certainly we are not the first couple in labor to prepare by packing a hospital bag?

I am finally wheeled to triage, after what is probably only two or three minutes of waiting in the emergency room. A cheery woman named Paula, who also looks like she has just partaken of baked goods, will be our labor and delivery nurse. The breeze of Paula casually whisking me through chilly hospital hallways feels nice on my face. I am *good*, clear of head, confident even, my contractions seeming to have stepped outside on break for a few minutes—maybe to squeeze in a quick cigarette or coffee, regaining their strength before the shit really hits the fan.

10:10: In triage. Scribbling something roughly resembling cat scratch or my signature on many official looking documents. IS THIS REALLY NECESSARY?

10:13: Wondering why the hell nobody has called the doctor to evac this baby already.

10:15: Finally being "checked." Moment of truth. Seven centimeters dilated. SCORE.

10:16: Nurses and other personnel moving quicker, taking me more seriously when I blurt things like "I'm telling you, this baby is COMING!" Overall bewilderment and skepticism whenever Alex communicates my desire not to be medicated.

10:17: Needing to vomit again. Paula fumbles, unprepared. Alex hands me garbage bag from our hospital bag.

Who's picking on our preparedness now?!

10:18: Alex continues to be my champion.

The next two hours are a blur of severe pain and indescribable pelvic pressure. I am moved to a room that is adjacent to an area of the hospital under heavy construction. Abrasive jackhammer noises accompany my contractions, almost metaphorically, every three to four minutes. Paula just giggles about the construction. Alex is enraged. I am unclear as to why everyone is focused on the construction instead of the baby that is rather quickly making its way out of me.

I denounce God and all his people. My blood pressure is too high (my hands look like inflated doctors gloves) and so Paula makes me lie on my left side, which seems to throw the contractions into a torrential, pulsating frenzy. I constantly feel the intense urge to urinate, without the ability to do so. On my way to the bathroom I pee on the floor, but mistake it for my water breaking. Alex, God bless him, has yet to rehash that detail (although I'm sure it got on his shoe).

I panic, I fight to take control of the situation, limping around the room, snapping regrettable words at Paula, begging Alex to TAKE MY PLACE.

Finally, after any effort proves futile, I give up. I let go.

God, if now is my time, take me.

HELP.

And the next hour is like being in some kind of a voodoo trance. As I am on no pain medication, my body completely takes control over my will. Anything I do to move or resist what is happening makes the pain significantly more horrific. At some point in the future, I'll think about that as a metaphor.[14] The only real way through this "situation" is to surrender, and dive through the many feminine and fertile tsunamis one-at-a-damn time.

11:30: Water actually breaking. Meconium (baby poop) in my amniotic fluid. Intensive care team called on the scene in case baby chokes on meconium. Nobody seems too worried, so neither am I.

Just minutes later my legs are in the stirrups and I'm ready to push. The doctor is nowhere to be found. I try feebly to conjure visions of enjoying Hogwarts at Christmas time, wand in hand, drinking butterbeer with my Quidditch teammates in the oaken halls of Gryffindor common room. Where the hell is the doctor? The doctor arrives. She is like an Amazon. Sturdy. Capable. I don't feel afraid. I begin to push as she adeptly slips on gloves. Ten centimeters.

Zero hour.

As I push, I'm not sure if progress is being made. Alex, the doctor, and Paula bravely stand at the business end of things. They are encouraging but unclear on the ETA of the baby. I continue to push under the assumption this could be a while.

"Push like you're going number two!" yells Paula.

I'm grateful for the helpful visual and still hoping it's just that: *a visual.*

Several minutes later—Mother of God!

Ford's head is born, but the umbilical cord is wrapped around his neck. The doctor has the situation under control in a matter of seconds. My beautiful boy is all the way born. Seven pounds and thirteen ounces. Lots of dark, curly hair. A newborn-clone of his dashing father.

I don't remember if the baby cries or not, as I am mostly

14. Maybe write a chapter in a book about it.

watching *Alex* cry while he carefully makes his way around the bed (on which I am still splayed like da Vinci's Vitruvian Man), over to our perfect, newborn son who is being tended to by the intensive care team.

Alex carefully passes Ford to me and as I hold him for the first time, staring into his baby-dark eyes, yet to be colored, I am both a new kind of terrified and yet utterly captivated. This baby is no accident. Unwashed and still covered in it-doesn't-matter-what, he is perfect. He is a masterpiece. And it shames me to think of how easily I tend to forget that God is good, that he is with me, and that so often what feels like punishment is actually the Maker making.

It took nine uncomfortable and exhilarating months to make Ford into a person who could survive in the world, outside my womb. And it took six unbelievably awful, drug-free hours to deliver him. I think it's important to note that scholars believe six hours is exactly how long Jesus hung on the cross before he died. And we all know what happened after that.[15]

Six hours for my richest gain.

---

15. Raise da roof.

PART SEVEN

HOW TO
FIND WINE
IN THE WILD

RECOVERED TRANSCRIPTS FROM LIFEBOAT 815

EXTERIOR: MORNING—SOMEWHERE IN THE PACIFIC.

The PHILLIPSES *and* GETZES *have officially dropped their oars, in both the literal and the spiritual sense. They are exhausted. They are floating in no particular direction at all. And they consumed their final rations of bread and wine the night before.*

CHARLOTTE (*becoming angry*): What are we *doing* out here?

STEPHANIE: Slowly turning into pretty over-cooked fish food (*she looks meanly toward the hot sun*).

CHARLOTTE: God has literally brought us out here to die.

STEPHANIE: God?? *What God??*

CHARLOTTE (*stops dead in her rant-tracks*): Oh Lord Almighty...

STEPHANIE: What?

CHARLOTTE: What is *that*? (*She points, jaw to the ground, to a medium-sized wooden crate floating just feet from their lifeboat.*)

The crate moves right to the edge of the boat, as if on a mission, and Jason and Alex haul it out.

STEPHANIE (*reads the barely legible black writing stamped onto the wood*): "Chateau Margaux 1787."

The two women stare at each other, in utter disbelief.

CHAR AND STEPH
WANDER THE DESERT

ACT IV

STEPHANIE *and* CHARLOTTE *are now elderly women, their children grown. For forty years they've wandered. And there, in the harsh plains of Moab, just before crossing into the Promised Land,* MOSES *dies.*

STEPH: Seriously?

CHAR: You've *got* to be kidding me.

STEPH: Now what?

CHAR: I guess he was pretty old.

STEPH: I know, but I'm still super sad.

CHAR: Me too. We always trusted him.

STEPH: *Always.*

CHAR: At this point, I feel like we're not going to live long enough to see how this ends.

STEPH: No chance. We're *old.*

CHAR: We're *dying*.

STEPH: We aren't dying, Char. I mean, look at Herm. *He's* still going.

CHAR: Sweet Herm.

STEPH: But honestly, Moses was like 120. I don't know if I really want to live that long.

CHAR: NO.

STEPH: I mean, I love my family and all—

CHAR: But how sick does heaven sound?

AFTER SOME TIME, *it becomes clear that God has anointed* JOSHUA *to take over for* MOSES *and lead the Israelites into Canaan.* JOSHUA *addresses the people.*

JOSHUA: Remember what Moses said: "The Lord your God is giving you rest and has granted you this land."

He gestures to the expanse behind him, as if pulling back the curtain on some mind-bending magic trick.

STEPH (*underwhelmed*): Looks alright.

CHAR: How are we even going to get there? All I see is RIVER.

STEPH: Has God really led us out here, just so we might drown at the outskirts of Jericho?

CHAR: Dude, there is no God.

STEPH: I see no precedent for this turning out well for us.

CHAR: None at all.

Before the Israelites enter into Canaan, JOSHUA *secretly sends a group of spies into this new land.* ALEX *and* JASON *are among them. The men return talking of nothing but rescuing a "lady of the night" named* RAHAB.

STEPH: Do you think Jason cheated on me?

CHAR: Do *you* think Jason cheated on you?

STEPH: He will not shut up about this Rahab chick. (*Imitating* JASON) "Oh, she was so nice. Oh, she saved our lives. BLAH BLAH BLAH."

CHAR: Alex has been doing the same thing, *nonstop.* (*Imitating* ALEX) "Aw man, I hope she remembers to hang that scarlet cord in her window so we don't accidentally murder her." I'LL 86 HER MYSELF, *ALEX.*

STEPH: What kind of name is *Rahab* anyway?

CHAR: She's not even that cute.

STEPH: Oh, so now you've met her?

CHAR: GET ON BOARD, STEPH. SHE'S A WHORE.

SEVERAL DAYS LATER, *the Israelites cross the Jordan, in a similar manner as they crossed the Red Sea forty years before. The flooded waters of the river are miraculously held at bay. They follow the ark of the covenant and come into Canaan safe and dry.*

STEPH: Omg we made it.

CHAR: Yeah, we're in our 70s now, but we made it.

STEPH: My own grown children had to literally carry me across the Jordan, but we did actually make it.

The women observe their new surroundings.

CHAR: I have a confession...

STEPH: What?

CHAR: This place isn't at all what I thought it would be.

STEPH: I was *just* thinking the same thing.

CHAR: I thought it would be—

STEPH: Paradise.

CHARLOTTE: Like PINA COLADAS and PADDLE BOARDING!

STEPH: PALM TREES!

CHAR: GLITTERING OASES!

STEPH: BEACH READS!

CHAR: MEN IN SHORT SHORTS!

STEPH: Whoa.

CHAR: Sorry. I'm senile.

STEPH: I guess the best we can hope for is that it might just feel like home.

CHAR: How long do you think that will take? I mean, we still have to actually conquer the area.

STEPH: Couple of days?

The women shrug their shoulders.

SIX YEARS LATER. *The Israelites have finally conquered Canaan.* STEPH *is in her 80s.* CHAR *is still youthful in her late 70s. They have built homes for their growing families. The two women attempt a stroll through their neighborhood.*

STEPH: It took a while, but this place kind of seems like ours, doesn't it?

CHAR: Like God had set it apart all along, just for us.

STEPH: But my left knee is still giving me grief. I sort of thought the Promised Land would, you know, take care of all that.

CHAR: Yeah, that pain in my abs is definitely still nagging me.

STEPH: Your *abs*?

CHAR: Fine, my hernia.

STEPH: Now that we're here, do you think God's work is done? Like we don't need help anymore?

CHAR: I need help. My anxiety is through the roof and I'm pretty sure I have typhus.

STEPH: What? Why?

Char pulls down the back of her tunic.

STEPH (*cont'd*): Char, that's backne.

CHAR: Oh, thank God.

STEPH: Either way, I think you made your point.

CHAR: What?

STEPH: You need help.

CHAR: Yeah well that left knee of yours ain't gonna fix itself. I think you may require further assistance as well, sister.

Both women sigh.

STEPH: You don't think—

CHAR: It's almost like—

STEPH: That was the whole point?

THE END.

RIDING THE WAVES
FROM WITHIN THE
WHALE

Stephanie

Sometimes the world seems against you
The journey can leave a scar
But scars can heal and reveal just
Where you are.
                    – Moana

I DRIVE BY THE BEACH every day. Sometimes I get out of the car; often, I don't. Seeing it can be enough.

Before and after those placid beach visits, there is life: the hustle of everyday existence for a family of four living as expats in Australia.

There are the early-morning minutes, when both boys have taken to climbing into our bed with unbridled energy that can be contained temporarily by video-viewing but eventually erupts into the jumps and cacophony of childhood: Will's tears over James not pausing a video to tell him "hello" followed by James's laughter at Will's funny faces.

There are the before-school hours, when I attempt to get them and myself ready, Jason helping on his way out the door: teeth brushed, clothes shrugged into, cereal poured, fights mediated. There is the walk to James's school: I field their questions about why today is Monday and why some cars are hatchbacks while others are sedans, then attempt to override said questions with a prayer for everyone's day— *God, let them know how loved they are even/especially when I fail to.*

There is drop-off at James's school, where we wait for his therapist to arrive while we greet the other kids and their parents. James usually approaches everyone he knows to show them his latest favourite car. Will likes to stand on the kindergarten steps and sing the ABC song. I ride the con-joined waves of anxiety and joy, knowing we are in the right place even as my mind jumps ahead to what's next: How long will James need extra help? Will he be included by his classmates today? James grabs his therapist's hand after en-during my kiss and skips toward the classroom, an excited grin on his face to challenge my tense one.

Will and I may go to the gym, where the ladies who run the kids' area laugh at my jokes about wine consumption. Will has friends there, and at his preschool where we go on other days, even though he often cries at drop-off there. I leave him, battling guilt and anxiety and a fear over what kind of a parent the staff think I am. Whether they like me. What to get them for Christmas that will make them like me more.

I'm still myself here, it turns out. How disappointing; what a revelation.

There is the rest of life: trips to the local, world-class zoo with its koalas and kangaroos. Sunday morning ferry rides into the harbour for church. The amusement park fifteen minutes from our house. The water views at every turn. There are the dates, with other couples and with other mums, which start as bursts of anxiety on the calendar but become less awkward as they deepen into friendship over time. There is the local paper, with a crime section so tame that its typical entries involve online identity theft and drunken bar patrons.

I am growing to love it, this suburb where we've set up shop. I mean, it's not in the throes of the hard-knock life. As one acquaintance put it, we've "landed on our feet." There are quite a few expats here, as well as a striking amount of wealth. We fit into the first group while enjoying the housing benefits of the second thanks to a generous allowance from Jason's company. In fact, when I look around (without listening; the Aussie accents would throw this comparison off), it all feels very 1950s America. There has to be an underbelly, though, right? If it's too good to be true, then…it's probably not. True?

Maybe. But life here is sanding away at my cynical edges. That's softening my sarcastic bent. Not *doing away with*, mind you—I'll always be an American. But there is something fascinating about historical and geographical contributions toward a nation's psychological profile, and back in the States, our capitalistic American dream often translates into a performance-based culture in which no ladder is too high to climb. It's exhausting, and it doesn't end in the corporate world, but trickles all the way into Pinterest and unofficial parenting competitions. In Australia, parents don't rush through Target on February 13 in a mad dash to procure enough Valentines for their kids' classes, because *they don't hand them out here.* Slow clap. The birthday parties we've attended were informal affairs with hotdogs on the grill (sausages on the barbie) and homemade cakes, not a Frozen-themed ice-castle-replica-centered soiree inside an event space littered with a DJ, $50 party favors, and a life-sized Olaf who gave rides on his tagalong unicorn. An Aussie friend told me recently that the idea of a climb upward is a bit gauche here, as there's more appeal in the narrative of struggle. Interesting contrast to our American sensibility that seems to outlaw such a prospect.

I guess what I'm saying is that I'm used to looking for rest in all the wrong places—the next achievement, my kids' well-being, a suffering-free existence—and life in America was only too willing to affirm that search. Which makes life here in Australia…well, it makes it exactly what it was meant to be. It *reveals* it to be exactly what all things are when they come from the hand of a good God: a *gift*. Specifically, Sydney is a place where we seem, daily, to be called into rest. The kind that no longer relies on the sleeping pills that sent me into unconsciousness nights back in Atlanta.

Lest I appear out of touch (too late) or haughty (I'm not meaning to imply that God sent us to Australia because he loves us more/this is heaven and the rest of you are left behind as The Remnant, though it's a theory worth exploring), I am fully aware of some of the drawbacks of Aussie living. Everyone back home is, like, *really* far away. I have to wait hours before my texting buddies find out about 3AM presidential tweets (the wait is interminable until I fall asleep; then everyone talks without me). There's our tony enclave's lack of diversity (unless you count my Swedish hairdresser); I'm going to need to speak with someone about the real definition of *bacon*; and I am definitely not prepared for Christmas during the summer and the images of a speedo-clad

Santa that it evokes. Then there's the fact that we're actually *all* still the same people here that we were back in the States, inconveniently. For example, I am sure that most days my children would have enjoyed the benefits of a post-relocation Mommy Personality Change. Instead, James and I mirror each others' meltdowns in public settings, and the ambivalence that defines my parenting endeavors is alive and well every time a tiny voice shouts "Play with me!"—shooting both warmth through my heart and shivers down my spine.

Brokenness and sin don't need plane tickets to follow me across the world.

My children suffer constantly and cross-hemispherically from my inability to stay in the present, as well as the anxiety that drives this tendency. I struggle to delight in them, in so many moments, and I can't even get to the part where I know he's God because I am incapable, it seems, of just being still.[1] Always have been. But I am changing. I am being brought into each moment, through one part mindfulness techniques, one part helpful books, and all parts grace and its rescue strategies (which are also unconstrained by plane tickets). I am being captivated into stillness by panoramas that demand to be beheld, sweeping vistas of ocean, brilliant sunsets, lapping waves. By even more awe-inspiring images, like that of James being set free alongside me, incrementally and sporadically, from anxiety and the limitations of a spectrum diagnosis while becoming a treasured member of the mainstream kindergarten class at his lovely school and *thriving*. By Will's blossoming early-life friendships and developing Aussie accent. By...just *life*. Here.

"In returning and rest you shall be saved; in quietness and

1. Psalm 46:10. Working on it.

trust shall be your strength," Isaiah proclaims to us across the millennia, and never has the *rest* part of that promise been more resonant. In the strangest way even the *returning* part is true: it feels as though we are returning to a simpler way of life after a season of struggle and uncertainty back in the States. And as I write that, my cynical self wonders when things will fall apart .

Isaiah is ready for my cynicism. "But you were not will- ing, [girl]" he continues in the lesser-quoted second part of the verse, and cites how the Israelites arranged for their own rescues and, therefore, their own demise. Once again, across the millennia, I hear the echoes resonate through my own life. And I watch as grace, which because of what happened specifically two millennia ago on a hill, makes no room for my demise. There's no drowning, for the Israelites or me, despite all the metaphorical lifesaving gear I haul around.

I feel that grace on Sundays, when I hold my palms up- ward during the benediction and feel the weightless weight that presses into them week after week, Spirit and air. I feel it as I push endless pounds[2] of stroller and child uphill toward school and anxiety laps at my edges and frays my nerves. Then the view to our right opens to reveal moun- tain and sea, and the little one below me, in response to my frustrated pleas to his brother to hurry up, sings, "Silly Mummy!"

Silly indeed. Ridiculous, actually, to have prayed for years for a beachside home only to be given it decades later on another continent and to have feared it was anything oth- er than grace. To fear that, whatever may come to us here, it could ever be anything but grace. Pain is God's mega- phone, according to C.S. Lewis, but he also wrote that "God

2. kilos

whispers to us in our pleasures." For now, at least, we hear that whisper, the wind of a Spirit that answers my fears by teaching us a different way to breathe. One that, some days when I'm driving by the impossibly blue water of the Pacific Ocean that is now my backyard, comes in the form of having my breath taken away altogether.

The boys' favorite Bible story lately, when I remember to read them one, is Jonah and the whale, or as they call it, "The Fish Belly Story." They ask, every time, why Jonah got swallowed by the fish. And every time, I tell them that it was how God rescued him. Before this exodus, before grace entered my life, I would have given a different answer—I thought it was punishment, those dark three days and nights—until I learned that, prior to them, Jonah had been lost. And it was in the belly that he was found. Where he was rescued. What else could he do there, but breathe and wait and keep living?

So that's what I do. And every time I enter our home here, I see the wall-hanging that I schlepped[3] from the US that reads "I was once lost, but now I'm found." I feel both of those things every day. Out of place, and in it. Settled and not. Home and away.

Strange, but is it possible that's what being rescued looks like?

---

3. Fine, it was air-shipped over by my husband's company.

ALL THE LEAVES ARE BROWNISH

Charlotte

IT'S FALL IN CALIFORNIA.

In most of America, this is a distinct season characterized by college football, a slight chill, and the dying of all
natural life. This particular evolution of fall is a process that
is both beautiful with its reds and rusts, and mysterious in
the knowledge that several months later, all will grow back
in full. Fall in California, on the other hand, is marked by a
change in the air color, only a slight drop in temperature, an
upkick in the Santa Ana winds, and *wildfires*. Looking at it
through the overhead gaze of an aerial firefighter, I guess we
have our own sort of seasonal death, even here in the gold-
en state.

This fall brings with it our one year Cali-versary. What
began with bitterness and, admittedly, at least a small whiff
of devil-may-care, now has the distinct scent of design and
intent. Initially, we labored to break into this place. We
didn't know where or if we belonged. In our first week, I ran

full speed, skull first into a set of monkey bars (on a rescue mission towards my tripping Margot). A year later, the dent below my hairline is still visible. At the time, it felt like a punch from the west coast itself. A blow that meant I did not belong.

Things first began to change when we bought a house, still small but significantly larger than the first apartment. It was a foundational attempt to till out some earth and root here. The house sits about 200 feet from Mother's Beach, which has become our backyard in the absence of an *actual* backyard. We are there nearly every afternoon running and digging and climbing and splashing. I am re-learning to be a kid alongside my own children and the blessed water. How appropriate, how wonderful, a beach for mothers where the ocean is shallow and calm, where boats float by as if on parade, where there is space to breathe and to be. My Mother's Beach: a beach just for me.

Throughout this California transition, I have tended to stay stuck on what and who is missing out here, feeling sorry for myself and my defective body which now has a label: *Lupus*. But over time, God has given me new eyes, even if they go in and out of proper focus every other second of the day.

Once, with this new vision, I was standing on a broken sidewalk in front of my kids who were locked in yet another bickering match over who got what toy. I looked beyond the stroller, tears burning behind my exhausted eyes, to a pier that reached out into the ocean like an opened hand, as far as the eye could see. We walked there. As the stroller began to bounce along the weathered wooden planks, the kids turned silent. The wind blew through me. And the world was as wide and wild as I wanted it to be as a child. God was everywhere.

Or the wallpaper in our new master bedroom, chosen haphazardly for its beauty, painted with green oaks, limbs winding and entangled. While working from bed (my creative and productive place), this plainly "pretty" wallpaper began to look like blessed signs of life that surrounded me, hemmed me in like a sanctuary. Or at church, with the dull pangs of darkness sitting heavily on my chest, burning hot on my palms, and the worship leader sang, "It is finished! He has done it! Let your weary heart rejoice / It is finished, lift your head and weep no more." Church that day—not a triage tent for the dying—but a holy green room for a New Earth; a new, always *being made*, me.

Over time, California has made a space for us, such that I suspect there may have been a God-crafted, Getz-shaped vacancy here all along.

This place, while wildly imperfect—even the monkey bars too low—almost wants to keep us. And I have to confess that I might want it, too. There is a developing symbiosis.

I need the repetitive pounding of the waves crashing along Seal Beach. The booming woosh and swoosh reminds me how small I am and how big the world is. I need my double-double protein style burger from In-N-Out. I need the marine layer that hovers over our town in the mornings, making my coffee time cozy, dear, and slow like a waking cat. I need my specific doctors who have *listened to me*, and weeded through my many frustrating symptoms to finally identify my illness. I need the moderate temperature. I need the personal freedom allowed here to let my spicy Margot dress in whatever odd clothing she wants, because she refuses to wear the smocked and collared frocks of most girls raised in the South. I need my friends, the friends who live *here*. I even need Alex's job, which has provided for us financially and helped to grow him. I need our church, its people, and its loud and outpouring message of GRACE. I need my children's pre-school, a tender place that pours into them in ways I cannot. They are safe there. The teachers, parents, and other kids at this tiny school have become a critical part of our *place* here.

In the beginning, we did so much of our living in the space of social media and cellular devices. We primarily stayed connected to our long-lost loved ones by way of airwaves, phone lines, and the internet. This space, I suppose, is a sort of place in and of itself. But space just can't deliver like real, in the flesh, *place*. If you take a close look, God is deeply concerned with place. The first thing he did was to create one. It's called *earth*, people. Then he created another place, *Eden*, and he put us there. When Adam and Eve had to leave Eden, perfectly designed just for them, it was a punishment. No wonder our own leaving-times often feel like an actual amputation. We were not meant to leave. But ever since, God has continued to promise and provide place after place for his wandering people. Jesus was born in a particular place, he lived and ministered in particular places, died in a particular place, and the particularity of all these places held purpose and meaning. Jesus didn't operate from afar, observing people's lives from a safe distance. No. He had skin in the game and left blood on the field, literally. He continues to be so intimately "small & fond & local" to our lives as to be *united* with each of us.

With all the moving around of the past several years, I think it's been easier, safer, to live like a geographical and relational tourist—not particularly knowing and not particularly known. And that's exactly how I began my time out here.

After several misses, our family finally landed on a church to call home, Cross of Christ OC. A few weeks ago our pastor, the great Nick Bogardus, preached on this very subject. He said:

> Being in a place gives you roots. Being in a place enables you to be known particularly and to know particularly. Being a tourist gives you general superficial awareness... If you're a tourist, how can you be patient, or long-suffering, or bare other people's weaknesses, or forgive? If you're a tourist, how can you be loyal or faithful? How do you love your neighbor as a tourist? A placeless person cannot be a faithful person. A placeless person cannot love their neighbor. A placeless person cannot be long-suffering. A placeless person cannot be forgiven or forgive because they are not around long enough to wrong or be wronged.

He said that part of being made in God's image as human, as an embodied soul, is to be in a place. Being in a place means you're going to be among people and the culture they've created. And because of the gospel, we are free to live and lead with our chins.

I knew I was home in SoCal when my best friend and I had a terrible fight because she wanted to spend *more* time with me (imagine!); I felt I had nothing left to give and that she was being possessive and ridiculous. Over the next few hours and days it occurred to me that I'd possibly been self-protecting. What if she gets sick of me? What if she sees who I really am? And that pesky grace has since made way for me, yet again, to give more of myself—my *actual* self—when objectively I have nothing left to give. So my best friend has remained my best friend. That's what you do when you love someone. That's what you do when you know and are known *particularly*.

And particularly is exactly how we are known and loved by God.

As I've lived days and then months in this new place, God has revealed himself to me particularly. For all the minutes I've been here, he has rescued me ten times more. He is here. He is with me. He loves me. And it makes me want to bring myself, my real self, to the people he's placed around me.

Ultimately, everywhere we will live in this world is temporary—like a manger, a cross, or a tomb. Places have the power to deliver us into the world, take us to our breaking point, and also bring us back to life as someone altogether new.

I RECENTLY READ about a man who was sentenced to prison for thirteen years but, because of a clerical error, was never summoned to serve out his punishment. Because of his undeserved freedom, he spent every day afterwards trying to turn his life around, to become a better man. He married a good woman, had children, started his own business, all the while waiting for the dreaded knock at the door that would take it all away. Many years later that knock came. The man was taken to prison where he awaited a new ruling. The trial lasted all of ten minutes before the judge, to people's great shock, determined to set the man free.

And I think I know this feeling—going about my days

trying to be a "better person," neurotically thinking through the possibilities of future traumatic events (and how to avoid them), guarding myself from being *too* known, doing everything in my power to stay healthy, strong, and to escape the certain doom and judgment lurking just around the corner (because I know Who I Really Am and therefore what I really deserve).

But on a good day, when I'm looking to springtime and the breeze is just right, it feels like that shadowy moment of my reckoning has come and gone—the stakes were high, the situation dire—but I had received instead some blinding mercy. And I suspect it is that same mercy, not punishment, that brought me here to California and all the other people and places, far and wide, that have shaped me.

Like I said, it is fall here.

But God has made this place, even in a season of many small and large deaths, *for me*. It's as if I had been asleep on a pillow of stone, and then suddenly woke saying, "Surely the Lord is in this place, and I was not aware of it." We were not banished here, this was our *escape*.

We are locals now. We have found new life, maybe better life, in our deliverance here. This place, like all my places, is making me. I am all at once Chicago (my city of birth), Birmingham, Rhode Island, Bolivia, Malibu, Italy, Savannah, Auburn, Long Beach, and more. Ever and always I come face to face with the Risen Lord when I am set apart, away. These places we inhabit make space for us, pour into us, and let us pour ourselves into them. Like Paul when he was Saul, Christ meets us out on the open road: fallen, broken, bruised. And just like a forest needs a wildfire to stay healthy, God is healing me in this place, in body and in spirit. The cultural, relational, geographic, and spiritual soil in each of our places—sometimes sandy, sometimes loam—grows us; all along the way we stretch forth new and surprising limbs, certainly a lion's share of thorns, but ultimately petals upon petals upon petals of wild and breathtaking *life*.

Wrong will be right, when Aslan comes in sight,
At the sound of his roar, sorrows will be no more,
When he bares his teeth, winter meets its death,
And when he shakes his mane, we shall have spring
again.

C.S. Lewis, *The Lion, the Witch, and the Wardrobe*

HOME, AND HOME AGAIN

Stephanie

"They're called jacarandas," she told me, as we stared out the window after James's therapy session. "They have those purple blooms, and they all come out at the same time. You see them everywhere."

She wasn't lying. A couple of weeks prior, I'd pointed out the trees to the boys on a car ride. "Look at the purple flowers!" I told them, and we all stared. Now they notice them everywhere we go, Will pointing and exclaiming, "Look, Mommy! Purple flowers all over the ground!"

Because that's what the petals do: they fall, covering the ground beneath the trees, concrete and grass alike, in purple. A floor of purple, the same colour as the hydrangeas at my wedding. They're everywhere, and I love them.

Like the jacarandas, I'm falling too, in this season of spring, our first spring here in Sydney. I'm falling for the sea of purple outside my window that, from the corner of my eye, looks like yet another body of water next to the bay

335

that's always there. I'm falling for the kids in my boys' lives: the way Will's friend ran up to him at school and grabbed him into a bear hug, and they both fell to the floor laughing; the mum who told me through tears in her eyes about how her own boy came home and told her, "Sometimes I don't understand James," and as she wondered how to respond to his inevitable questions, he instead concluded, "because he's American."

I love that.

I love the rest of the mums, who all gathered around a table for dinner and way too many drinks the other night, discussing our kids and life and everything. For the friendships that were formed and continued and solidified, then and now. For the friends who read my writing (and like me anyway) and whose kids bounce toward me when I pick up James early and who call me by my first name and walk to school with us.

I love the speech James gave to his class last week—about his life thus far, because damn has it been a doozy—and I love how he giddily and shyly stood in front of them, and they all clapped, and he finished by yelling, "TA DA!" I love the tears in his therapists' eyes, overjoyed at his progress and accomplishments, to which they remain committed. I love the way James bounded into school this morning, when months ago he would have fought it, to pass out an invitation to each kid in his class for his birthday party, shouting some of their names across the school yard.

I love going to the movies (cinema) and not feeling compelled to immediately locate an exit in case a deranged gunman shows up.

I don't love hangovers, but I'm working on that.

I love seeing my kids grow here. Before they were born,

when people would say they were falling in love with their kids, I would gag on the sweetness of it. Then mine came along, and I knew I *loved* them, but *in* love? That was a stretch. But feeling James nestle into me on the couch, or hearing Will say, "I keep you safe, Mommy. I love you," I feel it: the falling in love that is so sporadic but true, fraught but there, interspersed among moments of insanity and irritation and discipline and fighting, but there. And it strikes me that the truest part of love isn't the falling, nice as that is (especially in New York, with Jason, over endless tapas and wine), but this:

The staying.

We love most not by feeling the fall but by relaxing into the staying.

And I wonder what that means for us here, when James told me over dinner the other night, "I want to stay in Australia forever." Will we? We have years to decide and progress to make. We have homesickness to endure and fights to weather and tears to dry and laughs to release. We have stories to tell, and chapters to add on to those stories. For now, though, there is so much life here. And I love it.

James's teacher told me the other day that she heard him tell to another teacher the thing I've been telling him for years: "My brain is different." She and the other teachers present all looked at each other and felt the beautiful weight of it, this difference and his awareness of it and pride in it. I think about the crepe myrtle outside our house in Atlanta and how much I loved it, how I dreaded missing it, and how it's been replaced by the jacaranda: something different.

I'm living, and loving, the different. The set apart. The home.

I REMEMBER THE DAY we left. Of course I do; it's been almost a year, and I'm only now getting to the point where I can think about it without ugly crying. Most of the time.

Speaking of crying, there was plenty of it that day. Three days after Christmas and one day after a nasty stomach virus felled me and my organizing/packing plans, leaving me banished to my bed by way of the toilet. There was frenetic packing all morning to make up for lost time, the shoving of our lives into either a storage bin or a suitcase: endless *staying* vs. *coming* choices. There was the goodbye with my parents, who couldn't take seeing us off at the airport and so left our house before lunchtime, my mom crying in the window with the dog in her lap as my dad drove, emotion threatening to seep through his stoic gaze. There was the group that came over to load our cars and follow us to the airport: my sister and brother-in-law and their two girls. A college bestie. My sister's in-laws. Our people.

After the cars were loaded and our imminent departure loomed, our friend Beth asked quietly if she could say a prayer. Believers and non-believers of all stripes nodded yes, and we gathered in a circle in the driveway, holding hands.

That's when the tears hit in full force: after our lives were packed away and "goodbye" was the only thing left.

When I moved to New York in a U-Haul, I felt the cord to home stretching tauter with each mile until I felt sure my heart would break. The cord to home as we now knew it, deepened by time and relationships, would have to stretch much longer over the next twenty-four hours of travel and years of life. Would it? Could it? I wondered. *What would happen next?*

We prayed.

Then we left.

I think that's a pretty good sequence of events.

A YEAR. How is that even possible? We've been here four seasons, arriving in the oppressive heat of summer that is coming back now, full-circle. Fifty-two weeks of feeling like an idiot, speaking the general language but not the local one: "How are you going" vs. "how are you doing." Arvo instead of afternoon. Rubbish, not trash. Thongs, not flip-flops. Air con, not A/C. Rosetta Stone for Aussie, anyone? Twelve months of driving, finally, after being forced to by the fact that James would have no other way to get to therapy. One banged-up passenger side and a few near-head-on collisions later, I think I'm finally getting the hang of this left-side-of-the-road thing...then I climb into my car and wonder where the steering wheel went. *Wrong side, dumbass,* I hear from the mean voice inside my head (and maybe a few passers-by). Then I start the car and switch on the windshield wipers instead of the turn signal.

For at least the first six months, it was as though I needed a special kind of map: the kind that helps people find their way when they feel lost even though they know where they are.

But I wasn't ever given a map. Instead, I was given manna.

THERE'S A DEEP UNSETTLEDNESS that comes from being between two places: America and Australia, old friends and new, the now and the not yet. It's like ambivalence writ large, and it made me wonder in those first months if I'd ever feel at home anywhere. And this...this sort of undid me. The unsettledness provoked by the move, though, tapped into something deeper: a feeling I've had my whole life of being an outsider, of not really fitting in anywhere. Growing up, I felt much more comfortable with my books than with other kids. I felt alone in every relationship I'd been in before I met my husband, and then I married him and…well, we all know it's possible to feel lonely within marriage, too. Especially when your spouse leaves the seat up after you've *repeatedly asked him not to*.

My sister told me recently about a work trip that sent her driving right by the neighborhood where we grew up: she had the sudden urge to pull into our driveway, open the front door, and climb into her old bed. All of which would have been very upsetting to the people who live there now, since my parents have moved. But our lives as mothers and grown-ups leave us feeling split and stretched and pulled tight. Unsustainable at times. Depressing at others. We are our children's home, and when I think this, it makes me want to become a better home for them: a safer one, with more comfortable seating areas and less yelling. But after only a few seconds of that, I'm exhausted. I can't sustain that effort. I canNOT keep that up. The more aware I am of my trying, the more aware I am of my failing. It makes me realize: *I* need a safe home. I need a place to come home to: a place my parents won't sell, a place where I am cared for, a place where I am known and loved no matter what I do. Where is my home?

Well, physically, now? It's Sydney. And this makes so much sense even as it doesn't. For one thing: it's a CITY that is full of BEACHES, which is perfect because those are my two favorite things, and Jason and I met in a city and were married on a beach. Sydney, right now, means my husband and our two boys. It's family picnics on the beach, daily walks to school. It's tension, and exhaustion, and failure and success, being over a dozen hours ahead, a day apart, and two days' travel away, and feeling connected and disconnected at the same time.

There's a beach two minutes from our house and we go there often. It's a harbor beach, which in some circles is looked down upon because it's not a big, exciting *surf* beach. But I like it: it's like our own little safe-feeling cove. But a harbor beach still has waves, and deep water, and rocks, and all sorts of dangers. And I still battle depression, and anxiety over my parenting, and fears for my children, even with faith and grace in the mix. The other day, my sons and I were on the sand discussing theology, by which I mean, my son had a scratch on his finger, and I kissed it and told him we could pray for it to be healed. He asked what Jesus was doing right then and I said, "Taking care of you and loving you." And he paused, then his eyes lit up, and he yelled, "That's him!" He was pointing at me. He said, "Mommy! You're turning into Jesus!"

This is my home. This Jesus, who is drawing us to himself and making us more like himself and is unseen but there, crucified but alive, invisible yet undeniable. Home is an unchangeable person, who loves us too much to let us cling to the changeable. He is the one who makes my life both a becoming and an arrival, who is with me in every moment yet will meet me in the end, which is the beginning, face to face.

This ambivalence, and unsettledness, that runs through us and even defines us, is an invitation. It's not a sign of insanity but a reflection of deep truth: sojourners with a permanent residence living in the now and not-yet as justified and sinner. We're home, and we're not, and we will be; and this is not ambivalence or paradox, but grace. It's a reminder of somewhere we've never been but were made for and somehow already know. Our true home, who is not a place but a person. The One who will meet us in the beginning with a feast—and wine is one of his signature dishes, thank God. He is the One who was there the whole time, bringing us home to him.

When we got to Sydney, I wanted directions. God told me to sit down and eat. The longer I live and the further I wander, the less in control and somehow more at home I seem to be, because he gives me mystery. Manna. Bread and wine. Himself.

RECOVERED TRANSCRIPTS
FROM THE BEACH

EXTERIOR: DAY—DRY LAND.

CHARLOTTE *and* STEPHANIE *stand on the banks of some foreign land. Their toes curl in the warm sand.* ALEX, JASON, *and* THE KIDS *are being tended to by a team of coast guard medics. The women are solemn as they take stock of each other after a long, tiresome journey.*

STEPHANIE: You look different than you did when we left. (*She tugs at the sleeve of* CHARLOTTE'S *rash guard.*)

CHARLOTTE: I was literally going to say the exact same thing about you. (STEPHANIE *is burnt to a crisp, after forfeiting all of the sunscreen to* CHARLOTTE *over the last weeks.*)

STEPHANIE: How long do you think we were wandering?

CHARLOTTE: Hard to say.

STEPHANIE: Felt like a decade.

CHARLOTTE: Yeah. Things got pretty rough.

STEPHANIE: I'd say.

CHARLOTTE (*apologetic*): I was not my best self out there.

STEPHANIE: Well, it was the wilderness! We didn't even have a map!

CHARLOTTE: I know. It's an uncomfortable thing.

STEPHANIE: What's an uncomfortable thing?

CHARLOTTE: To be carried through.

The girls sit in silence for a minute, letting the ground beneath their feet hold all of their weight. A large cloud moves to cover the blazing sun, so STEPHANIE *reaches over and removes* CHARLOTTE'S *hat.*

STEPHANIE: There you are.

CHARLOTTE, *exposed, smiles.*

STEPHANIE: Come to think of it, you don't look so bad after all.

CHARLOTTE: I was *just* thinking the same about you.

STEPHANIE: Better even.

CHARLOTTE: Red is a ridiculously good color for you.

STEPHANIE: I know, right? (*She showcases her fried arms.*)

The women begin to walk toward their families. STEPHANIE *turns to look back at the lifeboat—strong, trusty, capable. It delivered them all the way through.*

CHARLOTTE: Do you think we'll ever get lost like that again?

STEPHANIE: Probably.

CHARLOTTE: You just know my kids' sleep schedule is going to be thrown from all this.

STEPHANIE: Oh, totally. And did I mention that James's favourite therapist is contemplating another job?

CHARLOTTE: The guy you call Jesus?

STEPHANIE: Well he has a beard and loves my kid. What would *you* call him?

CHARLOTTE: He's leaving? That's rough. Come to think of it, the near future doesn't look so hot for us either. We're going to start potty-training Margot soon...

STEPHANIE: See you on the water?

CHARLOTTE: We won't lose our paddles next time.

STEPHANIE (*smiles to herself*): If we do, though, it'll be okay.

They turn to part ways.

CHARLOTTE (*calling over her shoulder*): Shotgun on stern.

LIL STEPH *and* LIL C *climb awkwardly out of the lifeboat, onto dry ground. They clamber to keep up with their respective elder-selves as they go their separate directions.* LIL C, *from head to toe, is "crispy"—an unspeakable color of blistered burnt rust. She has obstinately refused sunscreen these many long months. Her clothes are tattered and her hair is wild and crazed, a disheveled young Medusa of the lost-at-sea.* LIL STEPH *is hunched over and green with seasickness. She wobbles as she walks, her legs not yet used to land. Her prim white collared shirt from yore is worn, filthy, and marvelously lived in.*

LIL STEPH (*yelling across the beach to* LIL C): Don't go! I'm scared!

LIL C: Don't say that—you're freaking me out!

LIL STEPH: What if this place scars my kids for life??

LIL C: What if people don't like me here??

LIL STEPH: What if I get anxious??

LIL C: What if I get sad??

IN UNISON: *HELP.*

Maps can change a life, a person, returning us to dreams, to our childhood, to the poetic, to what is real. They can move us forward to what we didn't even know we were looking for. A map can change a god-awful day or month, ruin a rut, give us directions home and to everywhere else, near and far, to the golden past and today, to the center and then back to the periphery, to our true selves, our lost selves, the traveler, the mystic, the child, the artist. The point of life, a friend said, is not staying alive, but staying in love, and maps give us a shot at this, taking us to the wild brand-new, the old favorite, and back home.

Anne Lamott, *Hallelujah Anyway*

POCKET LITURGY FOR WHEN YOU'VE BEEN FED, RESTED, TENDED TO, AND ACTUALLY HAVE A SECOND

Lord Jesus,

We were lost. SO LOST.

Before we were lost, *you knew we would be lost.*

You planned it that way.

You also knew the means by which we'd be found.

You stayed with us through the whole thing.

You did not leave even when we doubted you were there and swore you off.

You did not leave even when *we* wanted to leave.

You did not leave even when we had that talk about eating our husbands and kids for sustenance and relief.

You did not leave even when we turned to so many other things (SO SO MANY) for our rescue.

You did not leave even when we were our very worst selves.

You did not leave even when we took matters into our own hands.

You did not leave even when we kind of wanted you to because you were so not working on our timeline.

You stayed.

You stayed.

You stayed.

You showed us yourself time and again, even when we didn't want to see it, or couldn't because our heads were so far up our own backsides.

You showed us yourself in the calm breeze, in the lapping water, in the blessed shade, in the friendships, in the wine, and even and especially in all the bad stuff. Go figure.

You carried us to where we were going.

Even though we kicked, screamed, and were heavy and burdensome from all the whining and queso.

You carried us all the way.

Until we reached this place.

We don't know how long we'll stay here.

And we don't know where we'll go next.

But we know that you are here.

And you have moved us from there to here.

For now, we are home.

ACKNOWLEGEMENTS

This project would be just a handful of quirky files on our computers if it weren't for Dave Zahl. Dave launched our writing on Mockingbird many years ago, and when we casually mentioned a book project, he offered a resounding *yes* to publish it without knowing much more about it than that. This man is like our Dumbledore, and we wouldn't be where we are today without him. We'd follow you anywhere, Dave.

Our editor, CJ Green, guided us through the writing process with grace, whimsy, and wisdom. He managed two fiery women with the poise and expertise of someone like an orca trainer. We love you CJ. Thanks for making us look good. Also critical to the editorial process were Margaret Pope, Anna Nott, and Jeff Dillenbeck. We are grateful for you.

Thank you to Maddy Green for all of the extraordinary artwork throughout this book, on the cover and beyond. You have truly brought our story to life, Maddy.

A huge chest bump to our fellow female contributors at Mockingbird. Sarah Condon, Carrie Willard, Margaret Pope, your writing has inspired us, challenged us, and supported us. "We answer prayers."

And above all, to the master shipbuilder and captain, the holder of the maps, and the One who sent us and sends us on these incredible journeys that all lead straight to him; the God who chose a nondescript town that was barely on the map to begin (continue) the journey that saves us all.

My mom and dad never suggested I should do anything other than follow my passions and my gifts. This freedom—and the accompanying encouragement and grace—has been the most privileged facet of my entire life. Thank you for loving me, for letting me sleep in your bed more times than I can count, and for holding me up during times I didn't think standing was possible.

To my siblings, Din and Bruce (+Katherine). We have spent decades now laughing and fueling each other's fierce and wild imaginations. In more ways than just writing embarrassing stories about you and our childhoods, you are my muses. And thank you for bringing Ross and China (+Sam) into our kooky nest.

Thank you to "the moms" and the rest of my extended family (who are in essence my immediate family), to my wonderful in-laws, I love you all.

Thank you to the many teachers and professors, from elementary to graduate school, who pushed me, encouraged me, and very often failed me. I have been blessed by some incredible educators over the years, even the ones who made me cry (YOU KNOW WHO YOU ARE).

A resounding thank you to the Cathedral Church of the Advent—Paul Zahl, and my dear Frank Limehouse—for spewing the gospel from the pulpit every Sunday I can remember. Gil Kracke, no matter our geography, you will always remain my most cherished mentor. You *showed* me the gospel. Cameron Cole, I always wanted a big brother. I am so very grateful for our friendship.

Thank you Nick Bogardus and Cross of Christ OC for rooting us in a church family in California. Thank you for speaking Jesus into our hearts and minds every week.

Throughout my life I am lucky enough to have made dear, lasting friendships far and wide. It would be impossible to name you all because I'm *that* popular. To my friends—thank you for putting up with me and for so very much laughter and joy and love throughout the years.

Helen, Susan, Kim, and Jo workshopped some of my essays in their most primitive first drafts. I still miss Wednesday mornings in my living room with you ladies.

Stephanie, to quote the classic film *Fools Rush In*, "You are everything I never knew I always [needed]." Thank you for your friendship, your partnership, and your camaraderie in these trenches. This adventure—both life and *Unmapped*—is better because we're doing it together. And damn it's been fun.

To Ford and Margot, my babies, you have made simple pleasures like afternoon strolls, a dog beach, cloudy days, Happy Meals, and morning snuggles—*my life*—seem like the best story ever told. I cannot wait to see how these chapters, long and short, beautiful and chaotic, continue to unfold.

Alex, thank you for the countless nights you've pondered aloud how much cash I could bring in as a writer. While wildly unrealistic and besides the point, your unwavering belief in my fiscal worth has been oddly motivating. What a life, babe. Thank you for being by my side and for loving us so well. "*The country ahead is as wild a spread as ever we're likely to see / The horses are dancing to start the advance--won't you ride on with me?*"

FROM STEPHANIE

My parents have always expected more of me than I thought I had to give, and have been nothing less than supportive as I struggled through figuring out that they were often right. Thank you for letting me switch schools my senior year when I was sad, for always reading and cheering for my writing, and for loving my own little family so well. Mom, your encouragement is unflagging and a constant source of support. Dad, your own wit and writing have so informed mine—thank God we're both so hilarious.

Thank you to Ashlee (Rash), my partner in my oldest memories. You made me an aunt to two amazing girls and a sister-in-law to a pretty cool guy, not to mention another daughter to his parents. You've also far surpassed me in coolness and confidence but put up with me anyway, and are always on my side. What a team. To quote Nanner: We "really ARE sisters."

Thank you to my islands of people—all over the world, now. To my Atlanta people—bitmojis, Signal texts, Voxer recipients, email partners, tea providers, cousins, etc.—and populated so heavily by VCV and all the men and women there who were, and are, a lifeline of grace and laughter and love. To my Alabama people, who have put up with me/counseled me/loved me more than I deserved. To my NYC people, most of whom have dispersed but who helped me grow up in my half-decade in the city. To my Sydney people, who have welcomed me into a fold that I'm so thankful exists. To in-laws and family and friends all over the map, and to the places themselves, channels of grace that have made me who I am.

Thank you to the People on the Driveway—some listed above, as well as Seth and Yankee Mom and Dad, who joined our hands and prayed with us then took us to the airport as we flew to our new life.

Thank you to Charlotte, my partner in this crazy idea that is now a continuing reality. From the moment I received your acknowledgement via Facebook friend request, through our early and awkward Skype interactions, through the process of telling our stories, I'm so thankful we're in this together. Lifejackets forever.

Thank you to James and Will, the boys I always dreamed of, for being more than I ever imagined by way of so much I didn't know to ask for. Your forgiveness and grace come straight from God, and being your storyteller, your advocate, and your mother is a hard and wonderful mercy. You have infused my life and writing with purpose, but beyond all that you just amaze me. I'm so happy I'm your mom.

Jason, thank you for existing. For continuing to stay. For seeing the best in me and everyone. For your kindness. A favorite novel of mine quotes a mother, upon seeing her daughter with (finally) the right man, saying that "the professionals have arrived." Thank God that, in you, he sent the professionals for me. You are the best thing.

ABOUT MOCKINGBIRD

Founded in 2007, Mockingbird is an organization devoted to connecting the Christian faith with the realities of everyday life in fresh and down-to-earth ways. We do this primarily, but not exclusively, through our publications, conferences, and online resources. To find out more, visit us at mbird.com or e-mail us at info@mbird.com.

ALSO FROM

MOCKINGBIRD

MORE THEOLOGY & LESS HEAVY CREAM
THE MAN WHO MET GOD IN A BAR
BED & BOARD
by Robert Farrar Capon

CHURCHY
The Real Life Adventures of a Wife, Mom, and Priest
by Sarah Condon

LAW & GOSPEL
A Theology for Sinners (and Saints)
by Will McDavid, Ethan Richardson, and David Zahl

THE MOCKINGBIRD DEVOTIONAL
Good News for Today (and Everyday)
edited by Ethan Richardson and Sean Norris

GRACE IN ADDICTION
The Good News of Alcoholics Anonymous
for Everybody
by John Z.

The Mockingbird Quarterly
edited by Ethan Richardson

A Mess of Help
From the Crucified Soul of Rock N'Roll
by David Zahl

Eden and Afterward
A Mockingbird Guide to Genesis
by Will McDavid

Mockingbird at the Movies
edited by C.J. Green and David Peterson

PZ's Panopticon
An Off-the-Wall Guide to World Religion
by Paul F.M. Zahl

This American Gospel
Public Radio Parables and the Grace of God
by Ethan Richardson

*Our books are available at mbird.com/publications or on Amazon, and our
magazine can be found at magazine.mbird.com.*

Made in the USA
Coppell, TX
08 February 2022

73128908R00215